LORENZO DA PONTE

Lorenzo da Ponte
from an old print

LORENZO DA PONTE

A Biography of Mozart's Librettist

by

April FitzLyon

John Calder · London
Riverrun Press · New York

First published in this complete edition with preface
1982 in Great Britain by
John Calder (Publishers) Ltd.,
18 Brewer Street,
London W1R 4AS

and first published in the USA 1982 by
Riverrun Press Inc.,
175 Fifth Avenue,
New York, NY 10010

Originally published as *The Libertine Librettist* 1955 by
John Calder (Publishers) Ltd., London and in the U.S.A. 1957 by
Abelard Schuman, New York.

British Library Cataloguing in Publication Data
FitzLyon April
   Lorenzo da Ponte
   1. Da Ponte, Lorenzo
   2. Librettists — Italy — Biography
   I. Title
   782.1′092′4   ML.423.D/

ISBN 0 7145 3783 7

Printed and bound in the Channel Islands by the Guernsey Press Co. Ltd.

CONTENTS

By the same author

The Price of Genius: A Life of Pauline Viardot

TRANSLATIONS

The Woman in the Case by Anton Chekhov

The Devil & Family Happiness by Leo Tolstoy

Ladies' Delight by Emile Zola

Blaze of Embers by André Pieyre de Mandiargues

Richard Strauss & Romain Rolland Correspondence

Nobody by Nikolai Bokov

ILLUSTRATIONS

'Youth is a blunder, Manhood a struggle, Old age a regret . . .'

DISRAELI

PREFACE

Over a quarter of a century ago, when I wrote this book, the growth of interest in opera amongst a wide public was only just beginning. Since then this interest has grown enormously, and the public which appreciates opera is not only wide, but very well informed. Many of the operas mentioned in this book had not, when I wrote about them, been performed since the 18th century; now, many people have heard them. Lorenzo da Ponte's name is now familiar to all opera lovers; and the number of reprints of his memoirs, both in Italian and in various translations, shows that there is no lack of interest in the life and personality of Mozart's librettist. Yet, so far as I am aware, there has been no full-length biography of Da Ponte published since mine appeared in 1955.

When this new reprint of my book was planned, I contemplated revising the text, but decided not to do so. Although some new information about Da Ponte's life and work has been published, mostly in learned periodicals, this information amplifies, but does not greatly alter the account of Da Ponte's life which I gave in my biography. Perhaps, the most important new discovery is that the libretto of *Cosi fan tutte* was not, apparently, quite as original as Da Ponte would have had us believe. (See A. Liviemore: '*Cosi fan tutte*; a well-kept secret' in *Music and Letters*, XLVI (1965), pp. 316-321, in which it is suggested that the libretto is based on Tirso de Molina's *El amor medico*). Other scholarly articles, although fascinating to the specialist, deal with aspects of Da Ponte's life and work which are probably not of great interest to the general reader, for whom my book was written.

To revise my book would have meant, to me, completely re-writing it; it has already acquired a period flavour. In a quarter of a century a writer changes and, one hopes, evolves; if I were to write about Lorenzo da Ponte today I would write a completely different, although not necessarily better, book. It would be more sober, more scholarly – perhaps more pedantic – much less care-free, as befits the times. But I greatly enjoyed writing this biography all those years ago, and people seem to have enjoyed reading it; I have therefore left it as it is.

April FitzLyon,
March, 1982.

FOREWORD

THE name of Lorenzo da Ponte is not well-known in this country, yet scarcely a day passes without one of his works being performed here, either in the theatre, on the radio, on television, or on gramophone records. He has conquered the cinema, too; and if he might have been faintly surprised to learn that the British Board of Film Censors considered his scandalous libertine, Don Giovanni, as suitable entertainment for children he would, at the same time, have been interested and flattered to know that his work has been adapted to a medium which would undoubtedly have appealed to a man of his temperament. Da Ponte's association with Mozart was not his only title to fame; his activities as a teacher and impresario in America were at least of equal importance, and it was his lot to be connected with many of the outstanding personalities of his epoch.

This is the story of da Ponte's life, not an analysis of his work as a dramatist and poet. Those who wish to learn more about his dramatic technique and his importance in the history of operatic development will find this aspect of his work discussed very fully in Professor Dent's *Mozart's Operas*, in Saint-Foix's *Mozart*, and indeed in most serious studies of the composer's work. This book— the first biography of da Ponte to be published in England—is not a work for specialists, but rather an attempt to weave an eighteenth-century tapestry, with da Ponte as the central figure, for the general public.

Those who have read da Ponte's *Memoirs* will find that the account which I have written of his life often differs very considerably from that which he gave himself. Da Ponte had his own reasons for concealing or altering certain facts about his past; in addition, he wrote his *Memoirs* in extreme old age, when his memory was not always reliable. I have attempted to verify and, if necessary, correct his statements whenever possible. I should also like to point out that all the conversations in this book are translations either from da Ponte's *Memoirs*, or from other contemporary sources, and not the products of my imagination.

I should like to acknowledge, first and foremost, my debt to two scholars, one Italian and one American, who have done more to elucidate details of da Ponte's life in their respective countries than any others: Fausto Nicolini, and the late Arthur Livingston. I should also like to express my gratitude to the American translator of da Ponte's *Memoirs*, Miss Elizabeth Abbott of New York, for her great kindness and help, and for her permission to reproduce a portrait of da Ponte by N. Monachesi and a print of the Italian Opera House in New York. I should like to thank Miss Fannie Ratchford, of the Rare Book Collections, University of Texas, for permission to reproduce a copy of one of da Ponte's manuscripts; the Directors of the Museo Civico Correr, Venice, for permission to reproduce two paintings in the Palazzo Rezzonico; the Directors of the Oesterreichische Nationalbibliothek, Vienna, for the reproduction of three prints; Harry R. Beard, for permission to reproduce two prints from his Theatre Collection; Messrs Macmillan for permission to quote from Emily Anderson's translation of *The Letters of Mozart and his Family*; the staff of the Venetian State Archives for their courtesy and help; the staff of the London Library; and the Hon. Mrs Slade, Mary Hamersley, and Jenifer and Felix Graham-Jones, who have all been of great assistance to me in various ways.

A.F.

PROLOGUE

THE date was 20th August, 1838, the scene was New York, and the occasion was a funeral. A number of distinguished people, representatives of both the social and the academic worlds of the city, had assembled to pay their last respects to the Professor of Italian Literature at Columbia College, who had died three days earlier. As funerals go, this was not a tragic one; the professor had died in his ninetieth year of old age, and had enjoyed a long, happy and successful career. He had been a popular and respected citizen of New York, and his last rites were performed with suitable pomp and ceremony; it was even rumoured that a monument was to be erected in his memory.

If they thought of the deceased at all—for on such occasions even the most devout mind is inclined to stray—the mourners probably remembered him as a scholarly old gentleman with a mane of long white hair, with dark, piercing eyes, and with a face which was still remarkably handsome and striking, in spite of his extreme old age and the loss of all his teeth. He had looked patriarchal, like some ancient and inspired prophet. In character, he had been a man of strong enthusiasms and in his youth, it was rumoured, of strong passions. His courtly, old-fashioned manners had impressed the Americans almost as much as his energy, his intellectual alertness, and his vigour. As they assembled in his house in Spring Street before the ceremony, the mourners thought of him as a typical European gentleman of the old school. He had retained all his faculties till the very end, and had even written a couple of sonnets to his doctor on the day before he died.

For the professor had been a poet—a poet of some standing in his own country, it was understood. Although he had been an American citizen for almost a quarter of a century, he had been born in Italy, and had latterly devoted all his considerable energy to promoting the knowledge of his native tongue and encouraging a love for Italian literature and music in the States. He had been remarkably successful in so doing: he boasted that he had had over two thousand American pupils; he had been largely instrumental in introducing Italian opera to America, and had been responsible for the building of the first Opera House in New York. Many of his former pupils, now eminent men in their own right, came to pay their last respects to the teacher who had introduced them to the beauties of European literature and art, and whose extraordinary personality had created an impression which they were never to forget.

As they listened to the strains of Allegri's *Miserere* in the Catholic Cathedral in New York, the mourners thought of the long life which had just ended, and of the many and varied events which must have occurred in it. Indeed, the professor had been most communicative about his past although, it was suspected, he had been inclined to embroider on it a good deal in his old age. He used to boast, for example, that Metastasio had praised his poems; that he had known Mozart well, that he had even written the words for some of his operas; that he had been on intimate terms with the Emperor of Austria; and he had even said (here the mourners' voices dropped to a whisper) that he had been friendly with Casanova. . . .

Those who had learned sufficient Italian to read the professor's *Memoirs*, which had been published in New York some years earlier, confirmed that all this information was in fact to be found in them, and hinted at a good many other strange stories about their teacher as well. Certainly, some very odd rumours had circulated about him, but they had probably been spread by his jealous and unscrupulous compatriots—Italians always loved gossip and intrigue. It had been said, for instance, that the old man had once been a priest of the Catholic Church—but how could that possibly have been true? Everyone knew that he had been a respectable married man; some people even remembered his wife, who had died some years previously; his children were well-known citizens of New York, and had married into some of the best American families. . . . And yet, and yet. . . . Travellers from Europe had sometimes addressed him as *Abate*. . . .

The mourners quickly changed the subject; it was not right to harbour such thoughts about a man whose body was even now about to be committed to the ground. Instead, while they waited for the end of the long funeral procession to reach the cemetery, they discussed the events of the day in undertones. The young Queen of England's coronation, for instance, details of which were only just reaching the States. . . . A fascinating new novel, *Oliver Twist*, which was being serialised in one of the newspapers. . . . The steam experiment—the *Great Western* had just sailed for Europe with many passengers on board. . . . The Russian menace—a Russian 'plot' to partition France had just been exposed . . . . it was in all the newspapers. . . . Paris and Lyons were to be made into model republics, 'Great Britain must be content with Calais and Boulogne', and as to the French—'all the discontented might join the Emperor of Russia's army to go and civilize the Barbarians in Asia. . .'. What an idea! Really, peaceful co-operation with a nation such as Russia was impossible. The mourners shook their heads gravely: 'Ah, yes, there's no doubt about it', they said. 'We live in difficult times, very difficult times.' The old man now being buried had been born in a happier age. . . .

He had certainly been born in a different age, almost in a different world. In the year of his birth—1749—America was a British colony, Columbia College had not been founded, and George Washington was a school-boy; when he died his own country—Venice—had long ceased to exist as an independent state, and had become an Austrian possession. The face of Europe had changed in his life-time, had changed out of all recognition. He had seen the fall of the French monarchy, and its restoration; he had seen the end of the Holy Roman Empire; he had seen the establishment of Holland and Belgium as independent states, and the emergence of Russia as a Western European power. In his lifetime there had been great rulers in Europe—Maria-Theresa, Frederick the Great, Catharine of Russia; there had been insignificant ones, too: George II of England, Francis II of Austria, Louis-Philippe . . .

In the world of art, the professor's life had spanned the gap between the lives of Johann Sebastian Bach and Max Bruch, between Rameau and Offenbach, between Gainsborough and Degas, between

Laurence Sterne and Jules Verne. In his lifetime Europe had witnessed the birth and death of Goethe, Napoleon, Beethoven, Walter Scott, Jeremy Bentham. . . . When he was born Voltaire and Rousseau were changing the whole basis of European thought; when he died Karl Marx was a young man of twenty. Although the professor had known many people who had been born in the seventeenth century, he himself had lived to travel by railway and to have his portrait painted by the inventor of the Morse code. The Americans who stood around his grave in the Roman Catholic Cemetery in New York can have had scarcely any idea of the Europe of his youth, of the changes he had lived through, and of the European cities he had known; they had no inkling at all of the emotions he had felt, the passions that had ruled him, the adventures he had experienced, and the joys and sorrows which had fallen to his lot.

In fact, as the mourners deposited an enormous laurel wreath on the freshly-covered grave of their colleague and teacher, as they walked away from the cemetery, thankful that the long, pompous ceremony was over at last and that they no longer had to talk in whispers, they began to think how very little they did know about the man who had just died—scarcely anything, in fact, except that by birth he was an Italian, by faith a Catholic, by vocation a teacher, and that his name was Lorenzo da Ponte. Had they but known it, even this information was inaccurate. They knew nothing about him at all—they did not even know his real name.

PART I

VENICE

'In Venice they do let Heaven see the pranks
They dare not show their husbands; their best conscience
Is not to leave undone, but keep unknown.'

SHAKESPEARE : *Othello*

CHAPTER I

THE STUDENT

I

WHERE the fertile Venetian plain begins to slope upwards to the Dolomites, a little old fortress town guards one of the most important passes through the mountains into Austria. For centuries Ceneda, this solitary Venetian outpost, kept watch on the gateway to the North, through which an aggressor might so easily have penetrated to the glittering, tempting prize of Venice on the Adriatic. Ancient, now crumbling fortifications with little Alpine cyclamen growing in their shade, straggle up the foothills of the mountains; but the Southern gateway of the town is already on the fringe of the plain, and the rich vineyards for which the region is famous, lie around it.

The little town of Ceneda waited a long time for its chance to defend the great Venetian Republic; but when the chance came the Republic was no more, and Venice formed part of an united Italy. At this spot, on 4th November, 1918, Austrian forces were defeated in battle by the Italians, and to commemorate this great victory the name of Ceneda was changed to Vittorio Veneto. Today a flourishing small modern town of this name has grown up beyond the walls of the old town, but Ceneda has retained its ancient character and, locally, its ancient name; tradition and custom die hard, and it is easier to choose a new name than to become used to it.

Ceneda changed its name; one of its most remarkable citizens changed his name too. On 10th March, 1749, a child who was to become known to the world as Lorenzo da Ponte was born in the little town's ghetto. His father, Geremia Conegliano, and his mother, Rachele, were both Jews; this child, their first, was given the name of Emanuele.

The Conegliano family was fairly well-known in Northern Italy;

it probably originated in the town of the same name which lies a few miles away from Ceneda. The family had produced a number of distinguished scholars in the past, notably a Dr Israel Conegliano, physician and statesman, who played an important part in Venetian-Turkish diplomatic relations at the end of the seventeenth century; he was rewarded for his services by being exempted from the severe Venetian anti-semitic regulations. Geremia Conegliano, however, belonged to a less successful branch of the family, the members of which were artisans rather than professional men. He himself was a tanner by trade, lived on a very modest scale, and had no pretensions to intellectualism. Indeed, Ceneda was very far from being an intellectual centre; it was little more than a village.

When Emanuele Conegliano was five years old his mother died, leaving him and two younger brothers, Baruch and Anania. It is never easy for a widower to look after small children, especially if he has to earn the money to support them at the same time, and Geremia Conegliano made no attempt whatever to solve this problem. The children ran wild, played in the streets of Ceneda, and climbed the beautiful mountains which rise up majestically towards Pieve di Cadore, the birthplace of Titian, not far away. By the time he was eleven years old Emanuele could scarcely read or write, and at last his father decided that he must do something about his boys' education. He engaged a tutor to teach his eldest son Latin and, feeling he had done his duty, awaited results. To his intense irritation, there were none. Everyone in Ceneda agreed that Emanuele was a bright lad, but he nevertheless appeared to be quite incapable of learning anything at all.

One day Geremia Conegliano decided to attend one of his son's lessons and find out for himself why the boy was making so little progress. He soon discovered the reason. The tutor whom he had engaged, a peasant turned schoolmaster, had his own method of teaching; he gave his pupil a copy of a Latin grammar, and encouraged him to study it by means of vigorous slaps and hard punches. Geremia dealt with this situation promptly and realistically; he seized his son's tutor by the hair, threw him down the stairs, and threw his inkstand and books after him.

After this incident no further effort seems to have been made to engage a new tutor, or to provide for the boys' education in any other way. Emanuele admitted in after years that he had suffered a good deal from his father's lack of interest in him. He had acquired the reputation amongst his father's friends of being the clever one of the family; but the other boys in the village, who were all better-educated than he was and knew it, jeered at him with the eternal cruelty of school-boys, and nicknamed him the 'clever dunce'.

The truth of the matter was that Geremia Conegliano was far too preoccupied with his own personal affairs at that time to think much about the welfare of his little boys. He was over forty, and had fallen in love with a girl of sixteen. To complicate matters still further, the girl, Orsola Pasqua Paietta, was a Christian. There was only one way out of this difficulty, and Geremia Conegliano decided to take it: on 29th August, 1763, he and his three sons were baptised into the Catholic faith. The ceremony took place with much pomp in the baroque cathedral of Ceneda, and was performed by Monsignor Lorenzo da Ponte, the Bishop. As was the custom in such cases, the converts took the name of their sponsor; Geremia Conegliano became Gaspare da Ponte, the eldest son, Emanuele, took the bishop's Christian name as well and became Lorenzo da Ponte, and his younger brothers, Baruch and Anania, became Girolamo and Luigi respectively. A fortnight later the newly-baptised Gaspare da Ponte married Orsola Pasqua Paietta who, in the course of time, was to bear him no less than three more sons and seven daughters.

At the time of his conversion to Christianity Lorenzo da Ponte, as he was always to be called from that time on, was fourteen years old. The step which his father had taken—in all probability without even discussing it with his children—was one of the most important events in Lorenzo's whole life. He seems to have accepted his conversion with equanimity, and almost never again referred to his Jewish origins or to his old name. But however hard he might himself try to forget his childhood in the ghetto, there were always other people to remind him of it. Throughout his life, wherever he went, rumours about his birth followed him, and were used by his enemies to annoy him whenever possible.

With his conversion and his father's second marriage, Lorenzo's life changed very fundamentally and, on the whole, for the better.

The acquisition of a stepmother was a mixed blessing, but the fact that the Bishop of Ceneda had become his sponsor and patron was a great asset, and now that he was a Christian new possibilities in education were open to him.

At fourteen Lorenzo was a quick-witted, intelligent boy, full of intellectual curiosity, but with no education whatsoever. He was intelligent enough to realise his ignorance, and had tried to do what he could himself to make up for his father's lack of interest. His efforts had not been altogether unsuccessful, nor were they without significance for his future career. One day, rummaging in an attic, he came across a pile of old books. His quick, young mind was starved of intellectual food, and he read the dusty volumes with avidity; amongst them he found several volumes of poetry. In adolescence, when minds are receptive to every new impression, and when everything seems a great discovery, it is, above all, the discoveries which one makes oneself which leave the deepest marks. No matter if, later on, the idols of our 'teens turn out to be banal commonplaces—something of the first impression remains, and the excitement never quite leaves us in after years. Lorenzo da Ponte's discovery was the poet Metastasio, the greatest librettist of all Europe, Caesarean Poet to the Holy Roman Empire, and at that time at the height of his powers and of his fame. Lorenzo read and re-read his works, and they opened up new worlds for him. If at that time, the village boy reading Metastasio's poetry in his father's attic had been told that one day he would meet the author in person, and that he would, perhaps, do more than anyone else to make that poet's libretti seem outmoded and to banish them from the stage for ever, he would scarcely have believed it; but as he turned the dusty pages and read the poetry which 'gave him the sensation of music', he was unwittingly laying the foundations for the destruction of that poetry, which he himself was to help achieve.

Lorenzo realised, nevertheless, that reading poetry alone in an attic was not, in itself, an education, and that he needed further advice and assistance. In those days schools were not only almost entirely in the hands of the Church, but an ecclesiastical education was also the surest—indeed, almost the only—way in which an intelligent boy of humble origins could rise in the world. Lorenzo was ambitious, and he therefore decided to apply to his patron, the bishop, for help. Monsignor Lorenzo da Ponte took a kindly interest in the Jewish family which he had baptised, and he also realised that all the three da Ponte boys were well above average in intelligence. He not only agreed to take his namesake Lorenzo and the younger brother Girolamo into his seminary, but even offered to pay for their maintenance himself. It thus came about that Lorenzo and his brother entered the old seminary of Ceneda, which had been founded in the sixteenth century by Bishop Mocenigo, a member of an illustrious family of Venetian patricians. Lorenzo remained at the seminary for about five years, during which time he learned Latin, read the great Italian poets, began to write poetry himself, made a friend he was to keep all his life, and fell in love for the first time.

II

It was decided by his father that Lorenzo should become a priest although, as he himself remarked in later years, such a calling was completely opposed to his temperament and character; his tastes inclined him to quite different studies. But his father and, no doubt, the worthy bishop too, did not take Lorenzo's temperament and inclinations into account. In those days education for the priesthood meant, above all, the study of Latin. At the seminary in Ceneda Latin was well taught—Lorenzo remained a fine Latin scholar to the end of his life—but every other subject, including Italian, was neglected. 'When I was seventeen', da Ponte wrote many years later, 'although I was able to compose a long oration and perhaps fifty not inelegant verses in Latin in half a day, I could not write a letter of a few lines in my own language without making a dozen mistakes.' Fortunately this situation was remedied by the arrival at the seminary of a new professor. The Abbé Cagliari was a young man, full of enthusiasm, and with the gift for passing it on to others. He came to Ceneda from the famous University of Padua, where Italian litera-ture was as much appreciated as the Classics, and it was he who first introduced da Ponte to Dante and Petrarch, Tasso and Ariosto, to that Italian literature which was to be his only true and lasting passion throughout his life, and with enthusiasm for which Lorenzo

—like the Abbé Cagliari—was to inspire so many pupils, both in Europe and America.

At this time da Ponte began to write poetry himself, fired by the example of another student at the seminary, Michele Colombo, with whom he was to maintain a close friendship for the rest of his life. Colombo was two years older than da Ponte, and was eventually to die only two months before his friend. Although in later years they met very rarely, they corresponded with each other frequently, and some seventy-odd years later da Ponte was to dedicate to the friend of his school-days a poem entitled *Storia Americana, ossia Il Lamento di Lorenzo da Ponte quasi nonagenario al nonagenario Michele Colombo.*

Colombo, unlike da Ponte, had received an excellent grounding, both in Italian and in Latin, before he entered the seminary, and by the time Lorenzo met him he was writing verse in both languages. He it was who urged da Ponte to try his hand at poetry too, who laughed at his friend's first crude efforts, and who was the first to praise him later on, when his verse was becoming more practised.

Apart from having a common interest in poetry, the two friends were both in love with the same girl, Pierina Raccanelli. Sixty-five years later da Ponte still remembered the sonnet which Colombo wrote for him at the time of this first love-affair, and Colombo, when he was almost eighty, used to think with nostalgia of his youthful escapades with da Ponte in Ceneda.

In about 1768 da Ponte's studies were interrupted by a serious illness which lasted over six months, and in July of that year his patron, Monsignor Lorenzo da Ponte, died. As the bishop had been paying for Lorenzo's education, for that of his brother Girolamo and also, apparently, helping the rest of the family financially as well, his death was a real calamity. Lorenzo was obliged to sell the books which he had been acquiring—not always in a strictly honest way— and even some of his clothes in order to help support his family. 'In addition', he remembered in after years, 'the state of poverty into which my family was plunged made me renounce the hand of a noble and pretty girl, whom I loved tenderly, and made me embrace a calling totally opposed to my temperament, my character, my principles and my studies, thus opening the door to a thousand strange happenings and dangers, which the envy, hypocrisy and malice of my enemies took advantage of for more than twenty years. Allow me, gentle reader, to draw a veil of mystery over this painful moment in my life, so that my pen may be spared the expression of untimely remorse by a heart which, in spite of everything, I revere and will never cease to revere.' This rather enigmatic and, alas! typical passage in da Ponte's *Memoirs* presumably refers to the fact that, in November 1770, he took minor orders. It was not a fact to which he liked to draw attention in later years.

About a year after the bishop's death, thanks to the good offices of a canon of Ceneda cathedral, da Ponte and his two brothers were able to enter the seminary at Portogruaro, a small town not far from Ceneda. During his first year at Portogruaro da Ponte read philosophy and mathematics, and continued to study the Italian poets, of whom Petrarch was his idol. He also wrote a good deal of poetry himself, and was apparently a stern self-critic, for over two thousand lines which he considered unsatisfactory were subsequently burnt. Towards the end of his first year in Portogruaro he wrote a poem in praise of St Louis, which he recited in public. The poem pleased the Bishop of Concordia and, as a result, da Ponte was offered a post as instructor at the seminary. He was twenty-one years old and, as he admitted later, still had a great deal to learn himself; nevertheless, he accepted the appointment, and soon began teaching some thirty young men who had been, until then, his fellow students. It cannot have been an easy task, but da Ponte must have acquitted himself reasonably well, for within a year he was promoted, and in 1772 he was appointed Vice-rector of the seminary. His duties included supervising discipline, giving the address at the beginning of the school year, conducting the public debate at the end of it, and teaching Italian to fifty-two of the best students. It was not unnatural that some of the more seasoned instructors at the seminary should view his swift promotion with mistrust and displeasure; he was criticised by them, probably with some justice, for not having studied mathematics and physics sufficiently—it is surprising that he should have found time to study them at all. But his reputation as a poet was growing, and he was especially praised for a dithyramb on scents, 'which,' he said, 'was thought to show a flash of Redi's fire'.

It was a peaceful, scholarly life—but it was not to last very long.

It seems that the brothers had already visited Venice in 1771, when they were recovering from an attack of malaria, and Lorenzo may have gone there again during subsequent vacations. Once he had seen 'the permanent fancy-dress ball that was Venice' he was not to be happy in Portogruaro much longer. He says himself that he decided to leave the seminary because of the intrigues and jealousies of his colleagues; it may have been so, but one of da Ponte's least admirable characteristics, and one which was to become more and more pronounced as he grew older, was his sense of persecution. He always liked to think that he was an innocent victim, surrounded by jealous and vindictive enemies; although no doubt this was sometimes true, more often than not his enemies and their machinations existed only in his own imagination. It seems much more likely that, having once tasted the pleasures of Venice, he was hungry for more. In any case 'after exercising patience with his enemies for two years', as he put it, he left the seminary. When he did so he was twenty-four years old, handsome, intelligent, ardent and—for he had celebrated Mass for the first time in the spring of that year—a priest. With such qualifications he went to live in the most dissolute and sybaritic city in Europe.

CHAPTER II

THE PRIEST

I

BY the middle of the eighteenth century the Republic of Venice, which for over a thousand years had been one of the great states of Europe, was great no longer. It had lost almost all its possessions, its political, naval and commercial supremacy, and had already reached that stage of splendid decadence which great states experience before their final extinction. At a time when the rest of Europe was fermenting with new ideas and looking to the future, Venice was living in the past; in an age in which the rest of the civilised world was concerned with progress, the main concern of the Venetians was pleasure. The once awe-inspiring Lion of St Mark had become a lap-dog. Paralysed by their ancient, rigid traditions and surrounded by magnificent, decaying palaces, the Venetians refused to look beyond the limits of the lazy lagoons in which, like some splendid becalmed galleon, the wonderful city seemed to float.

The rest of Europe might be discussing the new ideas of Rousseau, Voltaire or Kant; the Venetians discussed the rivalry between three convents, each aspiring to provide a mistress for a newly-arrived nuncio. While Frederick the Great was welding Prussia into a military power, the workmen employed in Venice's once-famous arsenal spent their time in idleness, drinking the unlimited wine which flowed from a fountain for their benefit, and only condescending to work occasionally on rush jobs for which their pay was doubled. Whereas the rest of Europe was beginning to take an interest in mankind, the Venetians were only interested in themselves. When Rousseau wrote 'Man is born free, but everywhere he is in chains' he spoke for the new age: but Rousseau's ideas penetrated to Venice slowly, and the Venetians, although they had chains like everyone else, did not find them irksome. The seeds of the French Revolution might be germinating in fertile soil, all over the civilised world men were awakening to the new ideas of democracy, of equality and freedom: but the ancient patrician that was Venice— very civilised, very cultured, very sensual—was unaware of, or chose to ignore, the signs of the times. The Venetians were too occupied with the rivalry between Goldoni and Carlo Gozzi, they were too busy attending the concerts at the *Mendicanti* or the *Pietà* to think of anything else. Too busy or perhaps, sensing that the end of the old world—their world—was at hand, the Venetians realised their impotence against the new order, and unconsciously decided to make the most of their last years of independence, to squeeze the last drop of pleasure out of life before the stern realities of the nineteenth century banished frivolity for good and all. The Republic of Venice was determined to die as elegantly and as aristocratically as it had lived.

In Venice nothing was taken very seriously, nothing was very deep. The Venetians themselves summed up their way of life in their saying: *La mattina una messeta, l'apodisnar una basseta, e la sera una donneta*—'A little Mass in the morning, a little gamble in the afternoon, and a little lady in the evening'. Although they were passionate, the Venetians reserved their passion for the trivialities of life; they had no ardour for ideas, for causes, for reforms. Indeed, after a thousand years of independence and security during the course of which only one attempt was made—by Charlemagne—to invade their Republic, the Venetians had very little left of that divine discontent which breeds great innovators and reformers. Much of the superficiality of eighteenth-century Venice can be explained by the fact that Venice had never known foreign domination; that she was governed by a relatively benign oligarchy; that she was rich, and had one of the highest standards of living in eighteenth-century Europe; and that the Venetians themselves were of a particularly sunny and happy temperament. If, in consequence, there was a certain boredom and emptiness, a certain lack of that spiritual anguish and growth which is to be found in less fortunate states, the pleasantness of life and the sense of security probably amply compensated for the lack of depth of feeling. Eighteenth-century Venice produced no El Greco, no

Beethoven, no Tolstoy, but it produced countless happy men. Baretti advised foreign tourists that they would be well received by the Venetians only if they were known to be prudent and joyous men; 'I say *joyous*', he explained, 'because without such a quality nobody is welcome to a Venetian.'

If, therefore, the Venetians were conscious of their approaching end, they were not depressed by it. It was a city of extravagances. Carnival reigned for six months out of twelve, and during carnival the only thing that was sacred was the anonymity of masks. Members of the government would hastily remove their masks and dominos in the ante-rooms of the Senate if some absolutely unavoidable duty called for their presence there, and even priests and monks were no exception to the general rule. 'Curates, they say, would be displeased with their parishioners and the archbishop with his clergy, if they did not have a mask in their hand or on their nose', a visiting Frenchmen recorded. The Venetians boasted that they burnt more wax for one night's illuminations than the rest of Italy burnt in a year and, at a time when Paris had only three permanent theatres, there were seven in Venice. It was a selfish, pleasure-loving and debauched city, a city of egoists and sybarites whose only thought was the gratification of their senses, and the foreigners who flocked to the pleasure-resort of Europe recorded their impressions with a mixture of fascination and disapproval.

What seemed to impress visitors most was not the amazing beauty of the city, not the fantastic wealth and splendour with which its citizens were surrounded, not the unique form of government, but Venetian morals—or rather, the lack of them. This was nothing new, Roger Ascham, preceptor to Queen Elizabeth, had noticed it already in the sixteenth century. 'I was once in Italie myselfe', he wrote, 'but thanke God my abode there was but nine days: and yet I sawe in that little tyme, in one citie, more libertie to sinne than ever I heard tell of in our noble citie of London in nine years.' Since Roger Ascham's time the immorality of the decadent republic had become a by-word throughout Europe, and travellers approached the city much as provincial business-men on their first visit to Paris today approach Montmartre. Venice lived up to its reputation better than Montmartre; a French visitor remarked that one should not believe all the ill that was said about Venetian morals, but only most of it, and even the most sophisticated, jaded and depraved tastes were not disappointed by what Venice had to offer.

English travellers, in particular, were deeply shocked by the fact that almost all married women with social pretensions in Venice had either an official lover or a *cavaliere servente*, though their relationship with the latter was often platonic, an eighteenth-century variation of the medieval *amour courtois*; Venetians did their best to try to explain the advantages and the subtleties of this particular Venetian speciality to visiting Britons, and were surprised when they were greeted with a stony and disapproving stare. Their attempts to excuse the loose morals of Venetian women did not fare much better; in former times, they assured visitors, the courtesans were a useful class of citizens, whose arms were always open to the wealthy, whether they were young or old, but by the 1760's this was unfortunately no longer the case—courtesans had become the very dregs, so that Venetian gentlemen were forced to seek from amateurs what the professionals had formerly provided. Nevertheless, in spite of their compatriots' opinion of them, the Venetian courtesans were world-famous, and almost every traveller had tales to tell of their beauty, their wealth, and their accomplishments. They could be caustic, too; when Jean-Jacques Rousseau had a humiliating experience with one of them she finally advised him to 'leave the ladies alone and stick to mathematics'. One of their precepts was that people should get to know each other before making love, so that they would only grant their favours at a second meeting—thus incidentally earning a double fee. The courtesans' humbler sisters, the prostitutes, had an excellent custom of hanging their portraits outside their houses, so that prospective clients could choose the type which most appealed to them.

Anything was permissible in Venice, except criticism of the laws and customs of the Republic; foreign visitors, who had heard bloodcurdling and no doubt exaggerated tales about the terrible Council of Three, about the swift and secret execution of justice which awaited those who offended it and who were led across the Bridge of Sighs to their doom, had little inclination to criticise anything. Indeed they found so much to praise that it was not difficult to keep quiet about what little they saw of the seamy side of the Republic.

The first sight of Venice was something never to be forgotten—and in the eighteenth century tourists were spared the modern approach to the city past the gas-works and the railway station, and had to travel by boat, either from Mestre, or better still, from Padua, in which case they passed the fabulous Palladian villas on the banks of the Brenta. On their arrival they were dazzled by the illuminations, entranced by the theatres, amazed at the wealth, and astounded by the unique construction of the city and its fascinating acquatic life. Their first impressions had not been spoilt by innumerable photographs and films, and what they saw in Venice exceeded their wildest dreams.

When they had recovered from the first impact which the city made upon them and could view the scene in more detail, the first thing that struck travellers usually was the beauty of the Venetian women. 'Venice was the paradise of women', one visitor wrote nostalgically in his old age, 'and the Venetian women worthy of a paradise at least of Mahomet's. They were perfect Houri; and the Venetian dialect, spoken by a lovely woman, is the softest and most delicious music in the world to him whom she favours. In short, a Venetian woman in her zindale dress well answers young Mirable's description in the play of the Inconstant, "Give me the plump Venetian, who smiles upon me like the glowing sun, and meets my lips like sparkling wine; her person shining as the glass, her spirit like the foaming liquor".'

Jean-Jacques Rousseau was, above all, impressed by the music, but he too remarked 'as for women, it is not in a city like Venice that a man abstains from them'. Nor did he—for he even went so far as to buy a little girl of about twelve from her mother with the intention of sharing her with a friend. It is true that in the end his relationship with her remained fraternal in spite of his original intentions, but he records that such commercial transactions were not at all uncommon in the Republic.

Not all travellers, however, fell under the spell of Venetian women. Goethe, who visited the Republic in 1786, devoted his attention to art, and remained impervious to the city's less intellectual attractions. He found the theatres interesting, the marine fauna even more so, but it is obvious that the spirit of the city and of her people was really alien to him. 'Here, however, I could not live', he wrote during his stay there, 'nor indeed in any place where I had nothing to occupy my mind.' And truly, though eighteenth-century Venice had many gifts to offer to her visitors, serious thought and intellectual stimuli were not among them.

Most visitors were agreed on the decadence of Venice; but it was a splendid and joyous decadence, with nothing shabby or seedy about it. Venice was frivolous, but happy. It contributed little or nothing to eighteenth-century philosophy and thought; but in a century which, in spite of many men of artistic genius, was more remarkable for philosophers and generals than for artists, it did contribute something to art. Eighteenth-century Venetian art was not art of the greatest kind—its intellectual background was too materialistic and negative for that—but it is art without which the world would be a sadder place, and it is all that remains to us of that vanished age. Through the eyes of Piazzetta, of Guardi, of Pietro Longhi, of Canaletto, we can still catch a glimpse of the Venice which da Ponte knew, of a world that has almost nothing in common with our own, and through the eyes of its artists we see that world at its very best.

There was, however, one art in which eighteenth-century Venice really excelled. With the possible exception of Naples, Venice was undoubtedly the most musical city in Italy, perhaps in Europe. And music in Venice was not an intellectual cult, reserved for the aristocracy and the intelligentsia, but a prime necessity for the whole population, for rich and poor alike. 'Music in Italy costs so little', says Rousseau, 'that it is not worth while for anyone who is fond of it to deprive himself of it', and the Venetians certainly did not do so.

The gondoliers, that considerable and very influential group of men—tough, quick-witted, discreet, and essential to almost every Venetian activity, whether it was a business deal or a love affair—not only sang at their work, but were admitted free to any empty seats in the theatres and opera-houses. They made good use of this privilege, showed their approval with boisterous applause, and their disapproval by pelting the stage with rubbish, and it was known that their attitude could make or break an opera or a play. Goldoni

realised this, and wrote many of his plays not only about them, but
for them.

The part-songs of the gondoliers thrilled every foreign visitor,
but by the time Goethe went there in 1786 the art was already
apparently beginning to die out. 'This evening I bespoke the celebrated song of the mariners', he wrote, 'who chaunt Tasso and
Ariosto to melodies of their own. This must actually be ordered, as
it is not to be heard as a thing of course, but rather belongs to the
half-forgotten traditions of former times. I entered a gondola by
moonlight, with one singer before and the other behind me. They
sing their song, taking up the verses alternatively. The melody, which
we know from Rousseau, is of a middle kind, between choral and
recitative, maintaining throughout the same cadence, without any
fixed time. The modulation is also uniform, only varying with a sort
of declamation both tone and measure, according to the subject of the
verse.' However, those who visited Venice some twenty years earlier
than Goethe record that the gondoliers' song was an integral part of
Venetian life, and by no means a forgotten tradition that had to be
artificially revived for the benefit of enquiring and intellectual tourists.

Not only the gondoliers, but the street singers and ordinary people
sang most of the time, and sang well. Dr Burney's comments on
Venetian street musicians are worth quoting, for they were written
by a learned and fastidious professional musician who had heard
almost all the great performers of his day, and was not the man to
suffer musical fools gladly. 'The first music which I heard here was
in the street', he wrote, 'immediately on my arrival, performed by
an itinerant band of two fiddles, a violoncello, and a voice, who,
though as unnoticed here as small-coalmen or oyster-women in
England, performed so well, that in any other country of Europe
they would not only have excited attention, but have acquired
applause, which they justly merited. These two violins played difficult passages very neatly, the base stopped well in tune, and the
voice, which was a woman's, was well toned, and had several
essentials belonging to that of a good singer, such as compass, shake,
and volubility; but I shall not mention all the performances of this
kind which I met with here; as they were so numerous that the
repetition would be tiresome.'

The operatic tradition in Venice—the first city in Europe to possess a public opera house, which was established there in 1637—was of course very strong. When Casanova for a time earned his living as a violinist at the San Samuele theatre, there were six other theatres in Venice—two usually showed *opera seria*, two for *opera buffa*, and three for comedy. The number of opera houses varied, but was always relatively high, and another professional foreign critic—Michael Kelly, the singer—was very favourably impressed with the standard of performance in them, if not with the behaviour of Venetian audiences.

Indeed, Venetian audiences were far from ideal, in spite of their love for opera. It was the custom to talk, eat, drink, make love and gamble during the performances, and only when the principal singers came forward to sing their grand arias did the audience turn its attention to the stage. Jean-Jacques Rousseau was even obliged to creep away from the box of his noisy friends and find another seat where he could listen to the music in peace. Indeed, the Venetians showed both their approval and their disapproval with such a deafening din that it was not always clear to the performers which was meant—unless, of course, they were pelted with rubbish. The audience's lack of attention can partly be accounted for by the lack of dramatic cohesion in the operas of the day. There were many, too, who, like Casanova, went to the opera 'much more in order to quizz the actresses than to listen to the music'.

Perhaps the most famous and the most curious musical institutions in Venice were the four conservatories or orphanages—the *Pietà*, the *Mendicanti*, the *Incurabili* and the *Ospedaletto*. Originally these had been charitable institutions, taking in foundlings and orphans of the female sex, and giving them a complete musical education, both vocal and instrumental. But with such teachers as Porpora, Jommelli, Domenico Scarlatti, Hasse, Galuppi and Sacchini, the orphanages became less charitable than artistic institutions, and eventually girls who were not orphans but who simply wished to have a musical education were admitted to them. The standard of performance at these schools was extremely high, and although now one school would be the foremost and now another, according to the merits of the various teachers in charge, the four schools were always much

Venice with the Lagoons frozen [1788]
By an anonymous Venetian painter. [*from The Palazzo Rezzonico*]

The Ridotto, Venice. School of Pietro Longhi

on the same level. In the 1770's, in Dr Burney's day, for instance, the *Incurabili* directed by Galuppi—who had 'preserved all his fire and imagination from the chill blasts of Russia, whence he is lately returned'—and the *Ospedaletto*, directed by Sacchini, were pre-eminent; but a few years earlier the *Pietà* was considered the foremost school. It was at the *Pietà* that the Président de Brosses praised the instrumental playing, saying 'C'est là seulement qu'on entend ce premier coup d'archet si faussement vanté a l'opéra de Paris.' Concerts both of religious and of secular music were given regularly at these four schools, and all Venice went to hear them. Apart from the purely musical attractions, the girls themselves, playing every instrument, even double-basses and bassoons—'bref, il n'y a si gros instrument qui puisse leur faire peur'—were a very pleasing sight. They usually performed behind a grille—although this is not the case in Guardi's picture of one of their concerts—were dressed in a white habit with flowers in their hair, and although on closer inspection Rousseau found that many of them were pitted with small-pox or had some other physical defect, most visitors only had occasion to see them from a kindly distance. Most of the pupils of the musical schools married eventually, when they were given a dowry by the state, or else they taught the younger pupils.

When he visited the *Ospedaletto* Dr Burney was particularly struck by one of the singers, La Ferrarese, who 'sang very well, and had a very extraordinary compass of voice, as she was able to reach the highest E of our harpsichords, upon which she could dwell a considerable time, in a fair, natural voice'. La Ferrarese was later on to be very intimately connected with da Ponte, and to sing the part of Fiordiligi in the first performance of *Cosi fan Tutte* in Vienna.

In private houses, too, music played an important part. There was music at every party and for every occasion, and it formed an integral part of social life. However, unlike the custom in England, not every young lady was taught to play the harpsichord, for reasons expressed in very cogent terms by a contemporary Italian: 'We conceive that music is not an eligible study for our young ladies, and this for a very important consideration. Our climate quickens our sensibility in such a manner, that music affects us infinitely more than it does other nations. Let your imagination represent to you an

C

Italian lady, young and beautiful, with all that warmth of constitution peculiar to her country, arrayed in the thinnest silk favourable to the sultry season, sitting at her harpsichord, her fingers in busy search of the most delicate quavers, and languishing to a *Mi sento morii* of one of our most feeling composers! Where is the judicious parent who would wish to see his child in so dangerous a situation?' A far cry indeed from one of Jane Austen's characters who considered music as 'a very innocent diversion and perfectly compatible with the profession of a clergyman'. But perhaps in England it was different; 'Music may be cultivated in the soil of England without any danger', the Italian already quoted wrote sarcastically, 'because, like an exotic plant, it will never spread so as to prove hurtful by its luxuriancy, but we must rigidly lop it in Italy, where it grows naturally so fast, as to make us tremble at the balefulness of its influence.'

Church music in Venice was, of course, very highly developed. Monteverdi, who in the seventeenth century had been Master of Music at San Marco, had founded a great tradition. Almost every state function, whether it was ostensibly religious or purely secular, was accompanied by music, and in the splendid procession in which, on Ascension day, the Doge went in the *Bucentaur*, the golden state barge, for the symbolic marriage of Venice with the sea, there were 'several bands of music on board'. During Passion Week there were six orchestras in San Marco when High Mass was celebrated, and in every church in Venice there were magnificent choirs, trained by the foremost musicians of the day.

This, then, was Venice. 'A paradise for friars and whores' as the Venetian saying went; a paradise for adventurers, for artists and musicians, a city of contrasts and enigmas, as unique in its social life as in its geographical position. Debauched, indolent, frivolous, shallow—Venice was all this; yet, with a thousand years of grandeur behind her, she remained magnificent to the end.

II

When Lorenzo da Ponte arrived in Venice in 1773 the end was drawing near, and Venetian life had reached a climax of hectic dissipation and indulgence. Nothing—or almost nothing—was sacred, and it would have taken a stronger character than da Ponte's to have resisted the temptations which Venice so liberally offered to her citizens. The village boy from Ceneda was completely bedazzled by the splendour, by the elegance, by the luxury and by the sophistication of a city which still today, even in its decay, has the power to overwhelm those who see it for the first time with amazement and excitement.

Of course da Ponte fell in love in Venice—normal young men of twenty-four could not remain there for long without doing so; the febrile, sensuous atmosphere of the city was like a hot-house, forcing a prolific, exotic growth of amorous intrigue—and da Ponte was, in this respect, an extremely normal young man, in spite of his cassock. 'Being then in the prime of youth and, as everyone said, attractive, I allowed myself to be carried away by habits, opportunity and example, and gave myself up to the pleasures of the senses and to amusement', he confessed in later years, 'to the almost complete neglect of literature and study. I had conceived a violent passion for one of the most beautiful, but also one of the most capricious ladies of the capital. . . .'

The lady in question was Angiola Tiepolo, a member, albeit of an impoverished branch, of one of the oldest and most aristocratic Venetian families. Da Ponte had probably met her when he had visited Venice for a few days in the previous year; he was completely captivated by her fair fragility, her milk-and-roses complexion, her charm, and her feminine helplessness, and he probably gave up his excellent job at Portogruaro in order to be nearer her. However, appearances can be deceptive, as da Ponte soon discovered. Although she gave the impression of being a helpless little woman, Angiola was in fact nothing of the kind; she was domineering, capricious, fickle and bad-tempered. But da Ponte was so much in love with her, her physical charms held him so strongly, and her tastes accorded so well with his own, that although she made him suffer, he could not free himself from her. She was, probably, the only woman who truly made da Ponte suffer; she taught him a lesson, and after he had finally broken away from her he did not allow himself to make the same mistake again; from then on it was the women who suffered, not da Ponte.

One of da Ponte's favourite haunts in Venice was the *Caffé de' Letterati*. This was the meeting-place of the *Accademia dei Granelleschi*, a literary society founded by such men as the two Gozzi brothers, ostensibly as an attempt to reintroduce the pure Tuscan style of an earlier age into Italian literature, and to oppose new and, especially, foreign influences; in fact the society was principally concerned with harrying Carlo Goldoni, of whom Carlo Gozzi was the chief rival and enemy.

The story goes that Goldoni and Carlo Gozzi met one day in a bookshop, and that Goldoni, who had been suffering from Gozzi's bitter attacks on his plays for some time, told his critic that it was much easier to find fault with plays than to write them. Gozzi agreed that it was not difficult to find fault, but said that it would be even easier to write plays which would satisfy the thoughtless Venetians. He added contemptuously that he 'had a good mind to make all Venice run to see "The Tale of the Three Oranges".' Now 'The Tale of the Three Oranges' was the Venetian equivalent to 'Jack and the Beanstalk' or 'Puss in Boots', an old fairy-tale that every Venetian child learned in the nursery. Goldoni challenged Gozzi to carry out his boast, and when 'The Love of the Three Oranges' was first produced all Venice did indeed run to see it out of curiosity, and stayed to applaud it from sheer delight. What Gozzi had written was something not unlike our own pantomime, except that it was written by a man of genius and taste, and performed by one of the best companies of the day. It was a mixture of fairy-tale and satire, using some of the conventions and characters of the old *Commedia dell'Arte*, and introducing an attack on Goldoni and his works which delighted the Venetian audience.

A great deal of Gozzi's success was due to the talents, more especially those of improvisation, of Sacchi and his company of actors, and this is probably also one of the reasons why his plays, unlike those of Goldoni, have not stood the test of time. When Sacchi's company broke up half the effect of Gozzi's plays was lost; they were written too much for specific actors to be a success when played by a different troupe. However, when they first appeared they completely eclipsed those of Goldoni, and Gozzi became the darling of the Venetian public. Nowadays he is scarcely remembered

at all, although 'The Love of the Three Oranges' has been resur-
rected by the music of Prokofiev, and both Wagner ('The Fairies')
and Puccini ('Turandot') used Gozzi's tales as a basis for libretti.

Carlo Gozzi himself was a strange, gifted, and embittered man,
an eccentric and a reactionary. He came from a large and impoverished noble family which lived in an immense, decaying yet once
magnificent house. Surrounded by dirt, disorder, squealing children
and importunate creditors, most of the family wrote—Carlo Gozzi
himself, his elder brother Gasparo, and their aristocratic and imprac-
tical mother, to mention only the best-known members of the
family. Gasparo Gozzi was a satirist and a journalist of talent; he
founded, in 1762, the *Osservatore Veneto*, a weekly journal rather like
Addison's *Spectator*, and his pictures of Venetian life have worn better
than his brother Carlo's plays. Although much older than da Ponte
—he was born in 1713—Gasparo Gozzi befriended the young and
unknown poet, and later on was to use his considerable influence to
help him.

Although he made his début in literary circles at the *Caffé de'
Letterati* and made some influential friends, da Ponte did not spend
much time there; his love-affair with Angiola Tiepolo was, he
found, a full-time occupation. It was a stormy and not particularly
happy love-affair, and at one point da Ponte decided to leave Venice
in order to bring it to a conclusion. He did go away, but after a few
days without Angiola he found that he only desired her more
strongly. Abandoning his good intentions, he not only went back
to Venice, but also went to live in the house which his mistress
shared with her brother Girolamo. Girolamo Tiepolo was a particularly disreputable and unattractive character, and later on da
Ponte had good reason to regret his decision to live in his house.

One evening, when da Ponte was at the *Caffé de' Letterati*, masked
as everyone was during carnival, a gondolier came into the café and
beckoned to him to come outside. Thinking that his mistress had
sent her gondolier to fetch him as she sometimes did, da Ponte
followed the man without further thought, entered the waiting
gondola to which he was taken, and sat down beside the lady who
was inside it. The gondolier let fall the curtain over the door, and
left the occupants of the gondola in total darkness.

It was not long before da Ponte discovered that there had been some mistake. As he kissed the lady's hand he noticed that it was decidedly plumper than that of his mistress, and that the owner of it did not speak with a Venetian accent. The lady discovered the mistake at the same time, and was not unnaturally alarmed to find herself in such compromising proximity with a total stranger. Da Ponte was curious to find out more about her and, more particularly, whether she was attractive or not. He persuaded her that if she would consent to take some refreshment with him in the gondola he would then leave her without asking any more questions.

The gondolier went to fetch some ices for them, and soon returned, bringing a lantern with him. The light revealed da Ponte's companion to be a girl of sixteen of marvellous beauty, elegantly dressed and obviously of noble family. Da Ponte was not the man to let such an opportunity pass, and he 'said all the things one usually says to pretty women on such occasions'; but although the girl did not seem to be averse to his company, she refused to allow him to take her home, and would neither tell him her name nor where she lived. She hinted vaguely at some mystery concerning herself, and promised that, if possible, she would send her gondolier to the café to fetch da Ponte to her again before long. Then they parted.

Days passed, and da Ponte spent all his evenings at the café, but the mysterious beauty's gondolier did not reappear. Finally Lorenzo gave up hope of seeing her again, and left Venice for a few days. On his return he was told at the café that a gondolier had been enquiring for him, but had been told that he had gone away. Da Ponte was in despair; thinking he had lost the beautiful girl for ever, he regretfully turned his attention to Angiola once more. However, one day as he crossed the Piazza San Marco, he felt a tug at his coat sleeve: he turned round, and to his joy recognised the young girl's gondolier. He arranged another meeting.

When da Ponte entered the girl's gondola for the second time she gave orders that they should be taken to her house. When they were seated there the girl told him that her name was Matilda, that she was a Neapolitan, and that her father was the Duke of M——a. She then proceeded to tell him the story of her life—a story which, if not true, only an opera librettist could have invented.

Her mother, she said, had died when she was a child, and her father had remarried, choosing as his second wife a grocer's daughter, who turned out to be as cruel as any fairy-tale stepmother. Matilda was sent to a convent at Pisa, where she remained for six years, stoutly resisting the nuns' attempts to persuade her to take the veil. At the end of this time her stepmother reappeared, apparently a changed woman, and with every sign of affection promised Matilda that she could leave the convent on condition that she was a dutiful daughter to her father and agreed to marry the man he had chosen to be her husband. In those days there was nothing at all unusual in such a request; most marriages were arranged by the parents, and girls often did not meet their fiancés until their wedding-day. Matilda joyfully left the convent, returned to Naples and, under the strict supervision of her stepmother, preparations for the wedding went ahead.

All went well until the day came for Matilda to meet her future husband. To her horror he turned out to be a repulsive and aged brute, a 'walking corpse', a voluptuary who, in spite of his rank and fortune, had not been able to find a bride because of his 'physical and mental abnormalities'. The unfortunate girl gave a cry of horror at the sight of such a monster, and fell at her father's feet begging for mercy. At this point the wicked stepmother showed herself in her true colours once more, for at her orders Matilda was dragged away, half-fainting, and she was imprisoned in some gloomy dungeon.

How long she remained there, terrified and half-starved, she could not tell; she had almost lost hope of ever leaving her prison alive when, in the middle of the night, she received a mysterious visitor. The visitor turned out to be her faithful nurse, and she it was who engineered Matilda's escape. The nurse's son was at the door of the prison with a coach and horses, with money and a box of jewels; when they had said farewell to the nurse, Matilda and the young man drove away.

They travelled across Italy at breakneck speed, and finally arrived at Padua, which was Venetian territory. Even there they feared that they might be discovered by the wicked stepmother or her agents, and so they determined to push on to Venice, where the anonymity of masks afforded a safer refuge. In order to be safer still Matilda decided to disguise herself as a man, but on the way from Padua to Venice she attracted the attention of a young man who was travelling on the same boat, and he soon saw through her disguise. Her desire to conceal her sex aroused his curiosity, and he could only be persuaded not to give her away to the other passengers by a promise that she would tell him at least part of her story when they arrived in Venice. The young man turned out to be a nobleman of the Mocenigo family, Matilda was attracted to him, and he even proposed marriage to her. She was inclined to accept his proposal, but the young man was a gambler; he borrowed money from her which he subsequently lost at cards, and as a result came to see her less and less frequently. Matilda explained to da Ponte that her gondolier had mistaken him for this young man, and that their original meeting was due to this error.

The story would be fantastic enough if it were to end at this point, but according to da Ponte this was by no means all. When she had finished telling him her adventures Matilda offered da Ponte her hand and her heart, not to mention her considerable fortune. She proposed that they should start a new life together in some foreign country where her enemies would be powerless to harm her. Even da Ponte was taken aback by this sudden proposal of marriage from a girl whom he had only met twice—presumably he had not informed Matilda that he was a priest. In addition, his liaison with Angiola Tiepolo was at this time at its height, so he answered diplomatically that he would like to have three days in which to consider her proposal. It was a difficult problem. Da Ponte cynically weighed up the various attractions of the two girls—the Venetian small, fair, appealing and ill-educated; the Neapolitan tall, dark, cultivated and rich. His heart, he says, inclined him to the former, his head naturally preferred the latter. Finally, after one of Angiola's frequent storms of jealousy, he almost made up his mind to choose Matilda—whom he had meanwhile been visiting regularly—and he promised that he would give her a definite answer the next day.

Presumably Angiola had learned of his visits to Matilda, for when next he went to see her she was in a fury of jealous rage and attacked her errant lover with a dagger. After a sordid and stormy scene he managed to pacify Angiola, and when she had gone to bed he crept out of the house, determined to run away to Geneva or London with Matilda. But the melodrama which seemed to be Matilda's natural element had not yet left her. When da Ponte arrived at her house a servant told him that shortly after he had left her that evening officers of the Inquisitors of State had dragged the unfortunate girl from her bed, and taken her and all her possessions away in a gondola.

It was not until some twelve years later that da Ponte heard what had happened to Matilda. He says that it was Sebastiano Foscarini, the Venetian Ambassador at Vienna, who told him that she had once more been shut up in a convent on her stepmother's orders, and that, he, Foscarini, had finally succeeded in obtaining her release after six years. As her stepmother had died, Matilda had rejoined her father in Naples where, as in all fairy-tales, she lived happily ever after.

Did Matilda ever exist outside da Ponte's imagination? She has defied all the attempts of learned scholars to discover her identity, and retains her mystery to this day. In any case she would have made a splendid opera of, say, the early Verdi style, and it is curious that da Ponte himself never thought of turning her into a libretto. Perhaps he only invented the story in his old age, when he was no longer writing for the stage.

Like all Venetians of their day, Angiola Tiepolo and her brother were gamblers; they initiated da Ponte into this pleasure and he soon became as much a slave to the card-table as they were themselves. They all three spent their evenings at the Ridotto, the famous gambling-rooms near San Moisè, but as they were none of them rich and were very often unlucky at cards, they were soon reduced to pawning their clothes in order to have some money with which to gamble. Once, when da Ponte had lost everything he possessed, a gondolier whom he had tipped handsomely on more fortunate days lent him fifty sequins. Da Ponte went back to the Ridotto, his luck changed, and he won a large sum. When he took the money home, however, Girolamo Tiepolo 'borrowed' it from him, and had soon lost every penny of it again. Angiola's brother was unscrupulous and rapacious; he was delighted to have da Ponte in his house when he

CX

was rich, but as soon as he was down on his luck Tiepolo had no compunction about turning his sister's lover out into the street. On one occasion da Ponte managed to persuade Tiepolo that he had a secret method of making gold—it was the kind of hoax that Casanova liked to bring off on a larger scale—but the joke turned against da Ponte, for subsequently Tiepolo, armed with a pistol, ordered him to make a hundred sequins; when da Ponte was forced to admit that he could not do so, Tiepolo took all the money he possessed, and pocketed it.

One night, when da Ponte had lost all his money at the Ridotto, he fell asleep in the 'Chamber of Sighs'—so-called because it was frequented by unlucky gamblers—and did not wake until the next morning. One or two other unfortunates like himself had spent the night there too, and one of them, in a mask, asked da Ponte if he could lend him a few pence. On searching his pockets da Ponte was surprised to find some sequins hidden under his handkerchief, and having no small change he gave one to the masked man. The latter agreed to accept such a large sum only on condition that he might return the money in his own house. He wrote his address on a playing-card and gave it to da Ponte, who put the card in his pocket and thought no more about it. Sometime later, having nothing better to do, he went to the address the masked man had given him. His host, an old man of seventy-eight, welcomed him courteously and, after some exchange of compliments, began to tell him the story of his life.

The old man had been born in Leghorn, the son of a rich merchant, and had inherited a considerable sum of money when his father died. However, his youthful extravagances were such that he was soon left penniless; he had to leave Leghorn as a result, and eventually went to Venice. Having no money or friends there he was forced to beg in the streets, and he found this to be such a pleasant and lucrative way of life that he continued to lead it for forty-seven years, during which time he amassed an immense fortune. He had married, but had been left a widower, with one daughter. When he had reached this point in his story the old man said that he would like to introduce da Ponte to his daughter, and he went to fetch her.

He soon returned with a girl of great beauty and, to da Ponte's amazement, he offered her to him as his bride. The old man knew, he said, all about his guest, and had chosen him as a possible son-in-law because of the generous way da Ponte had always given alms to him when he was begging near the Ponte San Gregorio. Seeing that his guest was rather taken aback by this sudden proposal of marriage, the old man led him into another room where he showed him chest after chest filled with gold coins, hoping that the sight of them might help his visitor to make up his mind to accept his daughter's hand. It very nearly did—but the thought of Angiola Tiepolo and of 'another great obstacle' made da Ponte tell the old man, with some embarrassment, that he was not in a position to marry. Later on, hearing that another young man had had the sense to accept what he had refused, and was living not only in luxury but with a charming wife, da Ponte regretted his scruples and felt that he had made a great mistake.

After reading of da Ponte's love affairs and the proposals of marriage which he not only received, but apparently seriously considered, the reader may have forgotten—as da Ponte certainly tried to do—that he was a priest of the Catholic Church. In this respect, da Ponte must be judged by the standards of his contemporaries and of his compatriots. The influence of Rome was not strongly felt nor particularly highly esteemed in the Venetian Republic, and religious vows were interpreted in the widest possible sense. One has only to look at Guardi's pictures of convent life or to read the accounts of 18th-century travellers to realise that entering a convent, for a Venetian girl, was hardly a more serious step than going to finishing-school nowadays, and that taking minor orders, for a young man, merely meant having a good education. During carnival friars went about Venice masked like everyone else, and it was only a foreigner who was surprised to see a man who was not only a priest but also a minister flirting in public with 'la plus fameuse catin de la ville', and earning a tap on the nose with her fan as a result.

The nuns were no less emancipated than the friars; 'though their trade be chiefly devotion, not many of them are truly devout'. They received their admirers and their friends in elegant convent parlours, and although they saw them through a grille or grating, Baretti said that 'the largeness of the Venetian grates has ruined the reputation of the Venetian nuns'. It was not at all impossible for a nun to escape from her convent to meet her lover or to attend the carnival. One young nun, who found herself locked out of her convent after such an escapade, appealed to the Patriarch for assistance. That eminent ecclesiastic disguised her as a priest and then made a tour of inspection of her convent together with his secretaries, thus enabling the disguised nun to slip into her cell unobserved while he held the Abbess in conversation. However, according to Baretti, the nuns had certain standards of behaviour—'When they are in love, they make it a point to be very faithful, and never coquet with other men'. Very often the object of their affections was a priest or a friar; when an abbess and another lady fought with daggers for the favours of a priest it created a certain sensation even in Venice, but mainly because this battle took place outside the convent walls. Amongst other more innocent diversions, the nuns were particularly fond of giving marionette performances, and they had a passion for taking snuff.

It is the priests and nuns who broke their vows who have been recorded for history, whereas the countless devout people who led pious and saintly lives have escaped the attention of the chroniclers; but there is no doubt that the licence of the religious orders in eighteenth-century Venice was very great. Da Ponte's behaviour was not, therefore, so extraordinary to his contemporaries as it would seem nowadays. He was not, however, merely in minor orders, but a celebrant priest, and there were limits, even in Venice, as he was eventually to discover.

In the intervals between his romantic adventures da Ponte earned his living as tutor to the young sons of a noble Venetian lady, gambled, and quarrelled with his mistress. Angiola's physical charms must have been truly remarkable, for her character was impossible. Although she made da Ponte's life a misery he was too enamoured of her or too weak to make a break, and it was not until she caused him to lose his job and his only source of income that he decided to leave her.

This came about in the following way: one evening, having

greeted her lover with a well-aimed ink-pot which cut his hand so badly that he could not use it for a month, Angiola, who was extremely jealous, contrived a scheme to prevent him from leaving her house at all. When he was asleep she cut off all his hair, in the hope that he would be ashamed to show himself in public until it had grown again, and would therefore be forced to stay with her. She was right; she had made him her prisoner. Shorn of his hair, and with an injured hand, da Ponte stayed at home with her all day, and only went out with her to parties, to the theatre, or to gamble when it was dark. After a few days the lady who employed him as tutor came herself to enquire why he had not come to work. When she saw the sort of people with whom her children's tutor was living she promptly dismissed him.

When he lost his job da Ponte decided to leave Venice. He was not, apparently, lucky at cards, his only other source of income, and Angiola was an expensive mistress. His younger brother, Girolamo, who was also a priest and was also working as tutor to a Venetian family, had been trying to persuade him to leave Venice and to lead a less dissolute life for some time. Now da Ponte was inclined to agree with him. He tells us that his final decision to leave the city was taken because he was so shocked when a fellow priest stole his cloak one day that he suddenly realised what a disreputable life he was leading himself, and resolved as a result to give up women, gambling and Venice and to turn over a new leaf. In view of subsequent events this resolution and the story which he tells in his *Memoirs* of how he reformed the priest fail to ring true, and seem an unlikely explanation for his departure. Da Ponte can hardly be taken seriously as a reformer of black sheep, although he often liked to pose as one; it seems much more likely that he left the capital because he had no job and no money, and also perhaps because he wanted to make a break with Angiola and felt that this was the only way to do so. In any case, he did leave Venice and went home to Ceneda, where he spent ten days with his family. This was in the autumn of 1774.

In fact, it was Angiola who made the final break, not da Ponte. After he had left Venice she wrote affectionate letters to him every day, although she had taken a new lover almost immediately after da Ponte's departure. Nevertheless, their correspondence dragged on for another three months until, on New Year's day, 1775, da Ponte received an urgent letter from her, summoning him to an address in Venice. Da Ponte, who was then in Treviso, immediately set off, and after a trying and expensive journey—it was so cold that the lagoons were frozen and he had to pay four gondoliers to break a way for him through the ice—he arrived in Venice late at night and went straight to the address his mistress had indicated to him. He was just about to knock on the door of the house when someone suddenly pulled him back violently, whispering: 'For Heaven's sake, don't go in there!' Da Ponte looked round and in the dusk he recognised his old servant. 'Why not?' he asked in surprise; but the servant refused to answer him until he had dragged his master away to a safer place. When he had done so, he told da Ponte that the letter which Angiola had written summoning him to Venice was all part of a plot; she had agreed to lure da Ponte to her house, and it had been arranged that when he knocked on the door her new lover would attack him.

In spite of his servant's warning, da Ponte decided to go back to Angiola's house and have it out with her. When he knocked the door opened silently, but there was no-one behind it; apparently a string had been attached to the latch so that it could be opened from upstairs. Cautiously da Ponte went into the house, but instead of being attacked by a jealous lover, he found Angiola there alone, as fragile and helpless-looking as ever. Apparently he had been so long in coming that Dondorologi, his rival, had grown tired of waiting for him and had gone off to the Ridotto to gamble. One last, sordid scene ensued, but this time all Angiola's charms and wiles were of no avail. She was delighted to see him, she said. She had missed him so much. . . . She begged him for forgiveness, cajoled him, implored him to stay with her, but in vain. Da Ponte had learned his lesson; he left Angiola for ever, and without regret. Did he, as he left her house and walked quickly along the dark, narrow streets beside the frozen canals, mutter under his breath: 'Così fan tutte—that's how they all behave!'? At the age of twenty-five he had lost all his illusions about women. That same evening he went back to Treviso.

CHAPTER III

THE LIBERTINE

I

WHEN da Ponte had left Venice in the autumn of 1774 he had gone home to Ceneda. It was while he was there, at the beginning of October, that he and his brother Girolamo managed to obtain appointments at the seminary at Treviso. In the case of Lorenzo the appointment was not made without some opposition; rumours about his conduct in the capital had already reached the provinces, and he was beginning to have a bad name. A priest from Ceneda—perhaps the 'rival' whom da Ponte had attacked in a poem published anonymously while he was in Venice—protested against his appointment on moral grounds. Amongst other things, the priest accused him of eloping with a girl from Ceneda—'a thing which, as of course you know', da Ponte wrote smugly to his friend Colombo, 'I never even dreamt of doing!' It may have been Colombo, who always tried to help da Ponte whenever he could, who managed—at least, temporarily—to clear his friend's name. The da Ponte brothers were, at any rate, finally appointed to the Seminary at Treviso—Lorenzo as a teacher of literature, and Girolamo as a teacher of grammar.

Treviso was a small town halfway between Ceneda and Venice, but quite unlike either of them. Compared to Ceneda it was an important, busy place: compared to Venice it was a sleepy little provincial backwater. Surrounded as it was with walls and a moat, there was something claustrophobic about Treviso, it was shut in, stuffy, very bourgeois and rather priggish. The arrogant winged lion of St Mark on its gates proclaimed it as a Venetian possession— and a possession it was, a vassal, a colony, certainly not a dominion, not on an equal footing with the great, glittering capital of which the honest, dull citizens of Treviso no doubt disapproved. But all the same, Treviso at that time was a stimulating intellectual centre, and the seminary there was well-known for its high standards, particularly in the teaching of Italian literature.

With a mixture of boredom and pleasure da Ponte turned once more to literature; there was not much else to do. His accaparating liaison with Angiola Tiepolo was over, and he was free; he had longed for freedom, but when he obtained it he found it rather boring. Nevertheless, he made the best of the situation, and acquired some new friends. Monsignor Paolo Francesco Giustiniani, Bishop of Treviso, took a kindly interest in the brothers and helped and encouraged them. They also became intimate with Giulio Trento, who was a literary man of considerable reputation in his own day; he not only gave da Ponte help and advice, but—even more important for a young poet—he introduced him into literary circles where he had an opportunity to find an audience for his poems. In this stimulating atmosphere da Ponte began to write much better poetry than he had written previously. His *Il Cecchino o sia la storia del cane e del gatto*, which he wrote at this time and read aloud to an audience in Treviso, shows talent, and remains one of his best—or, as one critic has unkindly said, the least bad—of his lyrics.

Both the brothers were apparently very capable teachers, and they were promoted to more important positions at the end of the Academic year. In fact, it seemed as if a new and creative era was opening for da Ponte, and that, having sown a few wild oats as young men do, he was now settling down to the sort of life for which his education had prepared him. It would be rather a humdrum life probably, he would grow older and fatter, would spend his time gossiping about his colleagues, gradually being promoted to more and more responsible positions in the seminary, acquiring a certain position in the literary life of the small provincial town, and from time to time publishing elegantly-bound volumes of mediocre verse. And indeed, for a time da Ponte was contented. He was exhausted after his hectic stay in Venice, had fallen out of love, and was in that mood of devotion to Art which young men sometimes pass through as a reaction after their first real love affair. But with da Ponte the mood did not last long. He was only twenty-six years old, and although he was genuinely interested in literature, he was far more interested in life. After he had tasted the life of Venice, Treviso must have seemed a dull provincial backwater. The seminary, with the petty gossip and jealousies which are the curse of all academic life, was intolerable to a young man who, in any case, had no religious vocation, but who had a fiery temperament and plenty of high spirits. He felt stifled, shut in by the high walls around the little town, fettered by the bourgeois prejudices and pruderies of its inhabitants, and bored—bored by the seminary, bored by his colleagues, and even bored by himself. He longed for the theatres, the carnivals, the Ridotto, all the gaiety of Venice; he may even have longed for Angiola, in spite of her scenes of jealousy and her infidelities. Yet in spite of all this he stayed at Treviso for two years, and when he left the seminary it was more or less involuntarily.

At the end of the academic year it was the duty of the Professor of Rhetoric to compose a series of poems to be read in public at the *Accademia*, a function roughly equivalent to our school speech-days. The professor was at liberty to choose his own theme for this occasion, and it was usual for the compositions to be in Latin, Italian, and sometimes in Greek. The *Accademia* was a solemn annual event, and was attended by all the most important local dignitaries, both ecclesiastical and civil. In 1776 da Ponte, who had by then become Professor of Rhetoric, had to write the poems which were to be recited by his pupils at the *Accademia*. In choosing his theme for the occasion he showed intellectual daring and a singular lack of tact, for he took as his subject 'Whether man is happier in an organised society or in a simple state of nature'. Nowadays it is difficult to understand how such a theme could shock anyone, but in da Ponte's day, when the new ideas of Jean-Jacques Rousseau and other advanced foreign thinkers were slowly beginning to penetrate to Italy, it was considered to be not only an advanced, but even a revolutionary subject, more especially when chosen by a professor in a seminary for his pupils to recite.

In writing his poems da Ponte adhered strictly to the accepted rules, and produced four Latin and eleven Italian compositions in various metres on his chosen theme, together with a prose preface to them in Italian. Although today his verses seem of a tedium and mediocrity which make them difficult to read, when they were read aloud for the first time at the *Accademia* the audience was electrified with horror. Sedition! Dangerous free thought! Radicalism! gasped the citizens of Treviso, as poem after lengthy poem was read, each one a more daring variation on an already scandalous theme. It must, indeed, be admitted that da Ponte's political ideas were well ahead of their time. Amongst other things, he expressed the opinion that no laws serve any useful purpose; that states should have no rights over their citizens, nor parents over their children; and, as if this was not enough, he then went on to launch a violent attack on the privileged classes. The Republic of Venice was hardly a democratic state, and the ideas he expressed were not likely to pass unchallenged in Venetian territory. It was as if a Communist agitator had read a speech at the prize-giving at Downside. When the storm broke, it was not only da Ponte who was called to account for his indiscretion, but the whole of the seminary and the Bishop of Treviso as well.

Da Ponte himself described his poems as a 'mere poetic caprice', and laughed them off as such; but very soon the whole affair ceased to be a laughing matter. He was denounced to the *Riformatori*, who referred the affair to the Senate, where the case was discussed on December 14th, 1776. At first the culprit showed little interest in the affair, and did not even trouble to go to Venice, but finally his friends persuaded him to go to the capital to defend himself.

When he arrived in Venice da Ponte found that his case was making a great sensation there, and that he was not without supporters. Venetian intellectuals took his side, and he suddenly found that he had become a minor celebrity—a rôle which was very much to his taste. His supporters included Bernardo Memmo, an intelligent and influential patrician; Pietro Zaguri, also a patrician; and Gasparo Gozzi, brother of Carlo Gozzi, the dramatist.

Gasparo Gozzi was a most valuable ally for da Ponte, for he was not only a well-known journalist and literary man, but he also had a great deal of influence with the authorities at that time. He tried to do what he could for his friend, but even he was powerless to avert the storm. Da Ponte sent him the poems which he had written for the *Accademia*, together with an ode addressed to Gozzi himself. Gozzi was suitably impressed, and said to the *Riformatori* 'This young man has talent which should be encouraged.' The *Riformatori* replied with a frankness which did them credit: 'So much the worse; we must deprive him of the means of becoming dangerous.'

The case was heard, da Ponte's poems were read aloud, and the Senate was scandalised. The theme of the poems and its development was bad enough, but even worse, in the opinion of the Senators, was a passing reference in one of the poems to 'golden horns'. These words were construed as an insult to the Doge and his little horned cap. However, when sentence was finally passed it was relatively light, much to the relief of da Ponte's friends, who had feared at least a term of imprisonment. Da Ponte merely lost his livelihood, but not his freedom. He was publically admonished, dismissed from the Seminary, and forbidden ever again to hold any teaching position whatsoever in the Venetian Republic. In spite of the leniency of the sentence, the Senators took a very serious view of the affair. Da Ponte's friend and patron, the Bishop of Treviso, received a rebuke; the member of the Seminary who had passed da Ponte's list of poems as suitable for the *Accademia*, was publically censured; a general investigation into 'Radicalism in schools' was ordered throughout the Republic; and an edict was issued that all copies of the seditious poems, either printed or in manuscript, were to be confiscated. On 23rd December, 1776, the Doge was informed of da Ponte's dismissal.

Da Ponte himself seems on the whole to have enjoyed the scandal and not to have taken it very seriously. If his 'poetic caprice' had lost him his job, it had at least ended his safe, dull obscurity in the provinces. For the next few years, at any rate, his life was to be anything but dull.

II

After his trial da Ponte stayed on in Venice. Far from doing him any harm, the publicity given to the affair had helped him to become known in literary circles as a poet, and he was taken up by Venetian society. Bernardo Memmo not only took him to live in his house, but helped him financially as well, and there is no doubt that his friendship and influence helped da Ponte to gain admittance to literary and patrician circles and gave him an aura of respectability which he badly needed. Memmo, who was some twenty years older than da Ponte, was a man of considerable standing. He came of a very old patrician family—one of his ancestors had been Doge in the tenth century—and he had himself been Inquisitor of State. His brother Andrea became, in 1785, Procurator of St Mark, the second highest office in the Venetian state, and had previously been Ambassador to the Holy See. Andrea Memmo was a close friend of Goldoni—who dedicated his *L'Uomo di Mondo* to him—and also of Casanova. In fact, it was as a result of a denunciation by the Memmos' mother that Casanova was imprisoned; she thought, with some reason, that he might have a bad influence on her sons. As a result of his trial, therefore, da Ponte found himself associating with the foremost Venetians of his day, who considered him to be a promising poet of advanced ideas.

Da Ponte was now twenty-eight years old—a mature man. What was he like at this period of his life? Physically he was striking: tall and thin, with a slight stoop, he had very pronounced features, an aquiline nose, and a humorous, sensuous mouth; his hair was dark, as were his curiously brilliant, penetrating eyes. He talked volubly and wittily, with a strong Venetian accent and a slight lisp. Altogether, he was handsome, had great charm, and was very attractive to women. Men, too, found him a pleasant companion, for he was extremely intelligent and amusing, and throughout his life he had a capacity for making friends with people of all kinds. He did not, however, always have a capacity for keeping his friends, for he was quick to take offence and quick to give it; his humble Jewish origins and his provincial education had given him a sense of inferiority which, in its turn, made him touchy and aggressive. By nature he was a true intellectual, genuinely and deeply interested in things of the mind—but not of the soul. In this he was a child of his time and his country; he was quite devoid of any spiritual yearnings, he was a materialist and a rationalist, had no conscience, very few scruples, and as far as one can tell, no faith in anything but his own abilities. Yet he had a constructive, not a destructive, mind; he had the great intellectual qualities of enthusiasm, curiosity and open-mindedness. He also had a keen sense of humour, although he was not always capable of applying it to himself. These very real qualities were counterbalanced by his lack of scruples, which amounted sometimes to dishonesty, his passion for intrigue, and his lack of a sense of proportion—he always went just too far, overstepped the limits, and thus spoilt his own chances. By nature he was a very sensual man; if he had not been forced to become a priest against his will, his life would have been far easier for him, and much of his conduct can perhaps be excused on these grounds. He was egocentric, ambitious, a social climber and an adventurer; he was not, perhaps, a very estimable character morally, but he at least never committed the sin of being dull. His was a fascinating personality, full of contradictions and contrasts, and he made a lasting, though not always favourable, impression on all who met him.

While he was staying in Memmo's house da Ponte began to make a name for himself as an improviser or extemporary poet. The art of improvising in verse on any given theme was very popular in eighteenth-century Italy, and it was developed to an extraordinary degree. As a boy, Metastasio is said to have improvised eighty stanzas at one session, and to have ruined his health as a result of frequent precocious and exhausting performances of this nature. Probably the most famous improviser in the eighteenth-century was Perfetti who, in 1725, received the Crown of the Capitol, the highest literary honour Rome could offer, in recognition of his art. Contemporary observers recorded that when Perfetti had been given a theme by his audience he would think for a few moments in silence, while soft chords were played on a harpsichord. He would then begin to declaim in verse, at first slowly, then with ever-increasing animation; as he became more excited, so the accompanying chords on the harpsichord became louder and faster, building up to a climax. When the performance was over Perfetti was completely exhausted, both mentally and physically.

It is evident that the quality of such verse cannot have been very high, and probably more often than not it was just sonorous nonsense. Eye-witnesses of such improvisations agree, however, that apart from being remarkable feats, they were musical and agreeable to listen to, and that the meaninglessness of the words only became apparent in retrospect, or if anyone was foolish enough to write the verses down. There seems to have been something almost trance-like about such performances; many improvisers could not write poetry in the seclusion of their study, but needed the stimulus of an audience, the gradual crescendo of excitement, to be able to compose at all. It was apparently an art that could be acquired, for da Ponte says that he and his brother deliberately cultivated it, and with success.

One of the best-known extemporary poets of da Ponte's day, and one whom he very much admired, was a woman—Maria Maddalena Morelli, better known under her Arcadian name of Corilla Olimpica. This remarkable woman achieved a mixture of fame and notoriety in her lifetime which is rather confusing to subsequent generations. She was extravagantly praised and sought after by kings and princes, the Pope himself even gave her permission to read books forbidden by the Inquisition; yet she was as violently attacked by her enemies as she was praised by her admirers. Corilla, like Perfetti, was given the Crown of the Capitol, but in her case the award caused such a storm of protest from her enemies and detractors that the ceremony had to take place at night, and even then it was the occasion for hostile demonstrations and scurrilous lampoons. In 1770 Mozart, then a boy of fourteen, and his father paid a visit to Corilla in Florence. The poetess graciously wrote a sonnet for the young musician, while he spent the evening playing the violin with a friend of his own age, Thomas Linley. Casanova visited Corilla too, and was impressed with her talents if not with her looks, for she had a squint.

Although he never attained the facility of such improvisers as Perfetti and Corilla, da Ponte did have some success as an extemporary poet, and the time which he devoted to the study of this curious art was certainly not wasted. As in the case of Metastasio, the practice of improvisation developed da Ponte's already considerable poetic facility. Although it is questionable whether facility is a quality which makes great poets, it was undoubtedly a quality which, in the eighteenth century, was absolutely essential for theatre poets. The remarkable speed with which both Metastasio and da Ponte could, if necessary, produce a libretto becomes more understandable when it is known that they were able to improvise verse —of a sort—literally to order. However, da Ponte had, as yet, no connections with the theatre, and his new accomplishments as an extemporary poet were only of use to him in that they increased his popularity, made him sought after in society, and pleased his host and patron Bernardo Memmo.

When da Ponte went to live in Memmo's house his host's mistress, a certain Teresa Zerbin, was already installed there. She was a girl of about twenty, the daughter of a workman at the Arsenal, and Memmo, who was then nearly fifty, was completely infatuated with her and under her influence. There seems little doubt that Teresa and da Ponte found they had a certain amount in common, that they became intimate, and that Memmo discovered it. Da Ponte's own version of the story, according to which he was the completely innocent victim of Teresa's wicked wiles, is more difficult to believe. That Teresa found da Ponte—who was young, amusing and attractive—a pleasing alternative to her elderly lover is not difficult to understand; that da Ponte, who owed so much to Memmo, should repay his friend's kindness by making love to his mistress seems scandalous but not, on the whole, improbable. In any case, da Ponte was obliged to leave Memmo's house, and in so doing he lost his only means of support. He decided to leave Venice and to go to Padua to visit his brother, Luigi.

Padua, with its ancient university, with its strange, almost Byzantine basilica in which the tomb of St Anthony is enshrined, with its lovely Prato and its ancient narrow streets, is a very beautiful place—but it left da Ponte quite unmoved. The reason for this was simple: he was penniless. Although his brother Luigi was a student at the University of Padua, he was in no position to help Lorenzo, although he was probably very pleased to see him, for the brothers were close friends. Lorenzo did have one other friend, or rather, acquaintance in Padua—a Dalmatian priest, whom he had met through Memmo; but the priest proved unhelpful, although—or perhaps, because—da Ponte had once been 'kind enough' to re-write a speech for him. The situation was desperate. Venice was so near, and yet Lorenzo had not even enough money to pay for the journey back to the capital. When he was away from it he felt like a fish out of water. Although he did make a few acquaintances in Padua, notably Cesarotti—an extremely prolific poet who, amongst

other things, translated Gray's *Elegy* into Italian—it was hardly a
satisfactory existence, especially for one on whom the rank and
beauty of Venice had lately 'showered favours and praises'. Indeed,
he was forced to exist on a diet of bread, coffee and olives for forty-
two days. He just managed to keep himself from starvation by
challenging people whom he met in cafés to games of draughts and
ombre; probably he cheated, for he finally did make enough money
for the fare back to Venice.

When he had been living in Memmo's house da Ponte had made
friends with Caterino Mazzolà, a poet who was later on to help him
very considerably, and without whom he might never have become
a librettist. On his return from Padua it was Mazzolà who persuaded
him to go and visit Memmo in an attempt to effect a reconciliation.
Memmo was apparently an extremely forgiving man or, more
likely, da Ponte was an extremely plausible liar; in spite of what had
passed between them Memmo welcomed his former guest with
every show of friendship, accepted his version of his relationship
with Teresa, and invited him once more to live in his house. This
da Ponte refused; instead he took a room on his own, and obtained
a job as secretary to his other patrician patron, Pietro Antonio
Zaguri. Zaguri had held important positions in Venice, had been a
senator, and was well-known as a patron of the arts and a man of
wide culture. He was the close friend and patron of Casanova, and
it was he who introduced da Ponte to that extraordinary man.

In 1777, when da Ponte first met him, Giacomo Casanova, self-
styled Chevalier de Seingalt, was fifty-two years old, and rather the
worse for wear. He was no longer the brilliant young adventurer
who had swaggered and bluffed and womanised his way across
Europe; who had been received by the royalty, by the aristocracy
and the intelligentsia of almost every country; and who had
charmed everyone whom he met with his good looks, his brilliance,
and his witty conversation. He was no longer even irresistible to
women; and the hero whose fantastic escape from the Leads of
Venice had made history was now reduced to acting as a police spy
for the very government which had imprisoned him. However,
although when da Ponte met him Casanova was down, he was by
no means out; he was still one of the most extraordinary men of his

day, and he still had the power to charm everyone, men and women alike. Da Ponte was no exception to the rule and, having once met him, he was fascinated, intrigued and puzzled by Casanova until his dying day.

Da Ponte has often been compared to Casanova, but although they did have a certain amount in common, the resemblance was a superficial one. They were both Venetians, both adventurers, both poets, both wrote their memoirs in their old age—but these are coincidences rather than resemblances. Their characters were fundamentally different, and nothing illustrates this difference more clearly than their respective memoirs. In an age of adventurers Casanova was proud to be the greatest adventurer of them all, whereas da Ponte was just an adventurer pretending not to be one.

The friendship between Casanova and da Ponte, which began in Zaguri's house, was a curious one, and lasted till Casanova's death. The two men met only occasionally, corresponded intermittently, and criticised each other a good deal. It was not, on the face of it, a very warm friendship. Da Ponte, writing after Casanova's death, described him in censorious and rather patronising terms; but his letters to Casanova are quite different—they are affectionate and even somewhat obsequious. Casanova, too, was inclined to be critical of his friend, but he was interested in him all the same. His correspondence shows that he was anxious for any scraps of gossip about da Ponte, and that he followed his career with something more than idle curiosity. And indeed, it is clear that, with all his faults, da Ponte was a fascinating person. Although in the course of his life he succeeded in making a great number of enemies, he had a far greater number of friends, and friends who were eminent men in their day, intelligent men, sometimes even men of genius. Zaguri, his new employer, summed him up as follows: 'A strange man; known for a scoundrel of mediocre calibre, but gifted with great talents for literature, and with physical attractions which win love for him!'

Some little time before da Ponte left Venice he quarrelled with Casanova. The friends' respective versions of this quarrel are conflicting. Da Ponte says that their disagreement was over 'some trifling point of Latin prosody'; Casanova alleged that da Ponte was annoyed with him for not sufficiently praising his poems, 'but', Casanova wrote to his friend Collalto, 'a flatterer is not a friend'. In any case, the quarrel was a minor one, and was forgotten when the two friends met again three years later.

III

'At this stage of my life', da Ponte wrote many years afterwards of the period he spent as Zaguri's secretary, 'I was loved by women, esteemed by men, favoured by patrons, and full of great hopes.' What more could a young man desire? Zaguri was an amiable, easy-going employer, he shared many of da Ponte's interests, and was inclined to turn a blind eye on his secretary's private life. All this suited da Ponte very well, and for some time the two men got on admirably.

Da Ponte did not live in Zaguri's house, but in April 1779 he took a room in a house belonging to a family called Bellaudi. The household consisted of Laura Bellaudi, a widow; her son, Carlo, and his wife, Angioletta; there was also her daughter Caterina who, although married to a certain Gabriele Doria, continued to live in her mother's house, while her husband lived with his father. At the time when da Ponte went to live in their house, the young Bellaudis were in their very early twenties. Angioletta, Carlo's wife, was a little younger; she was not a Venetian, but a Florentine who had come to Venice some years earlier with her father, who had opened a dancing-school in the city. She was, by all accounts, a precocious girl, to say the least. At the age of ten she had behaved 'immodestly' with a young man who lived opposite her; at fifteen she was pregnant by Bellaudi, who subsequently married her, and she had had several lovers since her marriage.

Her sister-in-law can hardly have been surprised, therefore, when she one day chanced to witness a highly compromising scene between Angioletta and the new lodger. Accusations were made, but da Ponte protested his innocence with such picturesque volubility— 'May God strike me down with a thunderbolt while celebrating Mass'—that he managed to persuade Caterina that she must have been mistaken, and the affair blew over, at any rate for the time being. However, in August of the same year Angioletta's mother-in-law, Laura Bellaudi, once more became suspicious. She hid herself one day, and from her hiding place witnessed a scene which left no doubt at all as to the relationship between da Ponte and her son's wife. This time all da Ponte's protestations were useless, and he was given notice to leave the house at the end of the month.

Da Ponte and Angioletta were kindred spirits, they understood each other perfectly, and they needed each other. It was not a romantic love affair—indeed, romantic love affairs were not in vogue at that time—but a strong physical and mental attachment between two people who had much in common. Da Ponte realised this, and when he was given notice to leave the Bellaudi house he decided that he would not lose Angioletta, now that he had found her, without a struggle. He therefore evolved a plan, and a plan which shows him in a most discreditable light, to take her away with him.

One of the Bellaudi children attended a school which was run by a young woman called Francesca Bertati. Now Francesca Bertati was on intimate terms with Carlo Bellaudi, Angioletta's husband. Whether she was actually his mistress, or whether it was merely a case of *amitié amoureuse* is not clear; but in any case they corresponded secretly, and da Ponte acted as courier and go-between for them. He did not perform these services for nothing, but extracted payment from Francesca in a way that is best left to the imagination.

One day Bellaudi gave some letters to da Ponte and asked him to deliver them to Francesca; da Ponte, who had no scruples at all, naturally read the letters, and was 'horrified' by what he read. He alleged that, in one letter, Bellaudi had been so indiscreet as to tell Francesca that he would marry her if he could only get rid of his wife—either if she died as a result of her coming confinement, or, if necessary, by means of poison. It seems very probable that da Ponte had, in fact, forged this letter himself. He was never able to produce the original, only a copy of it, and in any case Bellaudi was practically illiterate and could not have written the letter in question. Although he admitted having written other letters, Bellaudi always denied that he was the author of that one. The purpose of this complicated and sordid intrigue of da Ponte's was to persuade Angioletta to elope with him; when she read of her husband's infidelities and murderous intentions she very readily agreed to do so.

The elopement was planned for the evening of 30th August. It was arranged that da Ponte should find a pretext to entice Carlo Bellaudi away from the house, while Angioletta was to collect her things together and take a gondola to a pre-arranged meeting place, where da Ponte would then rejoin her. The first part of the plan worked very well, da Ponte took Bellaudi out for a walk, Angioletta escaped from the house without anyone noticing her, and took a gondola. It was when she was leaving the gondola at the place where her lover was to meet her that what had started as an adventure began to turn into a tragedy. As she stepped from the gondola her labour-pains began, and with such force that when da Ponte arrived a few minutes later she was already lying helpless on the ground. As quickly as he could, her lover made arrangements for her to be carried to the house of his cousin, Pietro Mariani; he was only just in time, for an hour after their arrival there a baby girl was born. Whether da Ponte was the father of this child is not clear; Zaguri and Bellaudi certainly believed that he was. In any case, da Ponte's position was not only scandalous but also extremely difficult. He had no house, very little money, and a convalescent woman and a new-born baby on his hands. What was he to do? What he in fact did was to behave with magnificent effrontery. The next day a triumphant procession—which included da Ponte in his cassock, the midwife, a washerwoman, and Mariani and his mistress—carried the new-born baby to Bellaudi's house. After a stormy interview, during which da Ponte had at least the good sense to stay outside in the street, Bellaudi refused to accept the child, and it was taken to a foundling home.

In no time at all news of the scandal was all over Venice. Zaguri, who usually took a very broad view on questions of morality, nevertheless felt that his secretary had gone too far. He summoned da Ponte who, when questioned about the affair, replied that it was 'the kind of incident that happens every day'. Zaguri was incensed by da Ponte's attitude. 'Too many incidents, Abate', he replied. 'Too many incidents! I hope that this latest one, of having to assist a woman pregnant by you in the public street, and whose child was born on the pavement, will be the last incident I hear from you while you are in my house!' And so saying, Zaguri dismissed his secretary.

It was at this singularly unedifying moment in da Ponte's career that Giorgio Pisani, a noble Venetian, decided to entrust his son's education to him. The fact that he did so already gives some indication of Pisani's character—after all, da Ponte had been forbidden to teach anywhere in the Venetian Republic, his dismissal from Treviso had been widely publicised, and his latest escapade with Angioletta was a public scandal. Pisani's own reputation was, in fact, far from spotless. He was a member of the Major Council, and the leader of a revolutionary faction in it composed mainly of the poorer members of the nobility—the *Barnabotti*, as they were called. It was not only a revolutionary faction, but it was also corrupt and venal, a turbulent element which caused the government a good deal of trouble. It was an element in which da Ponte immediately found himself quite at home, and he espoused Pisani's cause with all the enthusiasm and indiscretion of which he was capable. It was not long before he had published a very scurrilous sonnet—written in the Venetian dialect, so that all classes could understand it—in which he attacked Pisani's enemies in most virulent tones. The sonnet became the talk of Venice, it was read in every café and quoted in whispers in every drawing-room. The authorities took note of it, but for a time they took no action.

After their elopement da Ponte and Angioletta had to find somewhere to live. It was decided that Angioletta should remain at Santa Margherita in the house of da Ponte's cousin, and she did so for almost a year. Da Ponte himself took a room close to the Rialto Bridge in order to be nearer his church for, incredible though it may seem, he was still attached to the church of San Luca as a priest. He continued to say Mass there, despite his scandalous reputation, and despite the fact that he spent most of his time with Angioletta, behaving with a cynicism and an effrontery which even Casanova would never have contemplated. It was alleged, for instance, that a young girl, one of Angioletta's friends, was often present at the lovers' most intimate meetings, after which she would accompany da Ponte to church, he to say Mass and she to hear it. It is scarcely surprising that the vicar finally forbade him to enter the church, and a solemn reprimand was issued by the *vicare generale* of San Bartolomeo.

But solemn reprimands had no effect on da Ponte: he abandoned what little discretion he had once had, and together with Angioletta he led a life of sordid, scandalous debauch. He quarrelled with his cousin, and so was forced to move with his mistress from lodging to lodging, for no one would keep such a couple for long. Money was, of course, a problem—it was a problem which, at one time, he solved by running a 'dance hall'. By all accounts this establishment was in reality nothing but a brothel; da Ponte himself, still dressed in his cassock, played the violin—this is the only recorded evidence that Mozart's librettist was musical—while Angioletta's duties remained undefined. It was a life of continuous dissipation, of perpetual moves from one lodging to another, of poverty, squalor and brawls. Although da Ponte and Angioletta remained together they were by no means faithful to each other, and Angioletta, in particular, made herself very unpopular with other women because of her love affairs. On one occasion a woman threatened to disfigure her, and on another she was so badly beaten up that da Ponte, who had to intervene with a knife, wounded one of her assailants. The couple became so notorious that Angioletta was nicknamed 'The priest's tart'—although da Ponte naively assured everyone that she was his sister. Altogether three of their children were deposited at the Foundling Hospital.

It was obvious that even in Venice such a state of affairs could not continue indefinitely, and that the authorities would be forced to take action. They were, however, very slow in doing so, and for two whole years da Ponte and Angioletta did as they pleased. When finally some action was taken against them it was prompted from a most unexpected quarter.

On May 28th, 1779, an anonymous denunciation was placed in the mouth of the bronze lion—specially constructed to receive such missives—at San Moisè. Although the letter was not signed, its contents—and more especially its syntax and orthography—made it clear that Carlo Bellaudi, Angioletta's husband, had written it. What made him voice his grievances against his wife's seducer only after a period of two years is not clear, but it may be that there were political as well as personal reasons for his action. It may be remembered that Carlo Bellaudi's sister, Caterina, was the wife of a certain Gabriele Doria. Da Ponte himself always maintained that Doria was a spy of the Inquisitors of State, that he was responsible for the denunciation, and that he was Angioletta's lover into the bargain. There is no evidence that Doria was a spy, and in any case most of da Ponte's version of the story—which he transfers to the year 1798 instead of 1779—is an invention. (Amongst other things, he describes Angioletta as 'a very pretty and charming young girl of excellent character'!) But if Doria was not a spy, he was at least on the fringe of influential circles, his father was employed by Piero Barbarigo, a nobleman who was assistant at the Holy Office. It may well be that when da Ponte's political activities with Pisani were becoming a source of irritation to the authorities, a well-placed hint was dropped and transmitted, through the intermediary of Doria, to Bellaudi, to the effect that a chance of prosecuting da Ponte would be welcome. It may also be that Bellaudi, who had seen his wife again in January, 1779, after an interval of eighteen months—they met at her father's house—still felt attracted to her, in spite of the way she had treated him, and denounced da Ponte in an attempt to win her back. This second theory is strongly supported by subsequent events.

Bellaudi's denunciation, illiterate though it was, contained enough material to make the authorities take immediate action. After touching lightly on da Ponte's general crimes of libertinage, blasphemy and sacrilege, Bellaudi had gone on to accuse him specifically of 'seducing a married woman and living with her outside the sacraments', and of 'procreating illegitimate children with her'. When therefore the *Esecutori contro la Bestemmia* drew up their case against da Ponte it was *per rapto di donna honesta*, adultery, and public concubinage. The *Esecutori*, Benedetto Valmarana, Alvise Renier, and Marcantonio Diedo, although they investigated the affair very thoroughly, did not immediately order da Ponte's arrest. Instead, they settled down to hear the testimony of over fifty witnesses, who supplied them with a wealth of picturesque and, in some cases, unprintable information about da Ponte's crimes; his earlier sentence as a result of his indiscreet poems at Treviso was naturally not forgotten either. This all took some time, and was only completed at the beginning of September.

It seems as if the authorities wished for some reason to give de Ponte a chance to escape, but he did not immediately take advantage of their leniency, although he was perfectly aware of the proceedings against him. He continued to live with Angioletta in a room near the Ponte di Sant'Antonio during July, but at the end of that month he was seen in Treviso, from whence he went to Padua. At the beginning of September Angioletta, whose third child by da Ponte had been born on 24th August and taken to a foundling hospital, rejoined him in Padua. It may be that she brought him news that the proceedings against him were drawing to a conclusion and that he was no longer safe in Venetian territory. In any case, by the time the order for his arrest was given, on 13th September, da Ponte had already crossed the frontier into Austria. Sentence was finally passed on him in his absence on 17th December, 1779; it was published in Ceneda on Christmas Eve, and in Venice on 5th January, 1780. Da Ponte was sentenced to fifteen years' banishment from Venetian territory or, if he should be apprehended there during that period, to seven years' imprisonment in a dungeon without light.

Those who have seen the windowless dungeons below the Ducal Palace in Venice will well understand why da Ponte fled to Austria. He had been condemned to the Pozzi, the prisons reserved for those guilty of very grave crimes. In these cells no light ever penetrated, and food was passed to the prisoners through a hole in the wall. Casanova was imprisoned, not in these dungeons, but in those reached from the Ducal Palace by the Bridge of Sighs over a canal; these cells were for more privileged prisoners, and had windows— although perhaps the windows were a mixed blessing, for through them the captives could hear the gay voices of people enjoying themselves on the Riva degli Schiavoni only a few yards away, and the songs of the passing gondoliers.

And what, the reader may wonder, became of Angioletta? Did she accompany her lover into exile and comfort and support him? Far from it. When the trial was over her husband, Carlo Bellaudi, went to Padua to fetch her, took her home to Venice, and lived with her there happily ever after.

Francesco Benucci
The first Figaro

Silhouettes by Johann Hieronymus Loeschenkohl of four singers
in the first performance of LE NOZZE DI FIGARO

Announcement of the first performance of
IL DON GIOVANNI *in Vienna*

PART II

VIENNA

'In Vienna whoever is most *impertinent* has the best chance.'

MOZART.

CHAPTER IV

THE POET

WHEN the Abbé Lorenzo da Ponte, a fugitive from his own country, arrived in Gorizia in September, 1779, his luggage was very light. A suit, a few underclothes, and three books—Horace, Dante, and Petrarch—together with a small sum of money were his only material possessions. Nor did he have many assets of a less tangible kind, apart from good looks, quick wits, and some literary talent. He knew no German and had, so far as he was aware, no friends in Austria; at any rate, he carried no letters of introduction, those essential documents without which an eighteenth-century traveller might just as well stay at home. Although da Ponte had nothing to fear from the Austrian police, Gorizia was only a few miles from Venetian territory, and it would not take long for news of his trial and sentence to catch up with him. If his reputation became known in Austria—and it was the prudish and sanctimonious Austria of Maria-Theresa, where the Church was taken seriously, where religious toleration was unknown, and where the sins of the flesh were not regarded as lightly as they were in Venice—he had little hope of making good.

However, da Ponte's first impressions of Austria were favourable, and he took them as a good omen for the future. He arrived in Gorizia, tired and hungry, and put up at the first inn he came across. He was welcomed by the proprietress, an extremely personable young woman in her early twenties. She was dressed in the German fashion, with a little golden lace cap on her head, with a fine Venetian chain twisted several times round her white neck and hanging provocatively over her full bosom, with a tight-fitting waistcoat which showed off her attractive figure, and with silk stockings and little pink slippers. Da Ponte began to feel that Austria was not so bad after all. The proprietress of the inn was very affable, although she could speak no Italian; indeed, she was

67

so affable that it soon became clear to da Ponte, in spite of his
ignorance of German, that her intentions were of a highly amorous
nature. At any other time he would have been only too glad to
encourage her, but at that particular moment he was so hungry
that the only thing he could think of was food. In vain he tried to
explain what he wanted by gestures; she interpreted everything as
flirtation. Da Ponte was in despair, he had never been in such a
predicament before. As they were talking, a servant happened
to pass by, carrying a tray loaded with food; the sight of it was
too much for da Ponte—he seized a drumstick as the tray went
past, and at last the young woman understood what he wanted.

The proprietress of the inn was not at all affronted; she immediately
gave orders for supper to be brought to da Ponte's room, and while
he was eating she did her best to entertain him and to carry on a
conversation in mime. When this method proved inadequate for
her purpose she sent for an Italian-German dictionary, and having
written *Ich liebe Sie* on a piece of paper, she made signs to her
companion to look the phrase up in Italian. She was obviously a
woman after da Ponte's own heart; but he had had a long and tiring
day, and after a charming evening of mild flirtation with the help
of the dictionary, he made signs to his hostess that he would like
to retire for the night—alone. If she was a little crestfallen, she had
the good manners not to show it, and she left him immediately.
Da Ponte settled down to his first good night's rest for weeks, with
no fears of a knock on the door or a summons from the police,
and with the feeling that his stay in Austria had began quite well.

The next morning he woke up refreshed, to find an excellent
meal awaiting him in the adjoining room, and his hostess, as
amiable and forthcoming as ever, waiting for him too. When he
returned to his bedroom after his meal he was surprised to find two
or three women there. They were carrying baskets full of trinkets
and souvenirs which they were offering for sale to travellers. Da
Ponte, like everyone else, had heard of the stern measures which
Maria-Theresa had instituted in order to combat prostitution;
he was amazed to find that these female pedlars were permitted to
enter bedrooms in Austrian inns. 'Under pretext of selling pins and
needles, handkerchiefs, collars, ribbons and other trifles, it was only

too easy', he remarked cynically, 'to offer other things, not to be
found in baskets, for sale too.'

Da Ponte remained at the inn for about ten days, and only decided
to leave it because his money was running very short. His generous
hostess realised his predicament, and one day put a purse full of
gold under his pillow; but da Ponte refused to accept it. 'I have never
forgotten my dignity so far as to live on a woman's money', he
said, 'although many women have not had the same tact towards
me.'

When he left the inn da Ponte remained on the best of terms with
the proprietress who, amongst other kind deeds, had taught him
some German—'a little vocabulary of amorous words and expressions which', he admitted, 'was of great use to me later both in that
town and elsewhere.' It was a relationship which might even have
developed into something of a permanent nature, perhaps, had it
not ended tragically; seven months after their meeting the young
woman died of a fever, at the age of twenty-two. Da Ponte remembered her with love and respect all his life. 'She was, without
exception', he wrote when he was over eighty, 'one of the best
women I have ever met.'

After leaving the inn da Ponte had taken a small room in a grain-
merchant's house. His honeymoon with Austria was over, and he
began to consider the vital question of how he was to make a
living. He had almost no money left, no friends, and no prospects.
He considered this unsatisfactory state of affairs, and came to a
practical conclusion: if he was to earn his living by literature, he
must have a wealthy and influential patron; he also realised that the
way to obtain a patron was by flattery. It only remained to decide
whom to flatter, and to write some laudatory verses, and he would
then be well on the way to success. He was perfectly right; in the
eighteenth century poets and other creative artists could not exist
without patrons, and patrons found it hard to exist without flattery.
As a result, eighteenth-century literature contains a vast quantity
of dedications, poems, sonnets, letters and other works in which the
most extravagant and outrageous compliments are paid to wealthy
and, in many cases, totally insignificant men.

In choosing his future patron da Ponte showed discrimination, foresight, and a knowledge of human nature. He studied the local aristocracy, and his choice fell on Count Guido Cobentzl. Cobentzl's son, Johann Philipp, was making a brilliant career for himself in diplomacy, and had become the right-hand man of the Austrian chancellor, Kaunitz; indeed, a few days after da Ponte's arrival in Gorizia the young Cobentzl, on behalf of Austria, had signed the Treaty of Teschen, thus officially terminating the war of the Bavarian succession between Prussia and Austria. The poet rightly surmised that old Count Cobentzl was full of paternal pride, and would probably therefore give a kindly reception to any poet who praised his brilliant son's achievements. Without further ado da Ponte composed an ode entitled *La Gara degli Uccelli* (*The Rivalry of the Birds*—the birds referred to were, of course, the eagles of Prussia and Austria), in which he described both Maria-Theresa and Cobentzl in most flattering terms. It was not a particularly good ode, but it had the desired effect. The old Count was delighted with the poem; he had it printed at his own expense and gave copies of it to all his friends. In a few days da Ponte had ceased to be a penniless nonentity, and had become a literary lion. He was taken up by the local aristocracy, who invited him to their houses and gave him excellent dinners. Da Ponte showed his appreciation of their hospitality by writing more flattering odes, and his new-found patrons rewarded him with handsome gifts.

Life in Gorizia had suddenly become delightful, and da Ponte naturally considered the Cobentzls, the Coroninis, the Torrianis, and all the other local families to be delightful and intelligent too. Casanova, who had passed through Gorizia a few days earlier, and who had been received by the same families, had also noted that foreigners could have a very pleasant time there. He knew da Ponte's patron, Count Cobentzl, who was, he says, wise, generous, extremely erudite, and without any pretensions. Casanova, however, was less enthusiastic about some of da Ponte's other friends. He describes how Count Torriani's eldest son, for example, had only one quality—he told good stories; apart from that social asset he was 'an ugly and shady individual, a libertine, a braggart, a liar, brazen, spiteful and indiscreet'. Another acquaintance of his, Count Lantieri-Puriatico, was married to Aloisia von Wagensberg;

he is said to have told a friend that his wife had 'no temperament, but that she possessed the most beautiful behind he had ever seen'. This lady became da Ponte's patroness and later encouraged him to translate a play which was performed in Gorizia.

Another friend of da Ponte's, whom he described in glowing terms, was Count Luigi Torriani, who had invited Casanova to stay with him in 1773. According to Casanova he was, in reality, a most unattractive individual. 'Without being actually good-looking, one could not call him ugly in spite of his goal-bird's face, on which one could read cruelty, disloyalty, treason, pride, sensual brutality, hate and jealousy.' Da Ponte stayed in Torriani's house for some time, and seems to have enjoyed his visit immensely; Casanova, on the other hand, bitterly regretted having accepted the invitation. Unlike da Ponte, he had found that the Count's hospitality was of the meanest, and his visit ended with a sordid and undignified scene and a hand-to-hand struggle with his host—the quarrel, it need hardly be said, was about a woman. Torriani challenged Casanova to a duel, but was too cowardly to fight when it came to the point. This extremely disagreeable man made his wife thoroughly unhappy, and died insane not long after da Ponte met him.

Apart from being invited everywhere, da Ponte also received some literary commissions from his new-found friends. One of these, Count Rodolfo Coronini, was something of a scholar—or at any rate, everyone preferred to give him the title of scholar on trust, rather than take the trouble of reading his works to see if he really merited it. Coronini commissioned da Ponte to translate his *Liber Primus Fastorum Goritiensium* into Italian, and paid him generously for his work. The next two commissions which he received were of greater consequence in the long run, although they probably brought da Ponte less fame and money than his laudatory odes and sonnets at the time. A troupe of comedians had been engaged by the director of the local theatre, and da Ponte was asked to write something for the new company. He had never written anything for the stage before, and his first effort—a translation and adaptation of a German tragedy—was not a success. His initial failure as a dramatist did not discourage him, and his second attempt proved more successful. It was also a translation, this time of a French tragedy by J. F. de la Harpe; da Ponte made this adaptation in collaboration with his brother Girolamo, so he may even have begun work on it before he left Venice. *Il Conte de Warwick*, as the play was called, had some success; it was performed in Gorizia in 1779 and 1780, and was revived in Trieste in 1791.

In Gorizia da Ponte made friends not only in aristocratic, but also in intellectual circles. One of the most active, if not the most talented, men in the literary life of the town was a certain Guiseppe Coletti, whom he met at about this time. Coletti had received his education from the Jesuits, and had then served as a private soldier in an infantry regiment. When da Ponte met him he had left the army, and had been taken on by the local printer, Guiseppe Tommasini, as his assistant. Coletti was not a particularly intelligent man and he wrote a great deal of very bad verse, but he was not without certain qualities. He was a man of immense energy, and thanks to his efforts Tommasini's printing firm, which had been in a very bad way when Coletti joined it, had revived to such an extent that in 1778 it received an Imperial Authorisation to print school books and official publications, and in 1782 it opened a branch in Trieste. If he was energetic and forceful as a business man, Coletti displayed these qualities in an even more marked fashion in the literary world; literature was apparently his hobby and his passion, and he was one of those talentless but tireless literary busybodies who always exist in every community. He was for ever organising literary societies and lectures and evenings, for ever pestering people to take part in them, relentlessly pursuing his victims until they were forced to do what he wanted in spite of themselves. He was, in fact, a well-meaning bore.

The arrival of a new literary man in Gorizia was a great event for Coletti; it meant all sorts of new possibilities—literary discussions, the poet reading his own work to well-chosen audiences, slim volumes, articles in the press, and so on. He pounced on da Ponte, and did his best to monopolise him; but da Ponte found the aristocracy more remunerative, more hospitable, and much more amusing than Coletti and his earnest friends, and he soon grew to dislike the amateur man of letters heartily. His dislike was something more than irritation and boredom, and almost amounted to vindictive hate, but the reasons for it are obscure. After almost two hundred years it is not easy to unravel the various intrigues and personal antipathies which occasioned it, but it would seem that a business rivalry was really at the root of it all; da Ponte himself tried to make out that Coletti was jealous of him. The printer, so he said, was heard to remark that he did not believe that da Ponte was the author of *La Gara degli Uccelli*; what Coletti probably meant was that he did not believe him capable of writing such a bad poem, but as da Ponte had a very high opinion of the work in question he did not understand Coletti's remark in that way. At first da Ponte did not take Coletti's insult very seriously, and for once had not thought of retaliating, until another friend of his, Valerio de Valeri, told him that he should not let such insulting comments pass unchecked.

Now Valerio de Valeri was also a printer—indeed he had been entrusted with the printing of Casanova's *Istoria delle turbolenze della Polonia*—and looked on Coletti as a dangerous business rival. He no doubt saw a possible ally in da Ponte, and therefore did his best to ingratiate himself with the newly-arrived and much admired Venetian poet. It was not very difficult to do so; da Ponte, although favoured and sometimes paid by the local aristocracy, was all the same very badly off financially, and was at that time living in one miserable room in the house of a drunkard who was given to beating his wife. When, therefore, Valeri asked him to come and live in his house, da Ponte accepted his invitation with alacrity, and felt that the least he could do in return for such hospitality was to comply with Valeri's request that he should wage a literary war against Coletti. In spite of his protestations to the contrary, da Ponte was probably not at all averse to such a war; it would give him publicity, and all through his life he was all too ready to attack his rivals and his enemies in print.

In no time at all war was declared; da Ponte wrote a satire attacking Coletti, Valeri printed it, and the whole town talked of nothing else for weeks. From that day on, da Ponte alleged, Coletti was his implacable enemy, although he continued to pretend that he was his friend. If this had been so, it would have been perfectly understandable, but all the evidence goes to show that Coletti was

DX

only too ready to forgive and forget. He was the kindest and most Christian of men—indeed, not only kind, but positively naive—and for the rest of his life he always did all he could to help da Ponte and to be of service to him. As will be seen, he received very little thanks for his efforts.

At about this time da Ponte's old friend, Caterino Mazzolà, passed through Gorizia. Da Ponte was delighted to see him and to hear the latest news from Venice, although the news was not all good. Giorgio Pisani, da Ponte's friend and one-time employer, had been elected Procurator of St Mark, only to be arrested and imprisoned three months later for his revolutionary activities. Until he received this news da Ponte had, apparently, had hopes of returning to Venice if Pisani's party should have come into power, but he now realised that he must abandon this idea and find some other alternative. Mazzolà had just been appointed poet to the Court Theatre of Dresden, and was in fact on his way to take up his position there, so da Ponte asked him to look out for some suitable employment for him in Saxony. Mazzolà promised to do what he could to help him.

Soon after Mazzolà's departure for Dresden an Arcadian Academy was founded in Gorizia, and da Ponte was made a member of it. The Arcadian Academy, a literary movement which had been founded in Rome in 1690 by such distinguished men as Giovanni Mario Crescimbeni and Gian Vincenzo Gravina, had gradually spread all over Italy, and had eventually become a kind of eighteenth-century P.E.N. Club. Members were given Arcadian names—da Ponte was Lesbonico Pegasio—and literary evenings were held at which members read their works aloud. Of course, the moving spirit behind this society in Gorizia was Coletti; it was just the kind of thing which appealed to him, and he organised *L'Accademia Letteraria degli Arcadi Romano-Sonziaca*, as it was called, with all his usual energy and enthusiasm. He prevailed on old Count Cobentzl to accept the presidency, and he was secretary. Da Ponte was admitted to the club a month after its foundation and, although he may have laughed at Coletti, he was really rather flattered when he received his invitation.

Life in Gorizia was, in fact, so pleasant, and da Ponte had so much success of every kind that he was almost sorry when he received a letter from Mazzolà telling him that an excellent situation was awaiting him in Dresden. However, he decided that the offer was too tempting to be refused, and made plans to leave the pleasant little Austrian town where he had spent so many happy months, and to try his fortunes in Saxony.

The nobility of Gorizia rose to the occasion, and gave the poet a generous farewell present accompanied by many fine words; Count Cobentzl also gave him a letter of introduction to his distinguished son in Vienna. Da Ponte left Gorizia with many happy memories and with sincere regret—regret which, it is true, was softened by the thought of the important court appointment awaiting him in Dresden.

II

On his way to the Saxon capital da Ponte passed through Vienna. He found the city in mourning, for the Empress Maria-Theresa had just died; he stayed in the capital for only three days. He was, nevertheless, prompt in presenting Count Cobentzl's letter of introduction to his son. The great diplomat received da Ponte affably, was obviously flattered by his poem, and gave him 100 florins 'for his travelling expenses'. The poet completed his journey to Dresden in high spirits.

His spirits dropped, however, when he met Mazzolà, who was extremely surprised to see him. 'Are you on your way to the theatre in St Petersburg?' he asked him politely and, perhaps, a little coldly. Considering that Mazzolà had sent him a letter inviting him to Dresden in order to take up an appointment there, this was rather a strange greeting, to put it mildly. Although Mazzolà was kind and friendly, he made no reference to the letter, or to the job which he had mentioned in it. It was all very awkward; when da Ponte finally plucked up enough courage to refer to the matter indirectly, it was perfectly clear from Mazzolà's replies that he was totally ignorant of the letter which da Ponte had received and which had borne his signature.

If Mazzolà had not written the letter, who had? Obviously

someone who had wanted him to leave Gorizia, da Ponte decided. Immediately, and without any proof he made up his mind that Coletti must have forged the letter in a fit of jealousy, and he maintained that this was so until his dying day. It may possibly have been so in fact, but an action of such a kind was completely out of keeping with Coletti's character; he may have been a bad poet and an irritating person, but everyone agreed that he was the kindest of men. It was also unlikely in view of subsequent events— Coletti consistently praised and over-praised da Ponte's poetry, and reprinted it whenever possible in his newspaper, together with fulsome eulogies about the author. Whether the letter ever existed at all is open to doubt—the whole story seems most improbable— and in any case da Ponte had no evidence that Coletti had written it beyond the fact that he had confided in him about his hopes for a job in Dresden.

Whatever the true facts behind this story may have been, da Ponte's rancour against Coletti was very persistent, and in his *Memoirs*—written after Coletti's death, when he could not defend himself—he had some very harsh things to say about that kind and inoffensive busybody. In 1828, a close friend of Coletti's called Rossetti, who had just read da Ponte's *Memoirs*, wrote to their author and said that he could never believe Coletti capable of such a mean forgery. Da Ponte replied with an immensely long letter dealing with all sorts of other things, which he finished with the following phrase: 'I could say a great deal about Coletti, but this letter is too long anyway without dragging dead people into it.' It seems as if there was some deep-rooted reason for his hatred of Coletti, something more than the forged letter—real or invented —but what it was will now probably never be known.

Although Mazzolà was clearly taken aback by da Ponte's unexpected arrival in Dresden, he did his best to make his friend's stay there agreeable, and he also tried to find work for him. In this he was not successful, but as he was extremely busy himself writing for the theatre, he was not displeased when da Ponte offered to help him. Most of the work was translation or adaptation; da Ponte helped his friend by translating an occasional aria or duet for him, and sometimes he was even entrusted with a whole scene. He naturally received no pay for this work, but it was an excellent apprenticeship for him. He probably learned a good deal from Mazzolà, who was an experienced craftsman, and even more from the demands of exacting musicians, petulant singers, and harassed stage-managers. It was his first real contact with the theatre, with the perpetual hurry, the everlasting clash of rival personalities, the intrigues, the gossip, the love-affairs, and the atmosphere of tension and excitement that many people—and especially people like da Ponte—find so attractive. When Mazzolà complimented him on his literary skill and said that he should turn his attention to the theatre more seriously, the suggestion appealed to him; at the moment there was no theatrical opening for him, but the idea took root, and was later to bear fruit.

Da Ponte made several new friends in Dresden, notably Count Camillo Marcolini, who was a close friend of the Elector (and who later missed one of the biggest literary *coups* in history when he refused to buy Casanova's *Mémoires*), and Michael Huber, a learned ex-Jesuit (the order had been suppressed by Clement XIV in 1773).

Father Huber, who was about the same age as da Ponte, came from the German Tyrol, but had a perfect knowledge of Italian and of Italian literature. He was an extremely erudite man, and had translated some of Metastasio's works into German. He took a great interest in da Ponte, and may have tried to use his influence to persuade him to change his way of life and return to the Church. In any case da Ponte became very friendly with him, and dedicated to him a set of rather unusual poems which he wrote at this time. These were his seven Psalms (which were original compositions in various metres, and not translations of the Psalms of David) which contain some of the best poetry he ever wrote—in fact, they were praised by no less a man than Ugo Foscolo. These compositions are of such an unusual type and are so unlike da Ponte's other work, that it may be of interest to quote one of them in full. As will be seen, they are curious productions for a man who believed in little or nothing, for a priest who consistently broke his vows, but he was probably sincere at the moment when he wrote them, for he possessed a remarkable capacity for forgetting everything which he did not want to remember. His education in the seminary and

also, perhaps, his early Jewish upbringing—he had learned Hebrew
—had, in spite of everything, left their mark on him.

Salmo I

Miserere Mei, Deus, quoniam infirmus sum.

Signor, di fragil terra
formasti il corpo mio,
a cui fa sempre guerra
crudo nemico e rio,
che nutre il fier desio
del pianto de' mortali;
e danni a danni aggiunge e mali a mali.
   Ahi! quante volte, ahi! quante
il barbaro mi vinse,
e dietro il volgo errante
l'anima mia sospinse!
quante il mio core avvinse,
che non temea d'inganno!
onde servo io divenni, egli tiranno.
   Or ei guida i miei passi
per vie fosche e distorte;
ove per tronchi e sassi
si giunge a strazio e a morte,
Ma tu con man più forte
spezza il funesta laccio,
e me ritogli ancor a l'empio braccio.
   Veggo quant'io peccai,
quanto il tuo nume offesi:
però, Padre, tu sai
che a lungo pria contesi;
sai che a l'empio mi resi
per mia fralezza estrema,
non già perch'io non t'ami e te non tema.
   Su queste labbia spesso
suonò il tuo nome santo,

in quel momento stesso
ch'io ti fuggia dal canto;
e sparsi amaro pianto
su quei stessi diletti,
onde peccâro i traviati affetti.
    Ma, se de' falli miei
scusa non è che basti,
salvami, perché sei
quel Dio che mi creasti,
e l'empio invan contrasti
col tuo voler superno,
ch'osa sfidarti ancor fin da l'inferno.

Father Huber was delighted with these poems and with their
dedication—he may have thought da Ponte had really seen the
error of his ways—and he showed them to the Elector; the poet was
generously rewarded by both of them.

Da Ponte had also made friends with an Italian painter who
had settled in Dresden with his family. This painter had two
beautiful daughters and a wife who, although almost forty, was
remarkable for her grace and wit. All three women attracted da
Ponte, the girls by their youthful beauty, innocence and freshness,
and the mother by her more mature charms. On the whole, he was
inclined to favour the daughters—he was only thirty-three at the
time—but he could not decide which of the two he preferred.
He solved the problem by paying court to both of them, while
maintaining, at the same time, an *amitié amoureuse* with the mother.
This situation went on for some weeks, and probably no one found
it disagreeable. Both girls were in love with the handsome young
poet, and the mother, too, was not at all averse to him. She was at an
age when women need confirmation of their power to attract young
men, and da Ponte was quite willing to give it to her. It was the
mother who tried to bring things to a head; she had already told
him *Chi vuol bene alla figlia accarezzi la mamma* ('Who loves the
daughter should pay court to the mother'), but he had perhaps not
paid sufficient attention to her words. Finally she gave da Ponte an
ultimatum: he must either decide which daughter he loved and make

her an honourable proposal, or else he must cease visiting them. She
gave him a day in which to make up his mind, and meanwhile her
husband took both girls away to the country.

Da Ponte was in despair. Although, as he said, he would dearly
have liked to marry one of the girls—but which? he lamented, still
unable to make up his mind—he was in no position to do so. It was
not the fact that he was a priest which worried him—he had con-
veniently forgotten that—but the fact that he had no work, no
prospects, and no money. He was debating this difficult problem,
and repeating to himself aloud: 'Oh, Rosina! Oh, Camilletta! Oh,
Camilletta! Oh, Rosina!' when Mazzolà came into his room.

Mazzolà had come to bring him letters, and their contents made
da Ponte quite forget both Rosina and Camilletta. One letter was
from his father, and it informed him of the death of his brother
Luigi—the brother who had been a student at Padua. This was a great
grief to Lorenzo, who was deeply attached to his family, and more
especially to his two brothers. It was also a financial blow, for Luigi
had been the breadwinner of the family, the principal means of support of their father and their numerous half-brothers and sisters.
Da Ponte was overwhelmed by this news, and Mazzolà, who did his
best to comfort his friend, could do nothing to distract him from his
grief. Finally he told da Ponte that he would read him something
which would make him laugh; it was a letter from one of Mazzolà's
friends in Venice, who wrote as follows:

'There is a rumour in Venice that da Ponte has gone to Dresden
in order to take your appointment as Court Poet away from you.
Be careful, my friend, these da Pontes are dangerous, as you well
know.'

Mazzolà read this letter out with the best of intentions, and sincerely thought that it would make da Ponte laugh and forget his
grief for a minute or two. However, the effect it produced was of a
very different kind. Da Ponte, who was always ready to take offence
where none was meant, jumped to the conclusion that Mazzolà took
his Venetian correspondent's warning seriously, that he wished to
be rid of a dangerous rival, and that he had read the letter out aloud
on purpose in order to drive his friend away. At first da Ponte was
hurt and insulted; when Mazzolà left him he was dignified and silent.

Who knows? Perhaps the idea of supplanting Mazzolà in Dresden had crossed da Ponte's mind. He was not a man of high moral integrity, and on occasion he was capable of treating his closest friends and his benefactors in the most ignoble way. He needed money, he had been helping Mazzolà in his work, and he probably felt that he could have done Mazzolà's work just as well, if not better, himself. But when he learned that his ambitions, which he had thought safely hidden from the world in the dark places of his own heart, were being openly discussed in Venice and had been pointed out to Mazzolà, he realised that, once more, the time had come to move on. In any case, his departure from Dresden would solve the otherwise insoluble problem of the two beautiful sisters and their attractive mother. He therefore made up his mind to leave Dresden that very night.

Da Ponte wrote a note to Father Huber promising that he would come to say goodbye to him that evening, and he wrote another to the mother of Rosina and Camilletta in which he announced his departure. Next he booked a place on the Prague coach, which left Dresden at 10 o'clock in the evening. When he went to say goodbye to Father Huber the ex-Jesuit gave him provisions for his journey, warm clothing, and also a little leather pouch with a silver fastening. He made da Ponte promise not to open the pouch until he had left Dresden, embraced him, and then said: 'Now go: my heart tells me that everything will turn out well for you.' Da Ponte kept his promise, and when he opened the silver fastening, found that the pouch contained a copy of Boethius: *De Consolatione Philosophiae*, a volume of Thomas à Kempis, and a purse containing twelve gold coins.

Da Ponte had one more visit to pay before he left—to Mazzolà. 'My friend', he said, 'thank you for all that you have done for me. I am leaving for Vienna. Please write and tell your Venetian friends.' Mazzolà was genuinely surprised and distressed at his friend's departure—perhaps he was also rather relieved. He ran after da Ponte, caught him up at the coach-station, and thrust a sheet of paper into his hand just as the coach was leaving. It was a letter to an intimate friend of his in Vienna, and it was, if only da Ponte had known it, to be of far greater value to him than Father Huber's gold coins.

'Dear Friend Salieri', Mazzolà had written. 'My well-beloved da Ponte will bring these few lines to you. Do as much for him as you would for me—his heart and talents deserve it—he is truly "pars animae dimidiumque meae".'

Da Ponte took his place in the coach, the doors were closed, the horses whinnied, and he moved off on his journey to Vienna—to the unknown.

CHAPTER V

THE LIBRETTIST

I

WHEN da Ponte had passed through Vienna two years earlier the city had been in mourning. On 29th November, 1780, the Empress Maria-Theresa had died, and had done so with the same serene faith and simple dignity with which she had lived.

'Her piety has been thought to border on bigotry', Dr Burney observed, 'but if we may judge of its effect by the tranquillity, happiness and affection of her people, compared with their turbulence, discontent and detestation of her unprincipled, philosophical and disorganising successor, we may suppose that too much religion is less mischievous in a sovereign than too little.' Dr Burney was an intelligent observer, and there were a great many people who agreed with his estimate of the new Emperor. Maria-Theresa was sincerely mourned by her subjects, more particularly by the older and the more conservative; it was the younger generation and the progressive thinkers who welcomed the new reign with high hopes.

When da Ponte returned to Vienna, in the spring of 1782, the atmosphere had changed very considerably. The feminine spirit, the elegance and strict etiquette, the pious catholicism of Maria-Theresa's court had been succeeded by the bachelor austerity and the spirit of enlightened reform which dominated that of her son. Although he had been a most devoted son—indeed Maria-Theresa was one of the very few people whom Joseph truly loved—most of his mother's ideas had been completely opposed to his own. During the last years of the old Empress's reign their differences of opinion, both on home and on foreign policy, had been fundamental; Joseph had been in the difficult position of being subordinate to his own mother and in opposition to her, and yet responsible for much of the conduct of affairs of state. On his mother's death he immediately began to put into practice those reforms of which he had dreamed since his earliest youth, and he did so with a precipitancy which makes it almost seem as if he was aware that his reign was to be a short one. Before Joseph's accession the Prince de Ligne had foretold that his reign would be 'a perpetual desire to sneeze', and he was right; there was a sense of insecurity, of something just about to happen, of success almost, but not quite achieved. Like his life, the Emperor's reign was an unresolved chord.

The results of Joseph's programme, which was to all intents and purposes a revolutionary programme within the framework of absolutism, were soon felt throughout the whole empire. Everyone, from the highest courtier, who was forbidden to kiss the new Emperor's hand or to kneel to him, down to the poorest peasant who suddenly found that his cause was being championed by the Emperor himself—everyone was surprised and, on the whole, mystified by the strange machinations and manifestations of enlightened despotism. By no means everyone found the new régime to their taste. Civil servants, who were accustomed to work with the inscrutable slowness and procrastination of their kind, were pained and surprised to find that the new Emperor was in the habit of enquiring frequently and sometimes personally as to whether his orders had been implemented immediately or not. The nobility and landowning classes were naturally opposed to Joseph's policy of diminishing their power and of liberating the serfs. They were also unfavourably impressed by Joseph's ideas of economy, of austerity and simplicity of manners; by his energy, by his habit of seeing to things personally, and by the high standards of work and efficiency which he expected from his subordinates. They did not appreciate the Emperor's enquiring mind, his interest in all new ideas, and his willingness to listen to his critics' point of view. The Empress of Russia had once compared him to Peter the Great: 'He allows people to contradict him', she had said; 'he is not offended by opposition to his opinions, and wants to convince people before giving orders.' But Joseph did not succeed in convincing people. It had all been better in Maria-Theresa's time, they felt, looking back with the love and nostalgia which it is so easy to feel for something which is irretrievably gone.

And yet, although he lacked the quality of being able to inspire affection, and was sometimes inconsistent and often mistaken in his actions, Joseph was a very remarkable man, with ideas far ahead of his time. In many ways and for many people life was easier during his reign than it had been during that of his mother. Under Joseph the Jews received partial emancipation, religious toleration was introduced, the death penalty removed from the Statute book, serfdom abolished, the censorship was relaxed—to mention but a few of Josephs reforms. The fact that he was forced to cancel most of them before his death does not detract from their value; it merely indicates how little support and understanding his ideas received. The Emperor was always ready to receive his subjects personally, princes and peasants alike, to listen to their grievances, and to do what he could, or what he considered just, to help them. Yet Joseph was unpopular, misunderstood, and his very real qualities were not appreciated by the Austrians, who found his unsmiling and austere character unsympathetic and most of his ideas incomprehensible.

If the Emperor's character was austere, however, that of his subjects was not, and Joseph's attempts to impose his ideals of hard work and frugality on the pleasure-loving and indolent Viennese had but little effect on the life of the capital. Concerts, masquerades, picnics on the banks of the Danube, amateur theatricals and sledge-rides by torch-light were the favourite pastimes of the light-hearted city, if not of its ruler. The passion for dancing at this time—a quarter of a century before the birth of Johann Strauss the elder—was already a Viennese speciality. 'The propensity of the Vienna ladies for dancing and going to carnival masquerades was so determined', an English traveller recorded, 'that nothing was permitted to interfere with their enjoyment of their favourite amusement—nay, so notorious was it that, for the sake of ladies in the family way who could not be persuaded to stay at home, there were apartments prepared with every convenience for their accouchement, should they be unfortunately required.' The Viennese were also 'doatingly fond' of music, but they were inclined to prefer novelty to depth, and were more enthusiastic than discriminating.

When da Ponte arrived in Vienna he at once went to visit Salieri. The letter of introduction to the composer which Mazzolà had given him had not been a mere empty gesture. Salieri was a most influential person in the theatrical life of Vienna, for he was Court Composer, and enjoyed the favour of the Emperor himself. Salieri was a small, vivacious man, said by those who knew them both to have strongly resembled David Garrick in appearance. He talked volubly in a sort of jargon, composed of Italian, German and French words, which he supplemented with frequent and eloquent gestures. In character, as in appearance, he was neat, methodical, and lively. He was well-known as a wit and a teller of humorous anecdotes, was popular in Vienna, and had a wide circle of friends. Although he was of an explosive temperament, quick to take offence and quick to forget it, Salieri was an extremely kind man, and was always helping other people, either financially or through his considerable influence at Court. He showed his own gratitude to others in practical ways, as for instance, when he educated the children of his teacher and benefactor Gassmann after their father's death. After Mozart's death Salieri befriended his son and used his influence to secure him his first appointment.

As a composer Salieri was by no means negligible. He consciously and conscientiously studied Gluck's style, and Gluck personally encouraged and helped him. In 1784 Gluck arranged for Salieri's opera *Les Danaïdes* to be produced in Paris as their joint work; after the twelfth performance, when the opera's success was already assured, Gluck announced publicly that it was the work of Salieri alone. Salieri's pupils included Beethoven, who often asked him for advice, Schubert, and Liszt, and he was a close friend of Haydn.

Da Ponte and Salieri had a certain amount in common; they were about the same age—Salieri was the younger by two years—and Salieri knew Venice well, for although he was born in Legnano, near Verona, he was educated at the choir school of San Marco. They also had a common interest in Italian literature, which Salieri greatly admired, and they seem to have liked each other at their first meeting. Although at that time Salieri could do nothing practical to help da Ponte, he promised that he would do what he could for him if ever an opportunity should arise.

This did not happen immediately, and da Ponte was forced to live very frugally for several months. He still did not speak German well, but instead of trying to learn it, he spent most of his time with other Italians, of whom there were a great number in Vienna at that time. It was one of his new Italian friends who offered to introduce him to the oldest and most eminent member of the Italian colony in Austria, the man who had been da Ponte's hero ever since his childhood—the poet Metastasio.

It was a great day for da Ponte. Metastasio received him very graciously, and showed interest in his poetry. In fact, the great man even read part of da Ponte's *Filemone e Bauci* aloud at one of the informal gatherings at which he was wont to entertain his friends. The old poet—Metastasio was eighty-four—was too tired to read the whole poem, and therefore asked da Ponte to finish reading it himself. Such favour from the greatest poet of the day naturally much enhanced da Ponte's literary reputation, and no doubt had a decisive effect on his subsequent career in Vienna.

When da Ponte met him, Metastasio had already long since ceased to be a mere man, and had become an institution—one is almost tempted to say a factory. His output as a librettist was prodigious, and every composer of note from Handel to Mozart set his words to music—Hasse is even said to have set all his libretti, some of them several times—and there are altogether over a thousand settings of his plays. He had been in Vienna so long that scarcely anyone could remember a time when he had not been there, or when opera libretti had been written by someone else.

Metastasio's real name was Pietro Trapassi; he was born in Rome in 1698, and was the son of a grocer. He apparently developed his poetic talent at a very early age, and used to amuse the other children in the street by improvising verses and by singing for them. One day while he was thus engaged, sitting on the pavement and surrounded by a crowd of grimy urchins like himself, a Roman gentleman who was passing by happened to hear his performance, and was struck by the boy's remarkable talent. In fact, the gentleman became so interested in young Trapassi that he finally adopted him and took him to live in his own house.

The boy's benefactor was the celebrated scholar and jurist,

Gravina, one of the founders of the Arcadian Academy, and a man of immense, albeit of rather dry, erudition. Gravina changed the boy's name from Trapassi to the more Hellenic Metastasio, and then set about training him as a jurist and developing his poetic talent with a complete disregard for his health and happiness. By the time he was twelve years old Metastasio had translated the whole of the *Iliad*, to say nothing of performing extraordinary feats of improvisation, writing poetry and studying law at the same time. It is not entirely surprising that when Gravina died in 1718, leaving all his fortune to his adopted son, Metastasio showed but little emotion. Gravina's arid pedantry and relentless insistence on study do not seem to have earned him the boy's love or gratitude.

After his patron's death Metastasio, who had taken minor orders, moved to Naples, and was there apprenticed to a lawyer. The young man's new master was of a different type to his old one, for he agreed to accept him only on condition that he should write no verse while he was apprenticed to him. However, Metastasio's reputation as a poet had reached Naples from Rome, and he was approached by the Viceroy of Naples with a request that he should write the words for an opera to be produced in honour of a royal birthday. It was a tempting proposition for a young and ambitious poet, and Metastasio finally agreed, on condition that his name should not be revealed. He wrote *Gli Orti Esperidi*, which was set to music by Porpora. The opera proved to be an immense success, and the whole of Naples was consumed with curiosity to know who had written the words. At length the secret was discovered by the singer Marianna Bulgarelli, known as La Romanina, who had taken the part of Venus in the opera.

It was La Romanina who took Metastasio under her wing and introduced him to society. She was considerably older than he was, and a curious, semi-maternal, semi-amorous relationship ensued. From that time onwards Metastasio abandoned law entirely, and made his living by his poetry. He was extremely musical, and in Naples, which was then one of the great musical centres of the world, he was constantly in contact with great musicians. He himself took lessons from such men as Hasse, Pergolesi, and Leo, and he was a close friend of Farinelli, the great castrato singer.

This musical training was of the greatest use to Metastasio in his subsequent career as a librettist. His understanding and knowledge of music and of the composer's point of view—for he often set his own words to music himself—enabled him to write verse which was suitable for a musical setting and which did not hamper the composer's work, but rather simplified it.

In 1729 Metastasio was invited to Vienna, and he remained there until his death, that is, for over half a century. By temperament he was not an adventurous man, and his life was one of comfortable and boring security. He remained in the same lodging for over fifty years, rarely if ever went out except to go to Mass, never bothered to learn German, and suffered from chronic hypochondria. When it was suggested to him that he might pay a visit to his native Rome, Metastasio replied: '. . . I have been a bird of court, almost *immemorabili*; not one in the woods, but used to ease, comfort and repose; and unable to fly here and there at a venture, exposed to all the severities of the season. So that to be safe conducted, I must be transported in my cage, with my water-glass and keeper to supply my wants.' He was only forty-four years old when he wrote these words. Almost the only event during Metastasio's fifty years in Vienna was a calm and cautious liaison with the mistress of his royal master, Charles VI; Countess Althann, who was, like La Romanina, years older than Metastasio, is said to have become his wife in secret.

Apart from his timidity and weakness of character, there was a certain cloying sweetness about Metastasio, as there was in his verses. A contemporary wrote of him shortly after his death: 'He disseminated that sweet urbanity which his heart never failed to furnish', and Casanova said that he was so modest that it did not seem natural. Goldoni, comparing Metastasio with his predecessor in Vienna, Apostolo Zeno, said: 'Their geniuses resembled their characters—Metastasio was mild, polished and agreeable in company; Zeno was serious, profound and instructive.' Even Dr Burney, who was a great admirer of Metastasio and wrote a three-volume biography of him, described him with the annihilating adjective 'innocuous'.

As a librettist Metastasio had great merits. He thoroughly understood what was required of him, both by the composers and by the audiences of his day—that is, those of his youth and his middle age —and his craftsmanship and musicianship were impeccable. He did his work quickly, efficiently and neatly, with no nonsense about poetic inspiration—in fact, Dr Burney tells us that Metastasio laughed at such ideas, and 'made a poem as another would make a watch, at what time he pleased, and without any other occasion than the want of it'. He adhered to the accepted rules of the day for libretto-writing: the action of the drama was carried forward in blank verse, which was set as *recitative*, and this was interspersed with lyrics which were usually solo arias or duets. Choruses were employed, but sparingly, and quartets, quintets and so on were, at the beginning of Metastasio's career, virtually unknown. Dr Burney expressed the division of labour between poet and musician as follows: 'The poet and musician claim equal attention from an audience; the bard in the recitatives and narrative parts, and the composer in the airs and choruses.' But this equilibrium was not to be maintained much longer; by the end of Metastasio's life *recitative* was already diminishing, concerted ensembles were becoming more and more prominent, and the old operatic conventions were being swept away. Libretti had to be altered to suit the new demands of composers; Metastasio's own *La Clemenza di Tito* was very considerably altered for Mozart—by da Ponte's friend, Caterino Mazzolà—and Mozart's opera is rather the last work of the old school than the first of the new.

Towards the end of his life Metastasio lost contact with his public which, considering the life he led, was not surprising. Tastes were changing, the composers for whom Metastasio had written, such as Hasse, Porpora, Jommelli, were dying out, and were being replaced by a new generation, by Salieri, Paisiello, Mozart. At the end of the eighteenth century the public no longer wanted the classical tragedies with which Metastasio had so faithfully provided it for over half a century; they were sick of the heroes of antiquity, and wanted something lighter, more amusing, more modern and in keeping with the spirit of the times. Metastasio lingered on, a relic from the past, a faithful servant of the Hapsburgs whom Maria-Theresa would never have dreamed of dismissing; but her son, who always looked forward and was imbued with the spirit of the new age, the age of enlightenment, probably felt, like the public, that the Caesarean Poet was unable to supply him with what he wanted. Metastasio had become a problem, but the problem did not last long.

Metastasio himself made no effort to compromise with the new age, and heartily disapproved of the new music. As early as 1756 he had described Gluck as 'a Bohemian composer, whose spirit, noise and extravagance have supplied the place of merit in many theatres of Europe', and he had no sympathy with Gluck's reforms and theories about opera either. Metastasio never heard any of Mozart's operas, but if he had he would undoubtedly have been deeply shocked by them. He would certainly have heartily endorsed the opinion of another critic of the old school (Lord Mount Edgcumbe) who, writing about the rising generation of operatic composers, said:

'The construction of these newly-invented pieces is essentially different from the old. The dialogue, which used to be carried on in recitative, and which in Metastasio's operas is often so beautiful and interesting, is now cut up (and rendered unintelligible if it were worth listening to) into *pezzi concertanti*, or long singing conversations, which present a tedious succession of unconnected, ever-changing motives, having nothing to do with each other; and if a satisfactory air is for a moment introduced, which the ear would like to dwell upon, to hear modulated, varied, and again returned to, it is broken off before it is well understood or sufficiently heard, by a sudden transition into a totally different melody, time and key, and recurs no more: so that no impression can be made, or recollection of it preserved. . . . The frippery and meretricious style of modern music is like tinsel to the eye. . . . '

Metastasio died on April 12th, 1782, only a few weeks after da Ponte's visit to him, and died, so the rumour ran, of a broken heart. Joseph had decided, on his accession, to discontinue the innumerable pensions which his mother had granted to almost anyone who applied for one. For example, having granted pensions to the Bishop of Gorizia for his father, mother, brother, sisters and all their servants, Maria-Theresa is said to have allowed the bishop three hundred florins a year for two of his father's old horses as well. Joseph gave orders that all pensions should be discontinued, but that an exception should be made in the case of the Caesarean Poet, who was a very old man and who had faithfully served the Hapsburgs through three reigns. He wrote an affectionate letter to Metastasio, informing him of his decision, but the poet died of grief before the Emperor's letter reached him.

Metastasio had praised da Ponte's poetry, and had even read it aloud in public; that was a great honour, and more than flattering, but what da Ponte needed immediately was money, or some means of making a living. Although he may have made a little by teaching or by writing flattering sonnets to rich members of the nobility, his earnings did not amount to much, and he was almost entirely supported for several months by a young and philanthropic lover of Italian literature. It was a depressing period, one of those periods of bad luck which seem eternal while they last. Without work, in a foreign country, almost penniless and friendless, and for once not even in love, da Ponte must have wondered, as he sat alone in the little room he had taken in a tailor's house in one of the suburbs of Vienna, if, at the age of thirty-four, the future held anything for him except poverty and obscurity. He had tasted success, and those who have once tasted it pine and languish without it. Had he not been considered one of the most promising poets in Venice? Had he not been received by the great families of the Republic? Had he not been the friend of the Gozzis, of Zaguri, of Memmo? Had he not been considered a distinguished man of letters in Gorizia, a member of the Arcadian Academy, received by all the nobility there, the protégé of Cobentzl, the guest of Count Torriani? And now? Now he was nothing, a penniless refugee in a huge and unfriendly city. He was plunged in apathy and boredom, in that frame of mind which makes any recovery very difficult, for if nothing succeeds like success, nothing communicates itself to others so easily and so disastrously as a sense of failure. It was one of the darkest periods in da Ponte's life, but it was the darkness which precedes the dawn.

II

In the spring of 1783 it was decided to engage a company of Italian singers for Vienna where, for some time, there had only been a company of German singers and a troupe of French comedians. The Italian opera was to replace the French company of actors whom the Emperor decided to dismiss, it is said, because they had criticised the wine which he had provided for them. A singer who owed his engagement in Vienna to the French company's dismissal was told that one of the French actors had, 'with the innate modesty so peculiarly belonging to his nation and profession', accosted the Emperor as he passed by the actors' dining-room, and having complained about the quality of the so-called Burgundy which they were drinking, he asked the Emperor to taste it for himself. Joseph did so, and then replied: 'I think it excellent, at least, quite good enough for *me*, though perhaps not sufficiently high-flavoured for *you* and your companions; in France, I dare say, you will get much better.' The French company was dismissed forthwith.

Rumours that changes were about to be made in the Imperial Theatre at length reached da Ponte. He had not forgotten Mazzolà's suggestion that he should try his hand at writing for the stage, and also, as he himself modestly put it, 'it occurred to me that I might become Caesarean Poet'. It was an ambitious idea, to say the least. The post of Caesarean Poet to the Roman Emperor was probably the biggest literary sinecure in Europe at that time, and almost every Italian poet or versifier—and almost all Italians were versifiers in the eighteenth century, when a sonnet was the equivalent of a greetings telegram nowadays—would have liked to succeed Metastasio. They would have liked to succeed him, but they never, even in their wildest dreams, imagined that they had any chance of doing so. How could anyone succeed Metastasio? He had been unique, a great genius, the foremost poet of Europe, he was irreplaceable—or at least, so most people thought. Not so da Ponte who, in spite of the fact that he was quite unknown in Vienna, and that anyway what slight reputation he had as a poet was amply counterbalanced by his considerable reputation as a political intriguer, renegade priest and adulterer, felt that he would make a very suitable successor to the great Roman poet. Had they not both changed their names?—for rather different reasons, it is true—but nevertheless it was symbolic. Had not Metastasio praised his, da Ponte's, verse just before he died? It was an excellent recommendation. Modesty was not one of da

Ponte's qualities, and he decided—and decided rightly—nothing venture, nothing gain. Mozart had noted a couple of years earlier that in Vienna 'whoever is most *impertinent* has the best chance', and his observation proved to be correct. Da Ponte went to Salieri and asked him to use his influence to help him, and Salieri, who had not forgotten his promise, willingly agreed. He approached Count Rosenberg on da Ponte's behalf, and presumably gave him a very glowing account of the poet's abilities. Count Rosenberg, who was Grand Chamberlain of the Court and Director of the Imperial Theatres, was a very important and influential person in Vienna, not only by virtue of his high office, but also because he was a close personal friend of the Emperor. He was also on very intimate terms with Salieri, a fact which was later to cause da Ponte a great deal of trouble, but which now stood him in good stead, for Rosenberg readily agreed to help him because Salieri had asked him to do so. Da Ponte was not made Caesarean Poet, but he was made the next best thing—Poet to the Imperial Theatres, with a salary of 1,200 florins a year. His duties were to provide comedies and libretti, for which he would receive royalties in addition to his salary. Da Ponte obtained this appointment—one of the most important appointments for a poet in the whole of Europe—just three years after he had been banished from Venice.

On taking up his appointment da Ponte was received in audience by the Emperor. The newly-appointed Poet to the Imperial Theatres was overawed, as well he might be, at the prospect of being received by the head of the Holy Roman Empire in person; but Joseph, whose passion for simplicity and informality was a by-word in Vienna, soon put him at his ease. Da Ponte was impressed by the Emperor's natural manners, by the simplicity of his dress—in fact, Joseph usually went about with his sleeves patched at the elbows—and by the interest he took in his new poet's personal affairs. Perhaps he even took too great an interest; when the Emperor asked him why he had left his native country da Ponte was forced to reply with extreme brevity, but the Emperor seemed to be satisfied with his answer, and did not pursue the subject any further. Finally Joseph asked da Ponte how many plays he had written. With some trepidation he replied,

'None, Sire!'

But the Emperor only smiled, and said:

'Good, good! Then we shall have a virgin muse.'

In after years da Ponte was wont to describe his first meeting with Joseph as the happiest moment of his life; it was, at any rate, a moment which inaugurated the most successful period of it. Salieri told him that the Emperor had been favourably impressed by him, and this good impression remained with Joseph until his death, despite da Ponte's many shortcomings. The Emperor liked da Ponte, found him amusing and intelligent, and he liked da Ponte's work. For the next few years Joseph was to be his staunchest— sometimes his only—ally, and in so far as their respective positions admitted it, the two men were friends.

Joseph II was, in many ways, a tragic figure, both in his private and in his public life. His private life virtually ceased on the death, in 1763, of his first wife, Isabella of Parma, whom he adored, but who had never truly reciprocated his love. She died three years after their marriage, and when she died Joseph the man died too—all that remained for the next thirty years was His Imperial Majesty, Joseph II. Broken-hearted as he was, Joseph was persuaded to marry again for diplomatic reasons; his second wife was Josepha, daughter of the Elector of Bavaria, and it would be difficult to say who suffered most in this marriage—Joseph, from his wife's existence, or Josepha, from her husband's indifference. Fortunately this unhappy state of affairs did not last long, for Josepha died in 1767, leaving Joseph embittered, childless, but free.

The Emperor did not have the capacity for making friends, nor for making himself popular with his subjects, and he led a lonely, austere life centred entirely around his work. This, too, gave him little happiness. The majority of his contemporaries did not understand or appreciate his ideas, his ideals, or the reforms which he tried to introduce. His ruling passion was military strategy, and he consciously tried to model himself on the pattern of his hero, Frederick the Great. However, his military genius was considerably less than that of Frederick, and he had no personal success in the sphere which appealed to him most. Although Joseph was interested in almost everything, and more especially in new ideas of a social and political nature, his interest in the arts—with one exception—was cursory and superficial. The one exception was the great interest which he took in the theatre.

The Emperor's connection with the theatre had started early in life. When he was three years old he took part in a ballet which was given at a gala luncheon at Court, and by the time he was six he was given the leading rôle in a comedy. Maria-Theresa, who had herself been coached by Metastasio, in amateur theatricals when she was a child, considered that such performances helped her children to acquire the self-possession and poise which, as future rulers of Europe, they so badly needed. When her eldest son grew up she found that, in his case at any rate, her training had worked only too well; he had become not only self-possessed, but obstinate and domineering into the bargain. But his interest in the theatre increased, and it was not purely theoretical, either. When Joseph succeeded to the throne he applied his administrative ability and his passion for reform to the theatre, and more particularly to the opera, as he did to everything else, and in this sphere, at any rate, some of his reforms were successful.

Joseph had a genuine love for music, although the extent of his understanding for it was revealed by his famous remark to Mozart after the first performance of *Die Entführung aus dem Serail:* 'Excellent, excellent, only there are rather too many notes in it'—a remark which bears comparison with that of another royal art critic, Nicholas I of Russia who, after reading Pushkin's great tragedy in blank verse, *Boris Godounov,* suggested that it would have been greatly improved if it had been written as a novel 'after the manner of Walter Scott'. Joseph sang—he is said to have had a fine bass voice —played the clavier, the 'cello and the viola, and was particularly good at sight-reading. After he had dined—punctually at quarter past three, and almost always on a dish of boiled bacon which, as a result of his partiality for it, became known as *Kaiser-Fleisch*—the Emperor almost every day had a concert in his private apartments. At these concerts, in which the Emperor himself and his brother, the Archduke Maximilian, usually took part, he would often go through the scores of operas which were later to be performed in the theatre. Joseph is said to have been particularly pleased and amused when the professional musicians who were reading the scores from sight made mistakes. Salieri who, like his teacher Gassmann, was a great favourite of the royal family, usually appeared before the Emperor at more formal concerts which were given three times a week.

Like his hero, Frederick the Great, Joseph occasionally made attempts at composition himself. His musical education had been acquired and his taste formed in the Italian school, and although he made attempts to encourage the establishment of a national German opera, this policy was dictated more by his reason and his passion for economy than by his heart.

In 1776 Joseph 'nationalised' the theatre, which had hitherto depended entirely on private patronage; he also lowered the prices of admission, and as a result a new and more democratic audience came into being. These were important steps which had a far-reaching effect on the history of the theatre in Vienna, and which must be numbered amongst Joseph's more successful minor reforms. In general, the Emperor took an active and personal interest in his theatres, more especially in the opera, and his interest was of a very practical nature. When he was travelling abroad he looked for new talent, went out of his way to hear singers and, if they pleased him, engaged them for Vienna; he also collected and sent back to the Director of the Imperial Theatres any new scores or libretti which seemed interesting to him, and which might be suitable for production. When he was in Vienna he personally went into such details as the singers' salaries, their holidays, their accommodation and general welfare. He drew up directives about the ordering and management of the theatres, made suggestions about casting, frequently attended rehearsals, and occasionally intervened and gave orders or advice on artistic matters and questions of production.

However, in spite of all this practical and often constructive work, Joseph nevertheless remained of the opinion that a hundred grenadiers were worth more than three comic actors who would cost the same amount, and in consequence he was usually inclined to engage not the best, but the cheapest singers and musicians. His parsimony had become a mania; and parsimony and opera are two incompatibles. The example of his economy which has gone down to history was his meanness to Mozart, who, when Joseph did finally give him

E

an official appointment, was allotted a salary of eight hundred gulden instead of the two thousand gulden which his predecessor, Gluck, had received. Joseph's hero, Frederick the Great, was less short-sighted in this respect, and would have been willing to pay Mozart three thousand gulden if he had agreed to go to Berlin.

On the whole, Joseph was popular with his singers and actors—more popular with them, in fact, than he was with his courtiers. He was extremely accessible, anyone could go and see him without ceremony at a certain time each day, and he was always ready to listen to his artists, to discuss their problems with them, and to help them. In fact, Joseph treated actors and musicians as human beings and not, as most eighteenth-century rulers did, as low-grade domestic servants. When Mozart was in the service of the Arch-bishop of Salzburg, for instance, he ranked below the valets.

The news that the Emperor was planning to engage an Italian opera company spread quickly, not only in Vienna, but throughout Europe. Musicians, singers, poets, and everyone who thought that they might in some way, however remote, profit from the new enterprise began to converge on Vienna. At that time singers and musicians had already become one of the principal Italian exports; although the demand for them was great, the opening of a new market was always an event, and when the new market was Vienna, the capital of the Holy Roman Empire and the seat of one of the most brilliant courts in Europe, it was a major event. Hopes ran high; everyone felt that with a new Emperor and a new opera com-pany there would be splendid opportunities for new talent. In Venice and Naples, in Dresden and London and St Petersburg, plans were made, trunks were packed, and artists of fame who were dis-contented and artists of promise with nothing to lose set out for the Austrian capital. Those who were already there set in motion those intrigues and cabals which have been an essential part of the theatre from time immemorial.

Amongst the travellers converging on Vienna there were several who were to be closely associated with da Ponte in his new capacity of Poet to the Imperial Theatres. Some of them, like Benucci, the *basso buffo*, Mandini, and Nancy Storace, an English singer of Italian origin, came with contracts in their pockets. Others, like Giambattista Casti, a much-travelled poet and satirist, or Paisiello, fresh from his successes in St Petersburg, had nothing but vague hopes, even vaguer promises, and their not inconsiderable artistic reputations.

One of the more fortunate ones was Michael Kelly, a young Irishman with a fine tenor voice and great gifts as a comic actor, who, after a tedious journey from Venice, arrived in Vienna and put up at the sign of the White Ox. Kelly had already signed a contract with the Austrian Ambassador in Venice; he was engaged for a year, with a salary of four hundred Venetian golden ducats, with free board, lodging and fuel and 'four large wax candles per diem, which was the customary allowance'. He was to be closely associated with da Ponte for many years and will, consequently, figure frequently in these pages.

Michael Kelly was a very young man when he arrived in Vienna —about eighteen years old—but he had already had a good deal of operatic experience and an eventful and interesting life. He had been born in Dublin, the child of musical parents, and he himself showed talent at a very early age. When he was fourteen years old he was sent—alone—to study music in Naples, and was there befriended by the British Ambassador, Sir William Hamilton and his first wife, who was a very remarkable amateur musician, and who is not to be confused with his second wife, Nelson's Emma. While in Naples Kelly studied singing with Finerolli, and was introduced to another pupil of his, Cimarosa. Indeed, he was fortunate enough to be in Naples at a time when it was one of the most musical cities in Europe, and he had the opportunity of hearing there some of the greatest musicians of the day. For instance, he heard the almost legendary *castrato* Pacchierotti, who was one of, if not the finest singer of the epoch. Pacchierotti's *forte* was the deeply-moving way in which he interpreted tragic rôles; it is said, for example, that once during a performance of Bertoni's opera, *Artaserse*, he was surprised and annoyed to find that, after the words *Eppur sono innocente* . . . the customary orchestral accompaniment was not forthcoming. Pacchierotti turned in irritation to the leader of the orchestra and asked: 'Well, what the devil are you doing?' The musician, immensely moved by Pacchierotti's performance, replied simply for himself and his colleagues, 'We are weeping.' Anyone who has had anything to do with the hard-bitten race of orchestral musicians will realise that this was a compliment indeed. Kelly also met and was given free lessons by Guiseppe Aprile, another famous *castrato* singer and teacher. He went with Aprile to Sicily, spent some time there, and then went on to Leghorn.

On his arrival in Leghorn an incident occurred which, although trivial at the time, was nevertheless memorable for Kelly in after years. 'After we had been visited by the officers of health', he tells us, 'I went on shore to show my passport at the Custom-house; I had on a Sicilian capote, with my hair (of which I had a great quantity, and which, like my complexion, was very fair) floating over it: I was as thin as a walking-stick. As I stepped from the boat, I perceived a young lady and gentleman standing on the Mole, making observations; as the former looked at me she laughed, and as I approached I heard her say to her companion in English which, of course, she thought I did not understand, "Look at that girl dressed in boy's clothes!" To her astonishment, I answered in the same language, "You are mistaken, Miss; I am a very proper *he* animal, and quite at your service!" ' So began a friendship which was to last for the rest of their lives. The English travellers with whom Kelly thus became acquainted at Leghorn were also musicians, Stephen Storace, a composer, and his sister Nancy, a singer. They were to meet again very shortly in Vienna, where da Ponte too was closely associated with them.

The Storaces were only half English, in fact; their father was a Neapolitan and had been a good bass-player in his day. Their mother had been born in Bath, and it was probably through her that the Storaces became friendly with the Sheridan family. When Richard Brinsley Sheridan first married he went to lodge with the elder Storaces in Marylebone. Later on Kelly and Stephen Storace got to know Sheridan very well and worked with him when they were all three connected with Drury Lane Theatre. Stephen Storace was a gifted man, not only in his chosen profession of music, but in painting as well. His sister Anna, or Nancy as she was usually called, ultimately became one of the foremost singers in Europe. When Kelly first met her, although she was still in her 'teens, she was already *prima donna* of the comic opera in Leghorn.

Kelly spent a few days with his new friends in Leghorn, and then went on to Lucca, Pisa, and finally to Florence, where he made his operatic début in *Il Franchese in Italia* with great success. His performance was attended, though not witnessed, by the 'Young' Pretender, then a very old man, who visited the theatre every night and invariably slept throughout the whole performance.

After leaving Florence Kelly travelled all over Northern Italy, crossed the frontier and went to Gratz, and finally returned to Venice, where he was reunited with Nancy Storace who was then drawing crowded houses at the San Samuele Theatre, where she was appearing in comic opera. It was while he was in Venice that Kelly received news of the formation of the Italian opera in Vienna, and that he and Nancy Storace were engaged to sing in it.

Kelly was a young man of wit and of great charm, and when he left Venice he carried letters of introduction from the many friends he had made there addressed to some of the most illustrious and influential people in Vienna: to Count Rosenberg, for instance; to His Britannic Majesty's Minister at Vienna, Sir Robert Keith; to the two great Marshalls, Lacy and Loudon; and last, but by no means least, to 'Le Prince de L'Europe', the Prince de Ligne, the greatest wit of his day and an intimate personal friend of the Emperor. A young man of eighteen could scarcely have arrived in the city with more brilliant recommendations.

Meanwhile, as Kelly and Nancy Storace prepared to leave Venice, as Paisiello jolted his way along the appalling roads of Eastern Europe on his way to the Austrian capital from St Petersburg, in Vienna itself there were many rumours and much activity. Shortly before Christmas, 1782, a young composer had attended a party given by the Russian Ambassador, Prince Galitzine, and had there heard rumours that some Italian singers might be coming to Vienna in the spring. Count Rosenberg approached him at the party, and suggested that he might write an Italian opera. Although this suggestion was not, in fact, to bear fruit for another three years, Mozart immediately began to look about for suitable libretti. He wrote off to his father in Salzburg, and also to friends in Italy, and asked them to send him texts which might be used for a comic opera. Had he but known it, the man who was to supply him with precisely what

he needed was already living only a few streets away from him in
Vienna.

III

Da Ponte's first work in his official capacity of Poet to the
Imperial Theatres naturally had to be for Salieri, who had procured
the position for him. He was very conscious of his lack of experience
as a writer for the opera, and also probably rather over-awed by
Salieri's reputation, which was very considerable. In order to learn
something more about the craft of dramatic writing before undertaking it himself, da Ponte went to see a certain Varesi, who owned
a large collection of Italian plays. Varesi, who was such a miser that
he was reputed to procure his meals by pilfering fruit and sweetmeats from the parties which he attended, was not inclined to be
co-operative. He refused to lend da Ponte any of his books, which
he esteemed as 'pearls of great price', and would only allow him to
look at one or two of them in his presence. After glancing through
some of the plays in this way da Ponte had soon seen enough to
realise that Varesi's 'pearls' were, in fact, very poor stuff, with no
plot, characterisation, style or humour. 'Poor Italy!' cried da Ponte,
and decided that it would not be at all difficult to do something
better. Full of confidence in his own abilities, he submitted several
plots to Salieri, and when the composer had made his choice the
poet set to work.

It was not long before da Ponte discovered that writing an opera
libretto was not, after all, so easy. The subject which Salieri had
chosen was not particularly suitable for an opera, and for the first
time da Ponte came up against the practical problems of working
for a composer. The finale of the first act, in particular, caused him
great difficulties—the finale, in which, as da Ponte said bitterly, 'the
genius of the composer and the power of the singers must shine, and
the greatest dramatic effect must be achieved. There is no recitative
in it, it is all singing, and singing of every kind: *adagio, allegro,
andante, amoroso, armonioso, strepitoso, arcistrepitoso, strepitosissimo,*
with which the finale almost always comes to an end: in technical
musical language this is called the *chiusa* (close) or *stretta* (straits).

I don't know whether it is so-called because it draws the play to a close, or because it generally puts the brain of the poor poet who has to write the words into such straits not once but a hundred times. In the finale, according to theatrical dogma, all the singers must appear on the stage, no matter if there are three hundred of them, one at a time, or two, three, six, ten or sixty at a time, to sing solos, duets, trios, sestets, or sessantets; and if the dramatic interest does not allow of this, it's up to the poet to find a way of making it do so, despite better judgment, reason, and all the Aristotles in the world—and if it should then turn out badly, so much the worse for him.'

Da Ponte tackled this seemingly hopeless task to the best of his ability, and then, in fear and trembling, showed what he had written to Salieri. To his great surprise, the composer was most affable; he said that da Ponte's work was not bad at all, and that only a few small alterations would be needed. Da Ponte, who had no experience of musicians, went home delighted. He soon discovered what Salieri meant by 'a few small alterations'. He was asked to 'mutilate or lengthen most of the scenes, introduce new duets, trios, quartets, etc., to change the metre in the middle of an aria, to insert choruses (to be sung by Germans!), to take away almost all the recitative, and consequently all the plot and interest of the play, in so far as it had any, so that when the play was put on the stage I don't think a hundred of my original lines remained!' On 7th May, 1783, Mozart wrote to his father that da Ponte was being 'driven frantic with the alterations he has to make for the theatre'.

The production of *Il Ricco d'un Giorno*—for such was the title of the mangled remains of da Ponte's libretto for Salieri—was postponed for some time, for various reasons. In the meantime two formidable newcomers arrived in Vienna—newcomers who were to prove dangerous rivals to da Ponte, Salieri, and Mozart. The first to arrive was the poet, the Abbé Giovanni Battista Casti. He came to Vienna from Milan, where he had been recovering from a serious illness—an illness which, according to gossip, had been caused by the dissipated life he had been leading. In any case, his voice had been strangely affected—a fact which distressed him very much, as it prevented him from reading his poetry aloud. Casti was to be da Ponte's principle rival and enemy during the years he spent in

Vienna. When he arrived in that city he was a danger to him more because of his influential friends than because of his reputation as a poet; although he was almost sixty years old at that time, he had not yet written any of the works on which his reputation now rests, and like da Ponte, he had practically no experience of writing for the stage. His talent had developed late in life, and he had not turned seriously to literature until he was approaching forty.

Casti's education and early career closely resembled those of da Ponte. He was born in Acquapendente in 1724, educated in a seminary, and eventually took minor orders. At a very early age he became professor of Greek and Latin, and later a Canon of the Cathedral of Montefiascone. But Casti was a restless person, and could never stay in one place for very long; he went to Rome, where he became a member of the Arcadian Academy, and then visited France and Holland. In 1765 he turned up in Florence, where he found favour with the Grand Duke Leopold, Joseph II's younger brother, and made friends with Count Rosenberg-Orsini. Rosenberg, who had been Austrian Ambassador in Madrid, became Leopold's Prime Minister in 1766; he it was who later became Joseph's Grand Chamberlain and Director of the Imperial Theatres in Vienna. In 1766 or 1767 Casti was made Court Poet by Leopold —a title which he was to hold for the rest of Leopold's life, although he was hardly ever in Tuscany and never took his duties very seriously. In 1769 Joseph visited his brother, and met Casti, whom he found very amusing and witty, as everyone—or almost everyone —did.

Although Casti had an excellent position at the Tuscan court, he did not stay there very long. The urge to travel was on him again, and in 1772 he accompanied Count Rosenberg to Vienna; Rosenberg introduced him to many influential people in the capital, among others to the Austrian Chancellor, Kaunitz, the most influential person of all. The result of this meeting was that Casti accompanied Kaunitz's son, Joseph, on several journeys which took him all over Europe. During the next ten years he visited Prussia, Sweden, Russia, and Spain and Portugal; during all this time he remained on the best of terms with the Grand-Duke Leopold, who apparently had no objection to his Court Poet's wanderings. In 1782

Casti fell ill in Milan, and remained there until he went to Vienna in 1783.

As a poet Casti's reputation was, at that time, rather slender. He did not write his principal work, *Gli Animali Parlanti*, until twelve years later, and most of his *Novelle* were written between 1793-1795. He was a satirist, not a lyric poet, and had a reputation for writing witty, salacious verse. Professor Dent has called him the 'Gilbert of his day', and there is much truth in the comparison; but although Gilbert was certainly witty, in his libretti he never wrote a line which could not have been repeated in any Victorian drawing-room, whereas even the eighteenth century considered Casti's work very indecent. His biting social and political satire, often expressed in the form of fables, was nearer to George Orwell than to Sullivan's librettist. As one of his early English translators said: 'Passion, as exhibited in the softer affections, was not Casti's *forte*: his talent lay in the ridicule and an agreeable irony, to which he brought great learning, sound judgment, and an inexhaustible invention and humour: it cannot be too much regretted that in lighter points his taste was not of a more severe nature.' The same writer—the date was 1826—went on to say that his ' "*Novelle* or Tales in Verse", are of a character that entirely forbids their perusal to modest eyes.' Casanova's eyes could scarcely be placed in this category, and he was curious to meet Casti because of 'certain very blasphemous little poems of which he was the author'; but when they did meet, in Trieste in 1773, he was not impressed by the poet. Casti was visiting Trieste with Count Rosenberg, with whom he had formed an intimate and lasting friendship. According to Casanova, Rosenberg took Casti about with him because he was useful as a clown and also as a 'pourvoyeur de filles'—two functions, as Casanova justly remarked, well in keeping with his low character, but not with his ecclesiastical status. Nor did Casti's wit come up to Casanova's expectations. 'Instead of a man of wit', he said scathingly, 'I found that the Abbé was nothing but an ignorant brazen fellow, very insolent, and with no merits beyond a very great facility for versification.' Casanova never read Casti's masterpiece, *Gli Animali Parlanti*—if he had he might have written less harshly about him as a poet, if not as a man.

EX

It was not surprising that da Ponte learnt of Casti's arrival in Vienna with misgiving. Here was a formidable rival to the newly-appointed theatre poet, here was a man who was the intimate personal friend of the Director of the Theatres, who had been Poet to the Tuscan Court for years, even if he did neglect his duties almost entirely, who was the favourite of the Grand Duke Leopold, and was liked by Joseph II. That Casti came to Vienna in the hope of obtaining the title of Caesarean Poet—a title which da Ponte had not given up hope of getting himself—is certain; in fact, he had received a letter from Brambilla, Court Surgeon to the Emperor, informing him that he had a very good chance of succeeding Metastasio, and had promptly set off for Vienna as a result. With such influential patrons and friends it seemed very likely that his ambition would be realised.

If Casti's arrival in Vienna was a threat to da Ponte, Salieri was none too pleased by the arrival, seven months later, of Giovanni Paisiello. Paisiello came to Vienna from St Petersburg, where he had spent eight years at the court of Catharine II, and where he had probably already met Casti. Like so many other Italian musicians, notably Galuppi and Sarti, Paisiello had such a success in Russia that his influence completely stifled any attempts which the Russians themselves might have made to create a national opera. The Empress Catharine herself was no great connoisseur of music—'Un grand opéra est un peu dûr à la digestion', she wrote to Grimm—but she liked Paisiello both as a musician and as a man. It is said that when Marshal Beloselsky—a member of one of the greatest families in Russia—so far forgot himself in a fit of jealousy as to strike Paisiello, the musician retaliated by giving the Marshal a sound thrashing. When Beloselsky complained to the Empress and demanded Paisiello's dismissal, Catharine took the musician's side. 'It is in my power to make fifty marshals', she is said to have replied, 'but not one Paisiello.'

In 1782 Paisiello's *Barbiere di Siviglia* was performed in St Petersburg with extraordinary success—a success which drew attention to Beaumarchais as a source for librettists. A year later, in 1783, the same composer's *Il Mondo della Luna* was chosen to be performed at the opening of the new Bolshoi Theatre in St Petersburg. In the same year the composer was granted leave of absence to visit Italy, and he never returned to Russia.

When Paisiello arrived in Vienna the Emperor, who liked his music, wished to see him; he also wished to see Casti again, whom he had not seen for many years, and so the two men were presented to him on the same day. 'I think I may say', Joseph is said to have remarked at this interview, 'that I have before me two of the greatest geniuses alive, and it would be most gratifying to me to have an opera, the joint production of both, performed at my theatre.' Count Rosenberg had no doubt put in a good word for Casti, who modestly said that he was unwilling to branch out into what was, for him, an entirely new field; however, he of course allowed himself to be persuaded. He set to work, inspired, as he himself admitted, by Voltaire's *Candide*, and perhaps also by a hint given him by Joseph II. The opera, based on the story of Baron Theodore de Neuhoff who became King of Corsica in 1736, was called *Il Re Teodoro in Venezia*.

Meanwhile, Michael Kelly made the acquaintance both of Casti and of Paisiello; Mozart he knew already, for they had met at a supper given by Kozeluch, and had become friendly. It was in Mozart's own house that Kelly saw the two composers meet for the first time; although they were potential rivals in opera, Mozart and Paisiello were known to have a high regard for each other's work. Kelly saw a good deal of the two musicians; in the company of Paisiello and Casti he heard a string quartet performed by Haydn, Mozart, Dittersdorf and Vanhall, and the young Irish boy—for he was little more—amused them with his 'monkey anticks', with his high spirits, his charm, and his talent for mimicry.

One day, when a particularly gay party was in progress, Stephen Storace persuaded Kelly to give his famous imitation of the old miser Varesi, the poet who had refused to lend da Ponte his collection of Italian plays and whose stinginess and eccentricity were by-words in Vienna. Casti watched Kelly attentively throughout his performance. 'When I had finished', Kelly described the scene, 'he turned to Paisiello and said "This is the very fellow to act the character of Gafforio in our opera".' Gafforio, the King's secretary, was a character of some importance in the opera; Casti had been having difficulty in finding a suitable actor to play the part and had,

in fact, sent off to Venice to try to engage Blasi for it 'at any price'.
'This boy shall be our old man!' Casti went on. 'And if he keeps
Varesi in his eye when he acts it, I will answer for his success!'
Kelly took the part, and performed it so well that he was given a
rise of salary by the Emperor as a result. Wherever he went the
eighteen-year-old singer was nicknamed 'Old Gafforio'.

Il Re Teodoro in Venezia was first performed on 23rd August,
1784, and was received with acclamation by the public. Even da
Ponte was forced to admit its success. 'The singers were all excellent',
he said, 'the décor was superb, the costumes magnificent, the music
divine.' He was less lavish with praise of the libretto, and maintained
that the opera was a success in spite of, and not because of it. Nevertheless he was intelligent enough to realise that Casti's witty play
would put his own amateurish libretto for Salieri completely in the
shade. Salieri, too, probably saw the shortcomings in his new opera,
and considered that it would be a mistake to produce it immediately
after Paisiello's immensely successful work; the first performance of
Il Ricco d'un Giorno was, therefore, postponed for some time. In any
case, the music was not completed until the autumn of 1784, for in April
of that year Salieri had gone to Paris for the production of *Les Danaïdes*,
and this journey had interrupted his work on his opera for Vienna.

Il Ricco d'un Giorno was at last performed, on 6th December, 1784.
It was as outstanding a failure as Paisiello and Casti's opera had been
a success. Although the opera itself was a poor piece of work, everything conspired to make its first performance a veritable fiasco.
Nancy Storace, who was to have taken the principle part, was ill,
and the singer who took her place was totally unsuitable. In addition,
a certain Brunati, an aspiring librettist, had somehow obtained a
copy of da Ponte's libretto before the performance; he had the
bright idea of writing a scathing criticism of it, which he had printed,
and then sold in the theatre on the first night. Da Ponte always suspected that Casti had a hand in this plot, too. The failure was complete; the opera was hissed, and a spate of pamphlets and lampoons
appeared against da Ponte and his verses. Salieri swore that he would
never set another word by da Ponte to music again, and Rosenberg,
probably with his friend Casti in mind, said that he would have to
look for another poet for the theatre.

Amidst all this hostility da Ponte had only two allies—one very powerful, and one very stupid. After his failure he had not had sufficient courage to go to see the Emperor, but one day he met him by chance. Joseph stopped him, and said kindly: 'You know, da Ponte, your opera isn't as bad as they say. You must pluck up your courage and give us another.' The Emperor refused to take Rosenberg's hint that da Ponte should be dismissed and Casti appointed in his stead.

The only other encouragement which da Ponte received came from a rather unexpected quarter. On 15th January, 1785, that well-meaning bore Coletti published some verses by da Ponte in the newspaper which he was then editing in Trieste. He prefaced these verses with the following words: 'After the applause obtained in Vienna by the comic opera *Il Ricco d'un Giorno* of Signor Abate Lorenzo da Ponte, member of the Arcadian Academy of Rome and Gorizia, and Poet to the Imperial Theatres in Vienna, the said author has published a *Canzonetta* dedicated to the Fair Sex as an apology for his way of writing against the same and proof of the respect which he professes to have towards it. We give ourselves the pleasure of publishing it. . . .' Only a man as kind and as stupid as Coletti could have transformed the boos and hisses which had greeted *Il Ricco d'un Giorno* into applause. This was but one of the many attempts which Coletti made to render service to da Ponte, who nevertheless persisted, even after Coletti's death, in describing him as an unscrupulous intriguer.

Da Ponte did not pluck up his courage and write something new for the stage for a whole year. Composers were none too keen to collaborate with a poet whose first dramatic effort had been so disastrous, and in any case da Ponte was unwell for several months. His ill-health was caused by a rather curious chain of events, and a woman was indirectly and unwillingly responsible for it.

In the house in which da Ponte was living there was a beautiful young girl. He scarcely knew her, and was, in fact, in love with another woman at that time; but she, in order to repulse the advances of an unwelcome and unattractive Italian suitor, pretended to be in love with da Ponte. The consequences were most unfortunate for him. One day he chanced to meet the Italian in a café, and in the course of conversation told him that he had a painful abscess on his gum which would have to be lanced. The Italian who, unknown to da Ponte, was bitterly jealous of him, offered to cure the abscess without lancing it, if da Ponte would give him a sequin. Da Ponte gave him the money, the Italian went away and soon returned with a small bottle containing a liquid which, he said, should be applied to the abscess.

At first all went well; by the end of the week the abscess had almost gone, and da Ponte was full of gratitude to his benefactor. However, one day the woman who looked after his clothes for him saw him applying the liquid to his mouth. She looked at the bottle more closely, and then gave a cry of horror. She realised that da Ponte had been applying *aqua fortis* to his gums, and although she made him rinse his mouth out with all manner of antidotes, the harm was already done. Gradually all his teeth fell out, and the drops of *aqua fortis* which he had inadvertently swallowed seriously affected his health for some time. The jealous Italian who had thus injured his imaginary rival was prudent enough to leave Vienna before his victim could retaliate; but da Ponte saw him again eight years later in Gorizia. Seeing a crowd assembled, da Ponte, who was passing by, went to see what was happening; he saw the Italian who had been responsible for the loss of his teeth lying on the ground gravely injured and, as da Ponte recorded with evident satisfaction, with all *his* teeth knocked out.

When he had recovered his health and also his self-confidence da Ponte began to think about writing another libretto. But for whom should he write it? Apart from Salieri, who was clearly out of the question, there were several other composers of opera in Vienna just then, amongst them a Spaniard, Vincenzo Martin y Soler, who was usually known as Martin or sometimes as Martini. He was a young man of thirty-two who had already had some success in Florence as a composer of opera, but who was at that time scarcely known in Vienna. The Emperor suggested that Martin and da Ponte should collaborate, and although there was a good deal of intrigue on the part of Casti and Rosenberg to prevent their collaboration, the Emperor's suggestion was naturally obeyed. Da Ponte decided to adapt Goldoni's play *Le Bourru Bienfaisant* as a comic opera; in those days there was no such thing as copyright, and no one had the slightest scruples about 'adapting', altering, translating, or appropriating other people's works without any acknowledgment to the original author whatsoever. Casti, who of course, like every cultured Italian of the day, knew Goldoni's play well, did all he could to prejudice public opinion against the opera before it was produced. He maintained that the subject was not a suitable one for a comic opera, and even said so in the presence of the Emperor.

When he next saw his theatre poet Joseph said to him:

'Da Ponte, your friend Casti says that the *Burbero* won't make people laugh.'

'Your majesty', da Ponte replied. 'We must wait and see. It will be all to the good for me if it makes *him* cry.'

To which the Emperor replied: 'I hope it will!'

When the opera was produced, on 4th January, 1786, it was a great success. Joseph applauded throughout the performance, and when it was over, whispered to the author: 'We have won!' Casti and Rosenberg were naturally less enthusiastic about da Ponte's achievement, and greeted him coldly when he went to ask them their opinion of the opera. In fact, they were so obviously hostile that da Ponte felt that it would be useless for him to go on struggling against the Director of the Theatres, and decided to hand in his resignation. However, when he went to tell the Emperor of his decision, Joseph congratulated him so warmly and insisted so strongly that he should follow up his success as quickly as possible with another opera for Martin, that he was forced to change his mind.

Casti's criticism continued, but the success of *Il Burbero* had brought da Ponte a certain amount of fame, and composers were no longer so reluctant to set his words to music. Salieri, it is true, had joined the Casti-Rosenberg faction, but Guiseppe Gazzaniga asked da Ponte for a libretto. This time the poet decided to adapt a French comedy, *L'Aveugle Clairvoyant*, but for various reasons—one being that Gazzaniga was preoccupied with a love-affair with a lady of fifty at the time and could not devote his full attention to the music —the opera was not a success. It was out of date, being mostly a rearrangement of an earlier opera, *Il Finto Cieco*, which had been produced in Vienna in 1770; da Ponte's version was only performed three times. However, da Ponte was not particularly abashed by this failure; his mind was fully occupied with plans for the future, for he was already thinking of writing a libretto for Mozart.

CHAPTER VI

THE LIBRETTIST

Le Nozze di Figaro

LORENZO DA PONTE met Mozart at the house of Baron Wetzlar —when, it is not quite clear, but probably as early as 1783. Baron Raimund Wetzlar von Plankenstern was a close friend of the Mozarts', besides being, for a time, their landlord; in January 1783 the newly married couple—Mozart had married Constanze Weber in August of the preceding year—moved into Wetzlar's house, where they occupied a flat on the third floor. When Mozart's first child was born Wetzlar was godfather to him—he was christened Raimund Leopold, after his godfather and Mozart's father. How and when da Ponte met Wetzlar is not known, but as they were both converted Jews they had at least something in common. Perhaps Wetzlar took da Ponte to a party which the Mozarts gave in February 1783 and which must have been a very gay one, for it lasted from six o'clock in the evening until seven o'clock the next morning. Wetzlar attended this party with his wife, and he may well have taken the new Italian Poet to the Imperial Theatres with him, for he probably knew how interested Mozart was at that time in finding new libretti. Wetzlar, who was a rich man, apparently sometimes helped Mozart financially, and later on, when there were difficulties about the first performance of *Figaro* in Vienna, he offered to help da Ponte and Mozart on a generous scale.

Nothing is known about the first meeting of Mozart and da Ponte—a meeting that was to be momentous for them both, but which did not, apparently, make much impression on either, for neither recorded anything about it. Although they probably both realised that there were possibilities of collaboration, nothing came of the meeting for some months.

That Mozart and da Ponte were intimate friends is to be doubted;

they had very little in common, and were men of totally opposed characters and tastes. Their temperaments were strongly conditioned by their nationalities: education and environment had made da Ponte a typical Venetian; although Mozart's early life and upbringing had been cosmopolitan, he still remained very Austrian at heart. Da Ponte was principally interested in himself, and in literature; he had no spiritual yearnings, and was not troubled by problems of philosophy or morality—his philosophy, in so far as he had any, was the typically Venetian one of *carpe diem*. By temperament Mozart was gay and sunny, but on a deeper level he had a basically serious approach to life, and as he grew older he was increasingly concerned with the fundamental questions of life and death. He had been brought up as a good Catholic, and if he eventually evolved a philosophy of life outside the framework of the Church—he became a Freemason in 1784—he was nevertheless always an intensely spiritual and believing man.

Their early life, too, had been very different: while da Ponte had been whoremongering and gambling and revelling in the low life of Venice, Mozart had been touring Europe as an infant prodigy, had been working and studying and composing, and had had no real childhood and very little normal youth. When da Ponte, as a boy of fourteen who could scarcely read or write, had been received into the Catholic Church in 1763, Mozart, then seven years old, was making his third tour as a concert pianist and was already beginning to compose himself. In 1770, when da Ponte was enjoying his first love-affair, Mozart received the Order of the Golden Spur from the Pope, and was elected a member of the Philharmonic Society of Bologna. Whereas most of Mozart's life had been work, most of da Ponte's had been play, and play of a rather dubious kind. When the two men met da Ponte was still playing; Mozart, on the other hand, had just married, and was deeply engrossed in his new family life. It seems unlikely that they found much in common—and yet, as very different people sometimes do, they seem to have got on well together, for later on Mozart apparently seriously considered accompanying da Ponte to London.

Mozart may not have found a kindred spirit and boon companion in da Ponte, but he found something much more important, and something for which he had been searching for years: he found in him an ideal collaborator, a poet whose mind, artistically, was perfectly attuned to his own—not because it resembled his own, but because it provided the right foil for it. Before he met da Ponte, Mozart had had much to do with librettists, none of whom had really provided him with what he wanted; it was, perhaps, as a result of his unfortunate experiences that he knew so well precisely what he did want. He held strong views about theatre poets, as can be seen from a letter to his father, written on 13th October, 1781, when he was working on *Die Entführung aus dem Serail*:

'... I should say that in an opera the poetry must be altogether the obedient daughter of the music. Why do Italian comic operas please everywhere—in spite of their miserable libretti—even in Paris, where I myself witnessed their success? Just because there the music reigns supreme and when one listens to it all else is forgotten. Why, an opera is sure of success when the plot is well worked out, the words written solely for the music and not shoved in here and there to suit some miserable rhyme (which, God knows, never enhances the value of any theatrical performance, be it what it may, but rather detracts from it)—I mean, words or even entire verses which ruin the composer's whole idea. Verses are indeed the most indispensable element for music, but rhymes—solely for the sake of rhyming—the most detrimental. Those high and mighty people who set to work in this pedantic fashion will always come to grief, both they and their music. The best thing of all is when a good composer, who understands the stage and is talented enough to make sound suggestions, meets an able poet, that true phoenix; in that case no fears need be entertained as to the applause even of the ignorant. Poets always remind me of trumpeters with their professional tricks! If we composers were always to stick so faithfully to our rules (which were very good at a time when no one knew better), we should be concocting music as unpalatable as their libretti.'

There is no doubt at all that in Lorenzo da Ponte, Mozart met the 'able poet' for whom he had been searching so long.

Mozart believed that in opera the words should be entirely subordinate to the music; there have been many in history—including the earliest Florentine school of opera composers, Gluck, Metastasio and Wagner—who disagreed with him. The question always has been, and presumably always will be, a controversial one. Mozart wanted what, to a certain extent, an earlier generation had indeed found in Metastasio—a good craftsman; but Metastasio had written for the musicians of his own day, and by the time Mozart was writing, opera had developed in such ways as to render Metastasio's libretti quite unsuitable. Da Ponte was a good craftsman and, equally important, he was of Mozart's own generation—just seven years older, to be precise. He was not too great a poet, or at that time too pretentious a man to resent having to take second place, or to refuse to accept advice from Mozart, who had far more stage experience than he had. He was not concerned with writing masterpieces, he wished to please the public of his day, which is perhaps precisely why he did succeed in producing masterpieces, for the public, by and large, always wants the same thing—to be entertained.

In his letter to his father Mozart had stressed the great importance of collaboration between poet and musician. 'The best thing of all is when a good composer, who understands the stage and is talented enough to make sound suggestions, meets an able poet. . . .' How much Mozart himself contributed to the planning and execution of the libretti da Ponte wrote for him is not known, but in all probability it was a great deal. He certainly 'understood the stage' and had a remarkably developed dramatic sense. His comments on libretti and the alterations he made to various texts on which he worked—notably *Idomeneo*—reveal his deep insight into dramatic technique and his flair for theatrical effect. He never lost sight of the fact that operas are written for performance in the theatre, not in some idealised and theoretical theatre, but the ordinary commercial theatre, with all its limitations and restrictions, and that operas must therefore be conceived within the framework of the theatre, must conform to its conventions, and must make use of all its tricks. Although as a very young man Mozart had accepted unsuitable and even positively bad libretti and had made the best of them, as he became more mature as a composer of opera he became more critical and more sure of what he required from a poet. In fact, he ultimately became so critical that he had the greatest difficulty in finding suitable libretti at all, although he read through an enormous number of texts in his search for what he wanted. 'I have looked through at least a hundred libretti and more', he wrote to his father on 7th May, 1783, 'but I have hardly found a single one with which I am satisfied; that is to say, so many alterations would have to be made here and there, that even if a poet would undertake to make them, it would be easier for him to write a completely new text—which indeed it is always best to do. . . .' Mozart probably never completed several operas—*L'Oca del Cairo* and *Lo Sposo Deluso* among them—because the texts did not satisfy him. The older he was, the more part he took in the composition of a libretto, and he must have driven some of his librettists—for instance, Stephanie, who adapted the words for *Die Entführung aus dem Serail* from a play by Bretzner—frantic with the numerous alterations and omissions and additions which he required. But Mozart was usually right; almost all the alterations which he made or suggested to poets were improvements, and his insistence on the closest possible collaboration between poet and musician was amply justified by the results.

There is no reason to suppose that da Ponte was any exception to the rule and that Mozart made no criticism of his work—on the contrary, when da Ponte first offered him a libretto (*Lo Sposo Deluso* in 1783) Mozart wrote to his father that he would set it to music only if the poet would agree to make all the alterations to it which he might demand. The fact that da Ponte gives almost no information about the composition of the libretti he wrote for Mozart perhaps indicates that the composer contributed a great deal to them; da Ponte was not the man to acknowledge such help, even from Mozart. It may be, too, that one of the reasons why none of da Ponte's libretti for other composers—with the possible exception of *Una Cosa Rara* for Martin—ever had such lasting success as those he wrote for Mozart, is that Mozart himself contributed more to his libretti in the form of suggestions and advice than we know.

Da Ponte was able, then, to supply Mozart with what he required: good craftsmanship, willing subordination to the music, verse expressed in the contemporary idiom, and the whole work carried out in the closest collaboration with the composer. He supplied him with more—with wit, sound plot construction, good characterisation, and elegant verse. Yet all these qualities—which Casti, for example, could probably have supplied just as well as da Ponte, if not better—do not explain why da Ponte, the licentious, unscrupulous adventurer, the facile, mediocre poet, the very inexperienced dramatist, should be the man who, above all others, succeeded in providing Mozart with the perfect framework for his music, and in collaborating with him to produce three of the very few operas in existence in which the words blend so perfectly with the music as to produce a truly homogeneous work of art. The explanation for this probably lies in the unexplainable. Artistic collaborations are like love-affairs; they do not depend on similarity of character or temperament, but rather on whether two minds vibrate on the same wave-length, whether they are attuned to each other. This combination in art of two minds complementary rather than similar, is not necessarily the product of personal sympathy and understanding between two artists; it is a combination which takes place on a higher level than that of personal relations, in a purely intellectual sphere. Indeed, one of the most successful artistic partnerships in the history of operetta—that of Gilbert and Sullivan—was between two men of totally opposed character whose personal dislike for each other frequently led them to communicate only through a third person. In the case of Mozart and da Ponte there is no reason to suppose that they disliked each other—on the contrary —but it is reasonable to suppose that as men they did not have much in common. Yet, as artists, their respective mentalities and temperaments interacted in such a way as to produce works which, if not perfect (and, as will be seen, there have been numerous critics, and critics whose opinion is to be respected, to point out the imperfections in *Figaro, Don Giovanni* and *Così fan Tutte*) are at least aesthetically almost completely satisfying.

In this partnership Mozart was the active, da Ponte the passive, partner; Mozart provided the intellectual depth and thought in their work, da Ponte contributed the framework and the frills. Mozart could truly say to da Ponte, as Louis Bouilhet once wrote to a woman:

Ta lampe n'a brûlé qu'en empruntant ma flamme.

Comme le grand convive aux noces de Cana,
Je changeais en vin pur les fadeurs de ton âme,
Et ce fut un festin dont chacun s'étonna.

Tu n'as jamais été, dans tes jours les plus rares,
Qu'un banal instrument sous mon archet vainqueur,
Et, comme un air qui sonne aux bois creux des guitares,
J'ai fait chanter mon rêve au vide de ton coeur . . .

What, it may be asked, might have happened if da Ponte's first libretto for Salieri had been a success and if, as a result, he had not been free to write for Mozart? It would be futile to suggest that Mozart could not have written a successful comic opera without da Ponte, but it would be only too true to say that da Ponte's name would scarcely be remembered today if he had not collaborated with Mozart. However, such speculation is in no way profitable; now, over 150 years after their meeting, we can only be grateful that Mozart did in fact find da Ponte, a man who was nothing but an adventurer and an able poet, but who yet was capable of giving him what he wanted at the time when he needed it most. When they met, Mozart's immortality was already assured, but as a result of that meeting da Ponte, too, has earned a very small, yet nevertheless permanent, place amongst the Immortals.

Nowadays Mozart's name has become so great, whereas those of other musicians contemporary with him, such as Salieri, Paisiello, Martin and Sarti, have been so completely forgotten, that it is difficult for us to realise how little Mozart was known and esteemed in Vienna at the time of his meeting with da Ponte. When Mozart arrived in Vienna in March 1781 he was still in the service of the Archbishop of Salzburg. He did not succeed in freeing himself from this humiliating and unprofitable post until June of the same year, when he gave his resignation, and was literally kicked out of the Archbishop's ante-chamber by the chamberlain. Although Mozart was highly valued as a performer, and there was a small set of discerning people in Vienna who valued his genius as a composer— Haydn was among them—his first years as a free-lance in Vienna were very difficult. He gave concerts, took pupils, and thus managed to earn just enough to live on, but his ambition had always been to write for the stage, and in this respect there were many obstacles in his way.

Opera in Vienna at that time meant Italian *opera buffa*. Although Mozart had written two such operas—*La Finta Semplice* (when he was twelve) and *La Finta Giardiniera* (when he was nineteen)—to say nothing of an *opera seria*, *Idomeneo*, and various other operatic works both German and Italian, he was not an Italian composer and was scarcely known in Vienna as a composer of opera at all. When he arrived in the Austrian capital there were several Italian composers of opera already installed there, with established reputations in that field; they were well-known to the Viennese public and, as in the case of Salieri, were personally favoured by the Emperor. Mozart was to remain in Vienna for eight years before he received a commission for an Italian *opera buffa* (*Così fan Tutte*—neither *Figaro* nor *Don Giovanni* were commissioned for Vienna). But he always hoped for a chance to show his work as a composer of opera, and in 1783 he started work on a libretto—*L'Oca del Cairo,* by Varesco; the libretto was so inane, however, that Mozart never completed the music.

On 5th July, 1783, Mozart wrote to his father: 'An Italian poet here has now brought me a libretto which I shall perhaps adopt, if he agrees to trim and adjust it in accordance with my wishes.' It is now almost certain that the libretto in question was *Lo Sposo Deluso* and that the Italian poet was none other than da Ponte. Mozart never finished the opera—he probably saw no possibility of its ever being performed—but the first step had been made, contact between the two men had been established, and Mozart probably realised that, as a librettist, da Ponte had distinct possibilities.

In 1782 Mozart wrote a German comic opera for the newly-established *National-Singspiel*. Following his abolition of the Italian Opera and Ballet for reasons of economy, Joseph II had made an attempt to encourage German opera—an attempt governed more by the Emperor's head than by his heart, for he was himself a devoted admirer of the Italian school. The *National-Singspiel* was opened in 1778, and in 1781 Mozart received a commission from Count Rosenberg to compose an opera for it. *Die Entführung aus dem Serail* was first performed on 16th July, 1782, and was received with great enthusiasm, but in spite of the fact that the opera was frequently performed—not only in Vienna, but throughout Germany—Mozart received no further commissions as a result of it. It was clear that, in spite of the attempts Joseph had made to encourage a national theatre and opera, in spite of first-class actors and singers, and in spite of works such as *Die Entführung aus dem Serail*, the Viennese public as a whole had remarkably little patriotism or national feeling so far as the theatre was concerned, and what it still really wanted was Italian *opera buffa*. No wonder that when the news came in 1783 that the Emperor had decided to reopen the Italian opera, Mozart's hopes rose; but his chance did not come for another two years. He had to wait impatiently for an opportunity to show Vienna what he could do, while second-rate operas which, like their composers, are now entirely forgotten, delighted that fickle and not always very discriminating city.

On 7th May, 1783, Mozart had written to his father: 'Our poet here is now a certain Abbate da Ponte; he has an enormous amount to do in writing pieces for the theatre and he has to write *per obbligo* an entirely new opera for Salieri (*Il Ricco d'un Giorno*) which will take him two months. He has promised after that to write a new libretto for me. But who knows whether he will be able to keep his word—or will want to? For, as you are aware, these Italian gentlemen are very civil to your face. Enough, we know them! If he is in league with Salieri, I shall never get anything out of him. But indeed I should dearly love to show what I can do in an Italian opera!'

Two years later, after the failure of *Il Ricco d'un Giorno*, da Ponte was far from being 'in league with Salieri'; he went to Mozart and suggested that they should write an opera together. At the time it must have seemed to him that, in offering to write a libretto for Mozart, he was making the best of a bad job, and offering his services to an almost unknown, second-rate composer. Posterity has judged otherwise. Mozart was pleased by the suggestion but, knowing how strong his rivals were, he thought that he would have no chance of getting the opera accepted. Da Ponte, no doubt relying on the Emperor's favour towards him, promised to see to that side of the business.

It was Mozart's idea to adapt Beaumarchais' *Le mariage de Figaro* as an opera. The idea was a daring one, and had much to commend it. The original play, which had been banned in Paris for three years, was finally produced there in 1784. It had been an immense success —a *succès de scandale*, for Beaumarchais, apart from being a brilliant dramatist, was also a brilliant business man with a flair for publicity. The first performance had been the occasion for scenes unparalleled in the history of the French theatre; all Paris—not excluding the aristocracy, against whom much of Beaumarchais' satire had been aimed—flocked to see the play which had been banned for so long. There was such a crush to buy tickets for it that three people were crushed to death and onlookers were amazed to see 'society ladies, forgetting all decency and modesty, shutting themselves up in the actresses' dressing rooms from the morning onwards, dining there and putting themselves under the actresses' protection in the hope of getting in first; to see, finally, the guard dispersed, doors broken open, and even iron grilles unable to resist, and shattered by the efforts of the assailants.' Although Napoleon was to say later of *Figaro* that 'c'était la Révolution déjà en action', it was precisely those whom it helped send to the scaffold eventually who flocked to see it with the greatest enthusiasm when it was first produced. Writing of the first performance a contemporary observer remarked: 'More than one duchess considered herself lucky on that day to find a wretched little stool in the dress-circle (where respectable ladies never go) . . .'

Beaumarchais was not content that only the first performance should be sensational; he saw to it that, throughout the very lengthy run of the play, public interest in it was kept alive by one means or another. His publicity campaign was remarkably astute, but he gained the best publicity of all from an incident that was not entirely of his own making. On March 7th, 1785, when he was dining with several distinguished gentlemen, he was arrested and conducted to prison at Saint-Lazare. It seems that, in a particularly virulent news-paper correspondence which Beaumarchais had been carrying on in the *Journal de Paris*, he had offended the susceptibilities of Monsieur le Comte de Provence (later Louis XVIII). The King, who disliked Beaumarchais, and who was tired of all the trouble he had been causing, came to hear about it, and gave orders for his arrest. Beaumarchais was mortally insulted, but it must be admitted that it was only his *amour-propre* that suffered; he remained in prison for six days only, and ultimately received compensation from the King to the tune of 2,150,000 livres, to say nothing of the added publicity which his play obtained as a result.

When Mozart conceived the idea of adapting *Figaro* as an opera the play was still banned in Vienna, thus giving it the charm of forbidden fruit. But there were other reasons, too, for his idea. Paisiello's opera *Il Barbiere di Siviglia*, an adaptation of Beaumarchais' play *Le Barbier de Séville* (of which *Figaro* was the continuation), had been produced in St Petersburg in 1782, and in Vienna in August 1783, with immense success. Mozart had seen a German version of *Le Barbier de Séville* with music by Benda in Salzburg in 1780; on 19th October, 1782, he wrote jokingly to his father: '. . . The Barber of Salzburg (not of Seville) called on me, and delivered kind messages from you. . . .' Mozart probably thought, and rightly, that the public would not only be interested in *Figaro* because it had been banned, but also because it dealt with the same characters as Paisiello's opera which had been so popular, and was in fact a sequel to it.

The idea of adapting Beaumarchais' play appealed to da Ponte, but in view of the ban which the Emperor had very recently imposed on it he foresaw that it would not be an easy matter to have it produced. Baron Wetzlar was so pessimistic about this that he offered to pay for the libretto and to arrange for the opera to be performed either in Paris or London; but da Ponte, who felt confident that he would eventually be able to persuade the Emperor to give his permission for the opera to be produced in Vienna, declined this generous offer. Instead, so he says, he proposed that the fact that the opera was being written should be kept a secret—Martin, with whom da Ponte was also working at the time, was the only person to be told about it—so that the Emperor should be asked to give an opinion only after he had seen the finished score. In point of fact it was a secret which everyone knew, as Mozart's letters and those of his father show, and it is also to be doubted that the whole opera was completed in only six weeks, as da Ponte says. Mozart started work on *Figaro* in the autumn of 1785; in November of that year his father wrote to his sister that Wolfgang was 'up to the eyes in work at his opera *Le Nozze di Figaro*.' Leopold Mozart did not, apparently, share his son's admiration for Beaumarchais' play. 'I know the piece', he wrote to his daughter on 11th November, 1785. 'It is a very tiresome play, and the translation from the French will certainly have to be altered very freely if it is to be effective as an opera. God grant that the text may be a success. I have no doubt about the music. But there will be a lot of running about and discussions before he gets the libretto so adjusted as to suit his purpose exactly.'

Leopold Mozart was perfectly right about the translation, if not about the merits of the original. Da Ponte's task was far from being an easy one. He had to translate Beaumarchais' French prose into Italian verse, he had to make it suitable for setting to music, and he had to make the text sufficiently innocuous for the Emperor to sanction its performance, yet not make it dull. He did his work with great skill, and kept remarkably close to the original text in spite of all these restrictions.

When the opera was completed da Ponte took advantage of the fact that a new opera was needed at the theatre and that, for once, the prolific Italians had nothing new to offer; he went to the Emperor, told him about *Figaro*, and suggested that it should be performed.

'What!' Joseph exclaimed. 'Don't you know that Mozart, although splendid at instrumental music, has only written one opera, and that was not up to much!' (Joseph presumably referred to *Die Entführung aus dem Serail*—Mozart's other operas were not known at all in Vienna.)

'I, too, would only have written one play in Vienna, if it had not been for Your Majesty's favour', da Ponte replied diplomatically.

'That is true', Joseph agreed, 'but I have forbidden this *Nozze di Figaro* to the German company.'

'Yes', da Ponte said, 'but as I have written an opera and not a comedy, I have had to omit a good many scenes and shorten a great many more, and I have left out and shortened anything which might offend the delicacy and decency of an entertainment at which your Sovereign Majesty presides. As to the music, as far as I can judge, it is remarkably beautiful.'

Joseph allowed himself to be persuaded by da Ponte's eloquence, and replied:

'All right; if that is so, I will trust your taste as to the music, and your discretion as to the morals. Have the score given to the copyist.'

Soon afterwards Joseph sent for Mozart and asked him to play him extracts from the score; he was very favourably impressed, and realised that da Ponte had been right about the music, at any rate.

Figaro was put into rehearsal, not without a good deal of opposition from the Casti-Rosenberg clique. Rosenberg himself was a passionate admirer of all things Italian, and also he naturally regarded da Ponte as the main obstacle in the way of his friend Casti obtaining the title of Caesarean Poet. Indeed, as Salieri informed da Ponte, Rosenberg actually asked the Emperor outright to give Casti this title, but Joseph replied: 'My dear Count, I have no need of poets myself, and for the theatre da Ponte is sufficient.' Mozart's fears of intrigue against him and his librettist were not, therefore, unfounded; it was fortunate for him that he had the Emperor as an ally, as without his patronage his rivals' attempts to wreck the opera might have been successful.

It was pointed out to Rosenberg that da Ponte had introduced some dances into the opera. The poet was summoned and informed none too politely that the Emperor refused to allow ballets in his theatre. Da Ponte said that he did not know of this regulation, Rosenberg lost his temper, and even went so far as to tear the two pages in question out of the libretto and burn them. When Mozart heard what had happened he was in despair; it was clear that the whole point of the scene (presumably the end of Act III) would be spoilt if the dances were omitted. At the dress rehearsal, which the Emperor attended, da Ponte gave instructions for the dance music to be left out and for the singers to continue to gesticulate on the stage in total silence. The Emperor naturally wished to know the meaning of this curious spectacle; when he had read the full version of the scene, which da Ponte showed him, and when he had learnt why it had been left out, he gave orders for dancers to be obtained immediately from another theatre.

The original cast of *Figaro* was a strong one, and included two singers from the British Isles—Nancy Storace, the first Susanna; and

Michael Kelly who took two small parts—Don Basilio and Don Curzio. Benucci took the part of Figaro.

Since her arrival in Vienna, in 1783, Nancy Storace had been through a serious illness and an unhappy marriage. The illness had started during a performance of one of her brother's operas, in which she was taking the leading part. Storace suddenly lost her voice in the middle of the first act and could not utter a sound for the rest of the evening. 'This', as one of her colleagues understandably remarked, 'threw a damper over the audience as well as the performers.' She did not recover her voice for five months, which was a great blow to the opera company, for she was one of its greatest assets. In September 1785, Mozart and da Ponte collaborated to write a cantata to celebrate her recovery, but the text of it has been lost. Nancy's marriage did not last as long as her illness; her husband was a certain Dr Fisher who, Kelly said, 'was a very ugly Christian, and who laid siege to poor Nancy Storace, and by dint of perseverance with her and drinking tea with her mother, prevailed upon her to take him for better or for worse, which she did in despite of the advice of all her friends.' Her friends had been perfectly right; Dr Fisher so ill-treated his wife that the Emperor had to tell him to leave Vienna. When he did so Nancy reverted to her maiden-name.

Mozart was very friendly with Nancy Storace and with her brother, Stephen, who was his pupil in composition. Apart from the cantata he wrote for her recovery, he wrote the *Scena and Rondo for Soprano*, 'Ch'io mi scordi di te' (K. 505) for her— 'Composto per la Signora Storace dal suo servo ed amico W. A. Mozart'—and in the thematic catalogue which Mozart kept for his own private use he noted against this composition: 'Für Mselle Storace und mich'. When Nancy returned to England Mozart corresponded with her, but these letters have been lost. Whether this friendship was of greater significance than it seems—Alfred Einstein in his *Mozart—His Character, His Work* suggests that it may have been—will probably never now be known. Certainly Mozart admired her as a singer, and the part of Susanna, which he wrote for her, is an enduring tribute to her vivacity and charm.

Although Michael Kelly had only two small parts in *Figaro*, the fact that he did take part in the opera is of great importance, for he was the only member of the cast to record his impressions of the rehearsals and first performance for posterity. In 1826 Kelly published his *Reminiscences*—they were 'ghosted' for him by Theodore Hook—and they are one of the most interesting and entertaining documents in operatic history. Kelly was only about twenty-two years old when *Figaro* was produced, yet he had his own ideas as to how the part of Don Curzio should be performed; he had the courage to argue with Mozart about it and, what is more, he won his point. This is the story in Kelly's own words:

'In the sestetto, in the second act (which was Mozart's favourite piece of the whole opera), I had a very conspicuous part, as the Stuttering Judge. All through the piece I was to stutter; but in the sestetto Mozart requested that I would not, for if I did I should spoil his music. I told him that although it might appear very presumptuous in a lad like me to differ with him on this point, I did, and was sure the way in which I intended to introduce the stuttering would not interfere with the other parts, but produce an effect; besides, it certainly was not in nature that I should stutter all through the part, and when I came to the sestetto speak plain; and after that piece of music was over, return to stuttering; and, I added (apologizing, at the same time, for my apparent want of deference and respect in placing my opinion in opposition to that of the great Mozart), that unless I was allowed to perform the part as I wished, I could not perform it at all. Mozart at last consented that I should have my own way, but doubted the success of the experiment. Crowded houses proved that nothing ever on the stage produced a more powerful effect; the audience were convulsed with laughter, in which Mozart himself joined. The Emperor repeatedly cried out "Bravo!" and the piece was loudly applauded and encored. When the opera was over Mozart came on the stage to me, and shaking me by both hands, said, "Bravo! young man, I feel obliged to you, and acknowledge you to have been in the right, and myself in the wrong." There was certainly a risk run, but I felt within myself I could give the effect I wished, and the event proved that I was not mistaken. I have seen the opera in London, and elsewhere, and never saw the judge portrayed as a stutterer, and the scene was often totally omitted. I played it as a stupid old man, though at the time I was a beardless stripling.'

In general, Kelly was always outspoken. One day, after the first performance of *Figaro* at which there had been so many encores that the opera had taken almost twice as long as usual to perform, the Emperor came in while a rehearsal was in progress. He announced to the singers—who included Nancy Storace, Benucci, Mandini and Kelly—'I daresay you are all pleased that I have desired there shall be no more encores; to have your songs so often repeated must be a great fatigue and very distressing to you.' The singers of course all agreed with the Emperor, except Kelly who had the courage to speak his mind. 'Do not believe them, Sire', he told Joseph. 'They all like to be encored, at least I am sure I always do.' Joseph, who enjoyed flattery less than most monarchs, laughed heartily at Kelly's reply.

Kelly was probably the first person, apart from the composer, to hear the duet

'Crudel! perchè finora
Farmi languir così . . .'

which Count Almaviva and Susanna sing in Act II of Figaro. He went to visit Mozart one evening, when the composer told him: 'I have just finished a little duet for my opera, you shall hear it.' Mozart sat down at the piano, and they went through the duet together.

Meanwhile, although the rehearsals for *Figaro* continued, the intrigues against the opera continued too. In April 1786, Mozart's father wrote to his sister: '*Le Nozze di Figaro* is being performed on the 28th for the first time. It will be surprising if it is a success, for I know that very powerful cabals have ranged themselves against your brother. Salieri and all his supporters will again try to move heaven and earth to down his opera. Duschek told me recently that it is on account of the very great reputation which your brother's exceptional talent and ability have won for him that so many people are plotting against him.' Salieri had, in fact, recently completed a new opera himself—*La Grotta di Trofonio*, with libretto by Casti—which was first produced on 12th October, 1785, and which was greeted with much enthusiasm. Another Italian rival of Mozart's,

Vincenzo Righini, was also working on an opera—*Il Demogorgone*, with a libretto by da Ponte. Mozart said of Righini: 'He composes *very charmingly* and he is not by any means superficial; but he is a monstrous thief. He offers his stolen goods in such superfluity, in such profusion, that people can hardly digest them.' There was a good deal of speculation as to whose opera would be produced first, and people began to take sides about it. Mozart was 'as touchy as gunpowder', according to Kelly, whereas Righini was 'working like a mole in the dark to get precedence'. The singers took sides, too; some of them were staunch supporters of Salieri, some favoured Righini, and very few people—except the Emperor—favoured Mozart and da Ponte.

However, at the rehearsals the music and wit of *Figaro* began to win the singers and the orchestra round. 'I remember at the first rehearsal of the full band', Kelly wrote in his old age, 'Mozart was on the stage with his crimson pelisse and gold-laced cocked hat, giving the time of the music to the orchestra. Figaro's song, "Non più andrai, farfallone amoroso", Benucci gave with the greatest animation and power of voice. I was standing close to Mozart, who *sotto voce*, was repeating, "Bravo! Bravo! Benucci"; and when Benucci came to the fine passage "Cherubino, alla vittoria, alla gloria militar", which he gave out with Stentorian lungs, the effect was electricity itself, for the whole of the performers on the stage, and those in the orchestra, as if actuated by one feeling of delight, vociferated "Bravo! Bravo! Maestro. Viva, viva, grande Mozart!" Those in the orchestra I thought would never have ceased applauding, by the beating of their violins against the music desks. The little man acknowledged, by repeated obeisances, his thanks for the distinguished mark of enthusiastic applause bestowed upon him.'

Figaro was first performed on 1st May, 1786. It was a success, but perhaps not the immense success which Kelly, writing long afterwards when Mozart's genius was more fully recognized, tried to make out. The opera was performed nine times in 1786, and was then completely eclipsed by Martin's *Una Cosa Rara* which was performed in November, and for which da Ponte also wrote the libretto. *Figaro* was dropped from the Viennese repertoire during 1787 and 1788, but was revived on 29th August, 1789.

F

However, in Prague, the city which can claim the honour of being one of the places where Mozart was happiest and where he was most appreciated during his lifetime, it was quite another story. *Figaro* was first performed there in December 1786, and in Prague its success was overwhelming. The whole city became 'Figaro-mad', and music from the opera was played everywhere. Mozart visited Prague himself in January 1787; while he was there he went to a ball at which he '. . . looked on with the greatest pleasure while all these people flew about in sheer delight to the music of my "Figaro", arranged for quadrilles and waltzes. For here they talk of nothing but "Figaro". Nothing is played, sung or whistled but "Figaro". No opera is drawing like "Figaro". Nothing, nothing but "Figaro". Certainly a great honour for me!' Even the street musicians in Prague had to play 'Non più andrai' if they wanted anyone to give them a coin. Mozart was fêted everywhere, poems were written in his honour and, most important of all, Bondini, the manager of the Prague theatre, commissioned him to write another opera for the next season. Da Ponte was not in Prague to share in the success of *Figaro*; he had remained in Vienna, where he, too, was being fêted and applauded—but not because of his association with Mozart.

CHAPTER VII

THE LIBRETTIST

Don Giovanni

AFTER the production of *Figaro* da Ponte's position in Vienna became more secure—not because of his libretto for Mozart, but because his rival Casti had left the Austrian capital. After the success of *Il Re Teodoro* in 1784, Casti had paid a visit to Italy; but he had soon returned to Vienna, full of energy and malice, and had caused da Ponte a good deal of trouble in one way and another. Casti had next collaborated with Salieri; *La Grotto di Trofonio*, which was first produced on 12th October, 1785, was considered by da Ponte to be superior to *Il Re Teodoro*, but although it was very successful, not many critics shared his opinion. Casti wrote one more libertto for Salieri six months later—a short *divertimento teatrale*, *Prima la Musica e poi le Parole*. This very witty and amusing work was written for a fête given at Schonbrunn on 7th February, 1786, in honour of the Governor-General of the Netherlands. On the same day Mozart's one-act comedy with music, *Der Schauspieldirektor*, with a libretto by Stephanie, was also performed. In his libretto, which was a satire on the controversy aroused by Gluck's theories about opera and libretti (and which may be considered a forerunner of Richard Strauss's *Capriccio*), Casti took the opportunity of caricaturing da Ponte, and Michael Kelly used all his considerable talent as a mimic to portray the poet on the stage. 'My friend the poet', wrote Kelly in after years, 'had a remarkably awkward gait, a habit of throwing himself (as he thought) into a graceful attitude, by putting his stick behind his back and leaning on it; he had also a very peculiar, rather dandyish way of dressing; for in sooth the Abbé stood mighty well with himself, and had the character of a consummate coxcomb; he had also a strong lisp and broad Venetian dialect. The first night of the performance he was seated in the boxes, more conspicuously than was absolutely necessary. . . . As usual, on the first night of a new opera, the Emperor was present, and a numerous auditory. When I made my *entrée* as the amorous poet, dressed exactly like the Abbé in the boxes, imitating his walk, leaning on my stick, and aping his gestures and his lisp, there was a universal roar of laughter and applause; and after a buzz round the house, the eyes of the whole audience were turned to the place where he was seated. The Emperor enjoyed the joke, laughed heartily, and applauded frequently during the performance; the Abbé was not at all affronted, but took my imitation of him in good part, and ever after we were on the best of terms.'

Although da Ponte laughed at Kelly's performance, it was probably something of a *rire jaune*; he said that Casti's libretto lacked wit and style—which was not at all true—and that the poet in the play resembled Casti rather than himself—which was not true either. In his libretto Casti had ridiculed da Ponte's amorous intrigues with ladies of the theatre; da Ponte remarked spitefully that two of Casti's own mistresses took part in the performance of the opera, but this was simply a case of the pot calling the kettle black, and the audience had no doubts at all as to the identity of Kelly's victim. After the performance da Ponte went home and wrote a sonnet about Casti in which he described him in most unflattering terms. Later on, encouraged by the fact that the Emperor had laughed at Parini's even more violent attack on his rival, da Ponte showed his sonnet to Joseph, who was amused by it and rewarded him generously for it.

Not long after this incident Casti had to leave Vienna. In 1784 he had written and presented to the Emperor his *Poema Tartaro*, a biting satire on Russia, which Casti had visited some years earlier, and on Catharine the Great herself. Joseph did not have a particularly high personal opinion of Catharine—'She thinks only of herself', he wrote to Kaunitz. 'Russia interests her just as little as I do . . .'—and he was amused by Casti's *jeu d'esprit* at her expense; he rewarded the poet handsomely for it. However, eighteen months later, when Joseph was seeking an alliance with Russia—he was to visit Catharine in the Crimea some months later—he began to feel that it was, perhaps, tactless to keep a poet at his court who had attacked his future ally, even though he himself used to refer to her disparagingly as 'cette femme exaltée'. One night at the opera Joseph summoned Casti into his box, and pointed out to him that it might be as well for him to travel for a time. Casti was probably not particularly upset at this suggestion; he was an inveterate globe-trotter and had, for some time, been contemplating a journey to the Near East. As the Emperor gave him a handsome sum towards his travelling expenses and numerous other parting presents, the poet was able to realise his ambition. He left Vienna a fortnight after the first performance of *Figaro*—he annoyed da Ponte by telling him that the libretto was 'pretty'—and went to Italy. In June, 1788, Casti embarked for Constantinople, and he did not return to Vienna until 1791, when Joseph II was already dead and Casti's friend and patron Leopold had succeeded him.

With Casti safely out of the way, da Ponte had no serious rivals left in Vienna; the success of *Figaro* had done much to improve his reputation as a librettist and composers were now anxious to secure his services. His first obligation was to Martin, to whom he had already promised another libretto before he had written *Figaro*, and when his work for Mozart was completed da Ponte carried out this promise. For reasons of his own, he did so in secret. No one but Martin's patroness, the Spanish Ambassadress, and da Ponte's patron, Joseph, knew that he was writing a new libretto for the Spanish composer; in fact, Martin told everyone that he had received a new libretto from Venice.

As a compliment to the Spanish Ambassadress, da Ponte chose a Spanish subject for this new opera. He rarely composed his own plots, and this time he adapted a Spanish comedy—*La Luna della Sierra*. Da Ponte's new version was to be entitled *Una Cosa Rara*, with the quotation *Rara est concordia formae atque pudicitiae* added as an explanation. The poet himself admitted that he never enjoyed writing anything so much as *Una Cosa Rara*, and it certainly is one of his best works. Da Ponte and Martin were close friends; they enjoyed working together and, as a result, worked well together, and they completed the opera within a remarkably short period—about a month.

However, when *Una Cosa Rara* was put into rehearsal, trouble started. The fact that da Ponte had written the words was still a secret, and remained one until after the opera had been performed, and so it was Martin who had to bear the brunt of the singers' disapproval. For disapprove they did—mainly, it seems, because Martin had seduced the *primo buffo's* mistress. In any case, the singers went on strike, some complaining that they had too much or too little to sing, others asserting that the music was too difficult, or too high or too low. They all agreed that the music was bad, although one singer gave da Ponte a good deal of pleasure by telling him that he should study the libretto and learn from it how such things should be written. It was not until the Emperor intervened and personally ordered the singers to continue to rehearse that the strike ended, although the complaints continued in secret.

When the opera was first performed, on 17th November, 1786, it was a sensation. The singers, who had been so unwilling to appear in the opera at all, found that they had never received such applause, and everyone was consumed with curiosity to know who had written the sparkling libretto. No one guessed the secret, except Michael Kelly, and he promised da Ponte not to give him away. Da Ponte, indeed, thoroughly enjoyed listening to the wild guesses which were made about the author's identity, and to the extravagant praise with which all Vienna greeted his opera. When the fact that he had written the libretto for Martin did finally leak out, he had a wonderful time. The authors of *Una Cosa Rara* had become celebrities overnight, they were the talk of Vienna, and were inundated with invitations to parties, picnics, dinners and so on, to say nothing of presents, verses, and *billets-doux*. Although da Ponte later affirmed that this brilliant success only inspired him with some wry reflections about human nature, there is no doubt that he enjoyed his newly-found popularity just as much as Martin, and that he, like the Spaniard, took full advantage of all his new opportunities.

Una Cosa Rara was one of the most outstanding operatic successes that Vienna ever witnessed. Ladies even did their hair and dressed 'à la Cosa Rara'. Mozart's *Figaro* was completely forgotten as a result of it, and its production marked the peak of da Ponte's career. Although the opera, unlike *Figaro*, has long ago dropped out of the repertoire, it was frequently performed all over Europe until about 1823, and da Ponte's text was translated into many languages, including Russian, Polish and Danish. A performance of *Una Cosa Rara* was broadcast on the B.B.C. Third Programme in 1954; those who heard it will probably wonder how the Viennese could possibly have preferred it to *Figaro*. It is a work of charm and wit, but the music is lamentably thin and poor in comparison to Mozart's, and the whole work cannot be regarded nowadays as anything but an interesting museum-piece. Only a few bars of the music have been rescued from oblivion by Mozart himself, who quotes them in the final scene in *Don Giovanni*. *Una Cosa Rara* was undoubtedly da Ponte's favourite opera, as well it might be—he never achieved such fame and success with any of his other works.

As soon as it became known that he had written the libretto for Martin's opera da Ponte was besieged with requests from other composers for libretti. He had already written an adaptation of Shakespeare's *Comedy of Errors* for Nancy Storace's brother, Stephen. Storace himself chose the subject, but whether da Ponte could read English sufficiently well at that time to study Shakespeare's play, or whether he worked from a translation, is not known. This opera was performed on 27th December, 1786, as *Gli Equivoci*, with Kelly taking one of the principal parts, and was very favourably received. By this time da Ponte was no longer an inexperienced beginner, but an accomplished craftsman. Alfred Einstein wrote of this libretto: 'To follow step by step the methods by which da Ponte converts Shakespeare's five acts into two would be tantamount to writing a short study of the dramatic technique of the opera-libretto—a technique from which many a librettist of the twentieth century could learn much.'

At about this time da Ponte also wrote a libretti for Righini— *Il Demogorgone*—but this was a dismal failure. So was *Bertoldo*, written for Francesco Piticchio, a third-rate composer. After the performance of this opera the Emperor said to his protégé: 'Da Ponte, write plays for Mozart, for Martin, for Salieri! But don't write again for this Potacchi, Petecchi, Pitocchi, Peticchi . . . whatever he's called. Casti was cleverer than you: he only wrote libretti for a Paisiello or a Salieri.'

It was not long before da Ponte had an opportunity for following this advice. Salieri who, after the failure of *Il Ricco d'un Giorno*, had sworn never to set another word by da Ponte to music again, now, after the success of *Una Cosa Rara*, was only too keen to do so. He asked him for an Italian translation of his *Tarare* which had been produced in Paris in 1787, and which he wanted to adapt for production in Vienna. The original libretto was by Beaumarchais, and da Ponte's success with his adaptation of *Figaro* made him an obvious choice for this work. Martin, who naturally wanted to repeat the success of *Una Cosa Rara* as soon as possible, also asked him for a libretto; and finally Mozart, who had a commission for an opera for Prague, wanted another play from him too. It was a tall order to translate and adapt one libretto and to write two new ones at the same time, but da Ponte was always a quick worker, and he felt confident of his ability to do it. For Martin he chose *L'Arbore di Diana*, and he proposed the old legend of Don Juan to Mozart, who was very pleased with the idea. Having chosen his subjects, da Ponte's next step was to inform the Emperor of his plans. When he explained that he intended to work on three libretti at once, Joseph was sceptical.

'You won't succeed!' he said.

'Perhaps not', da Ponte replied, 'but I shall try, all the same. I shall write for Mozart at night, which will be like reading Dante's *Inferno*. In the morning I shall write for Martin, and that will be like studying Petrarch. In the evening I will write for Salieri, and he will be my Tasso.'

Da Ponte shut himself up in his room, and set to work. 'I sat down at my desk', he wrote many years later, 'and stayed there for twelve hours at a stretch. A bottle of Tokay was at my right, the inkstand in the middle, and a box of Seville tobacco at my left. A lovely young girl of sixteen (whom I would like to have loved as a daughter . . . but . . .) was living in the house with her mother, who was the housekeeper; she would come to my room whenever I rang the bell which, truth to tell, was pretty often, especially when it seemed that my inspiration was beginning to cool: she would bring me sometimes a biscuit, sometimes a cup of coffee, and sometimes nothing but her own pretty face, always gay, always smiling, and made to inspire poetic fancy and witty ideas. With only brief breaks, I continued to work twelve hours a day for two months, and for the whole of this time she stayed in the next room, either with a book in her hand or with her sewing, so as to be ready to come to me as soon as I rang the bell.' At first, as da Ponte admits, he rang the bell extremely frequently and wrote next to nothing; soon, however, the composers for whom he was supposed to be working began to enquire about the progress of their libretti, and he was forced to ration the time he spent with his mistress.

Lamartine, who 'discovered' da Ponte, and wrote a great deal of nonsense about him—he compared his *Memoirs* to the *Confessions* of Saint Augustine, to the *Memoirs* of Gramont and of Molière, to the *Confessions* of Jean-Jacques Rousseau, and finally added the *Memoirs* of Benvenuto Cellini to this imposing, if ill-assorted list—seized on this description of how *Don Giovanni* was written, and interpreted it according to the spirit of Romanticism. 'C'est ainsi que Don Juan devait être écrit', he wrote, 'par un aventurier, un amant, un poète, un homme de plaisir et de désordre inspiré du vin, de l'amour et de la gloire, entre les tentations de la débauche et le respect divin pour l'innocence, homme sans scrupule, mais non sans terreur des vengeances du ciel. D'Aponte' (Lamartine never learned to spell his discovery's name properly), 'D'Aponte, à l'impénitence près, écrivait le drame de sa propre vie dans le drame de Don Juan.'

Lamartine was not, presumably, aware that there was nothing original about da Ponte's libretto, and that most of it was stolen and hastily adapted from the work of another poet; he was also probably ignorant of many of the less creditable episodes of da Ponte's own life, or he would never have described him as 'a man without scruples, but not without fear of Celestial vengeance.' The sin of blasphemy plays an important part in *Don Giovanni*; it was a sin which, together with sacrilege, da Ponte committed with a frequency and a cynicism which, even in that age of unbelief, was exceptional. Da Ponte's lack of belief was one of the few perfect things about him; it was absolute and complete, not even clouded by a hint of superstition. In Venice, when caught *en flagrant délit* with Angioletta Bellaudi, he had sworn: 'May God strike me down with a thunderbolt when celebrating Mass . . .' that he was innocent; it was an oath worthy of Don Giovanni himself, but it was not an

FX

oath which any Catholic priest with a grain of superstition, let alone
faith, would have pronounced so lightly. Celestial vengeance did not
worry da Ponte at all at this stage of his career. In fact, it is doubtful
if it ever did. It may be that his early Jewish upbringing had a far
more lasting influence on him than he himself admitted, and that
his conversion took place after his philosophy of life had been
permanently formed; or it may be that he was a true materialist, an
agnostic, and really believed in no divine power whatsoever. However, at the very end of his life, unlike Don Giovanni, da Ponte did,
it seems, attempt a reconciliation with the Catholic Church. It was
better, he felt, to be on the safe side. One never knows, and, as the
Arabic proverb has it: There are no fans in Hell.

L'*Arbore di Diana*, with music by Martin, was the first of da
Ponte's three operas to be produced, on 1st October, 1787, to celebrate the wedding of the Archduchess Maria-Theresa with Prince
Anton of Saxony. The plot was one calculated to please the Emperor,
for da Ponte had chosen as his central theme Joseph's recent measures
against monasticism—the Emperor had ordered the dissolution of all
orders which, in his opinion, did no useful work such as teaching,
nursing the sick, or scientific research. It was not a theme which, at
first sight, seemed particularly suitable for a comic opera to be performed on the occasion of a royal marriage, but da Ponte transformed it into a complicated allegory about Cupid, Diana and an
apple tree. The tree, which occupied a central place in the plot, was
covered with fruit which had the unfortunate property of turning
black and falling on and injuring any unchaste female who might
walk under its branches. Needless to say, at the end of the opera the
tree was cut down and replaced by a Temple of Love.

Da Ponte himself considered that L'*Arbore di Diana* was one of his
best works—'voluptuous without being lascivious'—and the
Viennese public liked it too. Joseph, who doubtless appreciated this
delicate compliment to his religious policy, rewarded the author
with a hundred sequins. When Count Rosenberg complimented
the poet on his work and enquired where he had found such interesting ideas, da Ponte replied characteristically: 'In the backsides of
my enemies'.

II

Immediately after the first performance of Martin's opera, da Ponte left for Prague to prepare for the production of *Don Giovanni* in that city. He remained in Prague for about a week, but was not there for the first performance of Mozart's opera, on 29th October, 1787, as he was recalled to Vienna to complete the libretto which he was translating and adapting for Salieri.

Da Ponte's *Don Giovanni* was very far from being an original work. In fact, he probably suggested the play to Mozart because, having his hands full with work for Martin and Salieri, he thought that it would take him less time to adapt an old play than to write a new one. And the Don Juan legend was very old—it was, in fact, so old that it had become a joke, and a joke in rather bad taste at that. 'Everyone is acquainted with the wretched Spanish play which the Italians call *Il Convitato di Pietro*, and the French 'Le Festin de Pierre', wrote Goldoni. 'I have always looked at it, in Italy, with horror, and I could never understand how this farce survived for so long, how it drew crowds to see it, and delighted a civilized country. Even the Italian Comedians were surprised at it themselves; and either as a joke, or out of ignorance, some of them said that the author of "Le Festin de Pierre" had signed a pact with the Devil in order to gain his protection.'

However, in spite of what he thought about it, Goldoni finally could not resist the temptation to use the legend himself; his *Don Giovanni Tenorio* was produced in Venice in 1736, but is far from being one of his best works.

The story of Don Juan seems to have originated in Spain in 1630 with *El Burlador de Sevilla y Combidado de Pietra*, a play by Tirso de Molina. It may be that this play was not without some historical foundation. It is said that, in the Middle Ages, there was in Seville a certain Don Juan, who was a member of one of the great families of Andalusia. This gentleman, who was famous for his scandalous behaviour, did in fact seduce the daughter of a Commendatore, and did subsequently kill her father, who was then buried in the monastery of Saint Francis. The monks decided to make an example of Don Juan, and so, having enticed him into an ambush, they killed

him. Then, in order to discourage other libertines, they spread the
rumour that Don Juan had insulted the statue of his victim, and that
while he did so the ground had opened and he had been swallowed
up in the flames of Hell. Whether Tirso de Molina drew on this old
story, or on his own imagination, is not very important; in any
case, so far as can be ascertained, he was the first person to put the
story of Don Juan on the stage.

The story quickly became popular, not only in Spain, but in
France and Italy too, which was not surprising. The legend of the
profligate nobleman who commits murder and then blasphemy by
inviting the statue of his victim to dinner, and who is justly punished
when the statue does, in fact, come to carry him away to Hell, contained all the elements necessary to grip the attention of an audience,
and of a not very sophisticated audience. Love, debauchery, murder,
blasphemy, the supernatural element, and a moral ending which
nicely balanced the immoral beginning, were ingredients guaranteed
to appeal to crowds at fairs as well as to those in theatres, and soon
the story was taken up and spread all over Europe by strolling
players, by puppet shows, and so on. The great dramatists, too, who
were writing for the aristocracy and the courts, for audiences which
were, in theory at any rate, more sophisticated, realised that those
same elements in the Don Juan story which appealed to the masses
would, with a little adjustment, serve their purposes very well too.
Molière's *Le Festin de Pierre* was produced in 1665, Goldoni's Italian
version followed in 1736, and there were innumerable other plays
on the same subject both in French, Italian and German; in England
Thomas Shadwell's *The Libertine* was produced in 1676, and Purcell
later composed music for it.

Musicians had, in fact, been quick to realise the possibilities which
the Don Juan legend presented for musical setting. Purcell had been
one of the first to write music to the play; he was followed by Gluck,
who wrote his ballet *Don Juan* in 1761, and in 1777 Vincenzo Righini
(for whom da Ponte later wrote an unsuccessful libretto) composed
his opera, *Il Convitato di Pietra*—to mention but a few of the many
musical settings. However, it was an opera by Guiseppe Gazzaniga,
with whom da Ponte also collaborated later, which served as the
principle model for Mozart and da Ponte's *Don Giovanni*.

Gazzaniga's *Don Giovanni Tenorio o sia Il Convitato di Pietra* was performed for the first time in Venice in 1782, and was revived, with some slight alterations, for the carnival season of 1787. The libretto was by Giovanni Bertati, a poet whom da Ponte later met and cordially disliked—he described him as a 'frog blown up with wind'. The fact that da Ponte considered that Bertati was no poet and did not even know Italian, did not prevent him from appropriating a great deal of Bertati's libretto when he came to write his own *Don Giovanni*. Subsequently da Ponte grew to dislike Bertati even more, for when he eventually fell from favour in Vienna it was Bertati who succeeded him as Poet to the Imperial Theatres. Bertati's best known libretto, and one which is still performed nowadays, is *Il Matrimonio Segreto*, with music by Cimarosa.

Mozart and da Ponte's *Don Giovanni* was, like almost all its predecessors, presented as a comic opera—the original title-page bears the inscription *dramma giocoso*. Later generations, particularly in nineteenth-century Germany, tended to disregard these instructions, and tried to interpret the opera in the spirit of Romanticism —a spirit which would have been most alien, both to da Ponte and to Mozart. Yet, although *Don Giovanni* contains many of the elements of an ordinary Italian *opera buffa*, the incomparable depth and grandeur of Mozart's music have made it transcend the ordinary operatic categories and become a unique work which cannot be put in any category at all. In the same way, Chekhov's plays, described by their author as 'comedies', have so many subtle overtones and so deep and sensitive an understanding of humanity in them that later generations, moved to tears by the human tragedy of Uncle Vanya or the Three Sisters, are at a loss to understand how Chekhov could have imagined that he had written comedies. In *Don Giovanni*, as in Chekhov's plays, as in life itself, the action of the play moves from tragedy to farce and back to tragedy again, sometimes inconsequentially, and often unexpectedly, but never without dramatic effect. Each fresh spectator must interpret the opera individually, according to his temperament and his generation.

It may be, in fact, that Mozart originally intended to go against tradition, and to turn the Don Juan legend into pure tragedy. Da Ponte, in his old age, maintained that this was so, and that he suc-

ceeded in persuading Mozart to change his mind only after work on
the opera had already begun. Dr John Francis, a distinguished
American physician and amateur man of letters—who was, incidentally, one of the very few Americans to realise da Ponte's
potential value as a source of information about Mozart, and to
question him closely concerning his association with the composer
—was told by da Ponte that:

'Mozart determined to cast the opera exclusively as serious, and
had well advanced in the work. Da Ponte assured me', Dr Francis
continued, 'that he remonstrated and urged the expediency on the
great composer of the introduction of the *vis comica*, in order to
accomplish a greater success, and prepared the rôle with *Batti, batti,
Là ci darem*, etc.'

If da Ponte's statement is true, and not just another attempt on his
part to make himself seem more important than he really was, it
gives rise to fascinating speculation. Did da Ponte make or mar a
masterpiece? Taken at its face-value, his remark to Dr Francis
amounts to no more nor less than a claim that the dualism in *Don
Giovanni*, the almost Shakespearean introduction of the comic element in it which has for so long intrigued and perplexed the critics,
the mixture of tragedy and farce which, to so many people, makes
Don Giovanni the greatest of Mozart's operas—in fact, that all the
most important dramatic ideas in its construction are the products
not of Mozart's brain, but of da Ponte's.

This is too much to believe, and the very nature of the music
denies it. The history of the Don Juan legend denies it, too; the idea
of introducing comedy into the play was not new, and Mozart was
certainly aware of this. Yet perhaps he may have considered the
possibility of writing an *opera seria*, and da Ponte may have persuaded him to change his mind. That some drastic alterations were
made to the opera when work on it was already well advanced has
always been evident; whether these alterations were made at da
Ponte's suggestion, and whether they were changes for the better
or for the worse, we shall probably never now know.

What were da Ponte's other contributions to the opera, apart from
his hypothetical insistence on the introduction of the comic element?
In an article in the *Sunday Times* (3rd October, 1954) Ernest New-

man described the libretto as 'one of the sorriest pieces of stage joinery ever nailed together by a hack in a hurry', and one cannot altogether disagree with him. The plot was not original, and much of the actual text was taken straight from Bertati's libretto. However, a comparison of the two texts shows that da Ponte did polish Bertati's lines and improve them very considerably—Leporello's 'catalogue' aria, for instance, which da Ponte took from Bertati, has been improved almost out of all recognition in Mozart's opera. Da Ponte also had the gift for making his characters come to life, although he exercised this gift less in *Don Giovanni* than in any of the other operas which he wrote for Mozart. Leporello, Don Giovanni himself, Donna Elvira, Zerlina and Masetto are all three-dimensional figures, but it takes singers of remarkable gifts to make Donna Anna and Don Ottavio anything but lifeless puppets. The construction of the plot, too, lacks the smoothness and clarity which characterises so much of da Ponte's other work; the libretto was hastily written and much altered at the last moment, and this is all too apparent in the results.

Yet, with all its imperfections, to many people *Don Giovanni* is still the greatest of all operas, and it has a power to move audiences which few other operas possess. It would be unfair to da Ponte to suggest, as many people do, that Mozart's music alone is responsible for the opera's greatness, and that it is great in spite of the libretto. As always, Mozart composed the music in the closest collaboration with da Ponte, and the music fits the words like a glove—the two cannot be separated, and the opera can only be judged as a whole. In fact, in this opera, more than in any other, if the words are inaudible or incomprehensible, half the effect of the music is lost. Volumes have been written analysing the opera's greatness and its imperfections, and mostly to no avail; in the last analysis, like all truly great works of art, *Don Giovanni* eludes the critics. When it is dissected in the cold light of criticism, the glowing colours of the opera fade away, like those of a dead butterfly transfixed on a pin.

To some generations, particularly in the nineteenth century, it was not so much the technical shortcomings of da Ponte's libretto which shocked the critics, as its moral shortcomings. Indeed, it was on moral grounds that all da Ponte's libretti for Mozart were most

severely criticised. The serious-minded nineteenth century considered *Figaro* as frivolous, *Don Giovanni* as licentious, and *Così fan
Tutte* as positively immoral; both Beethoven and Wagner failed to
see how Mozart could have composed music to such texts. (*Così fan
Tutte*, which was quite devoid of any purpose or meaning apart from
its entertainment value, was of course, the worst offender in this
respect.) Ruskin, for example, frankly considered *Don Giovanni* the
'foolishest and most monstrous of conceivable human words and
subjects of thought'. He went even further, and said of Mozart's
setting of da Ponte's words: 'No such spectacle of unconscious (and
in that unconsciousness all the more fearful) moral degradation of
the highest faculty to the lowest purpose can be found in history.'

These are strong words, but there were a good many people in the
nineteenth century who agreed with them. Otto Jahn, the author of
what was for many years considered to be the standard biography of
Mozart, had much the same opinion, but went into more detail—in
this case, he is discussing *Figaro*: 'The omission of political satire is
the more serious because it leaves as the central point of the plot an
immorality which is not exactly justified, but not by any means
severely punished; only treated with a certain frivolity. The noble
libertine is opposed by true and upright love, honest devotion to
duty and honourable conduct; but these moral qualities are not
made in themselves effective; the true levers of the plot are cunning
and intrigue employed as weapons of defence. The whole piece
appears in a doubtful light, the atmosphere surrounding Count
Almaviva is impure, and the suppression of those circumstances
which could alone make the phenomenon natural affects more or
less the whole spirit of the plot, and deprives the dialogue of much
of its point and double meaning.' Jahn, who was writing in the
1850's, went on to say that 'A later age is disgusted by the contrast
between semblance and reality, and at the representation of immorality in all its nakedness; the taste of the time demands that it
shall be shown after another form and fashion.' Nowadays, an even
later age considers these opinions as curious expressions of the nineteenth-century mentality.

It was probably in September 1787 that Mozart left Vienna to
supervise the first performance of *Don Giovanni* in Prague. In the

months preceding his departure from Vienna, while he had been working on the opera, two events worthy of note had occurred. The first, probably in April of the same year, had been Beethoven's visit to him. Beethoven was, at this time, just seventeen. It is not known precisely what occurred at these, his only meetings with Mozart, but it does not seem that any very warm friendship grew up between the two men.

A month later, on 28th May, 1787, Leopold Mozart died. The loss of his father was undoubtedly a great blow to Mozart; they had had many disagreements, it is true, particularly over Mozart's marriage and his decision to leave the service of the Archbishop of Salzburg, but Leopold Mozart had been such an important influence in his son's life that his death could not fail to make a deep impression. It has been suggested that the grief Mozart felt at the loss of his father is reflected in the music of *Don Giovanni*.

When Mozart arrived in Prague the music of *Don Giovanni* was not finished; at least four numbers, including the overture and the last finale, seem to have been written after Mozart's arrival in the Bohemian capital. There are many versions of the story of the composition of the overture—how Mozart was locked into a room by his friends in order to force him to complete it in time, or how his wife told him fairy-stories while he was writing it down in order to prevent him from falling asleep. The only thing that is certain is that the overture, although conceived long before in Mozart's brain, was written down in a great hurry at the last moment.

The libretto, too, may very well not have been completed when da Ponte left Vienna; he had been working hard for Salieri and Martin as well as for Mozart, and when he arrived in Prague he may still have had the finishing touches to put to *Don Giovanni*. There are, indeed, indications that he called in an assistant.

Casanova was in Prague at the time of the first performance of the opera—he was there on business in connection with his novel *Icosameron*; no doubt da Ponte heard that his friend was in Prague, and on his arrival in that city sought him out. He may have been put in touch with him by a mutual friend, Guardassoni, who was co-director with Bondini of the Prague theatre. Da Ponte was

recalled to Vienna by the Emperor a few days before the first performance of *Don Giovanni*, and it seems as if he may have asked
Casanova to put a few finishing touches to the libretto for him. In
any case, in recent years some lines have been discovered among
Casanova's papers, lines which are undoubtedly sketches for an
alternative version of Leporello's air just after the sextet in Act II of
Don Giovanni, and which are also, it seems, undoubtedly in Casanova's handwriting. Did Casanova actually contribute anything to
the libretto as we now know it, or were these lines just jotted down
idly one day for his own personal amusement? The fact that the lines
in question contain a great many corrections—also in Casanova's
handwriting—makes the latter alternative seem very unlikely. What,
in fact, probably happened is that when da Ponte was suddenly
recalled to Vienna he asked his old friend to make any last-minute
alterations to the text which Mozart might require, and to supervise
the rehearsals from the librettist's point of view.

It will probably never be known just how much Casanova contributed to *Don Giovanni*, if indeed he did contribute to it, but the
theory that he may have done so has great fascination. Casanova
who, in his youth, used to reel off lists of his conquests' names in the
cafés of Venice, may have given a wry smile in his old age when he
heard Leporello's 'catalogue' aria, and even Leporello bears a certain resemblance to Casanova's own servant, Costa. But although
superficially Don Giovanni and Casanova seem to be very alike,
fundamentally they had little in common. Their reaction to women
was different, and women reacted differently to them. Casanova was
only concerned with pleasure, both with the pleasure which he gave
and with that which, as a result, he received. Don Giovanni, on the
contrary, wished to humiliate women, to expose their weaknesses,
and found his pleasure in so doing. Women flocked to Casanova,
but they fled from Don Giovanni, and those who had been vic-
timised by him, such as Donna Elvira, warned other women against
him. It was a fundamental difference, and one which Casanova
probably noticed himself with some satisfaction.

There were a good many delays before *Don Giovanni* was finally
performed. 'You probably think that my opera is over by now',
Mozart wrote to a friend on 15th October, 'If so, you are a little

mistaken. In the first place, the stage personnel are not so smart here as those in Vienna when it comes to mastering an opera of this kind in a very short time. Secondly, I found on my arrival that so few preparations and arrangements had been made that it would have been absolutely impossible to produce it on 14th, that is, yesterday. So yesterday my "Figaro" was performed in a fully lighted theatre, and I myself conducted.' This performance of *Figaro* was given in honour of Prince Anton of Saxony and his bride, the Archduchess Maria-Theresa, who were passing through Prague on their honeymoon.

The performance of *Don Giovanni* was further postponed by the illness of one of the singers; the Prague company was a very small one, and when a singer fell ill it was a major disaster. Mozart also complained that the singers were lazy and refused to rehearse on days when an opera was being performed, and that the manager was too timorous to force them.

Don Giovanni was performed for the first time on 29th October, 1787. Legend has it that there had been no time to rehearse the overture, but the orchestra played it so well at sight that Mozart is said to have whispered during the introduction to the first act to the musicians nearest him: 'Some of the notes went under the music-stands, it is true, but the overture went capitally on the whole.' The opera was received with tremendous enthusiasm; da Ponte, who no doubt anxiously scanned the reports in the Viennese press, must have been delighted to see, in the *Wiener Zeitung*, that '. . . Musicians and and connoisseurs are agreed in declaring that such a performance has never before been witnessed in Prague. Herr Mozart himself conducted, and his appearance in the orchestra was the signal for cheers, which were renewed at his exit. The opera is exceedingly difficult of execution, and the excellence of the representation, in spite of the short time allowed for studying the work, was the subject of general remark. The whole powers, both of actors and orchestra, were put forward to do honour to Mozart. Considerable expense was incurred for additional chorus and scenery, which has been generously defrayed by Herr Guardassoni. The enormous audience was a sufficient guarantee of the public favour.'

Da Ponte also received news of the performance from his friends.

Mozart wrote to him and told him of the wonderful reception of their opera, and Guardassoni, co-manager of the theatre, wrote as follows: 'Long live da Ponte! Long live Mozart! All impresarios, all performers, should bless your names. So long as you two are alive the theatre will not know hard times.' An attempt was, in fact, made to persuade Mozart to remain in Prague and to write another opera, but he reluctantly refused.

The first Don Giovanni was Luigi Bassi, who was twenty-two years old when he took the part. Leporello was played by Felice Ponziani, who had played the part of Figaro with great success; he was that rare combination, a fine singer and a talented actor, thus combining qualities essential to both parts. Antonio Baglioni was the first Don Ottavio; he was later to appear in Mozart's *La Clemenza di Tito*. The first Donna Anna, Teresa Saporiti, was not only a fine singer, but a beautiful woman as well; she lived to be 106 years old, and died in Milan in 1869. She was the only person intimately connected with the original performance of Mozart's opera who outlived da Ponte. The first Zerlina was Caterina Bondini, wife of the director of the theatre, and a great favourite with the Prague public.

Da Ponte had missed all the applause *Don Giovanni* had received in Prague, but in Vienna his adaptation of Beaumarchais' *Tarare* was occupying most of his time. The opera, renamed *Axur, Re d'Ormus*, with music by Salieri, was first performed on 8th January, 1788, in honour of the marriage of the Archduke Francis of Austria, Joseph's nephew, with Elizabeth of Wurtemberg. This marriage, which was to end most tragically two years later, was the occasion for some of the most splendid celebrations of Joseph's reign; they were also to be the last that he attended, for he was already a sick man, and a month later Austria was to declare war against the Turks. Princess Elizabeth was one of the very few people who succeeded in breaking through Joseph's hard protective shell of reserve and touching his heart; she was his only joy in the last, bitterly disappointing years of his life, and he who was usually so parsimonious and austere spared no expense for her marriage. The ceremony was performed by Joseph's brother, Maximilian, Prince Archbishop of Mayence, who told the Emperor jokingly before the wedding: 'I should be ashamed

if my benediction were to be less effective than that of the Archbishop of Trèves who married Leopold.' Joseph replied that he did
not think it would matter if the benediction were to be a little less
effective, for Leopold had had no less than twenty children. After
the ceremony, which was truly magnificent, Joseph gave a dinner
on the same scale; on the next day there was a gala ball, and on the
day after that Salieri and da Ponte's opera was performed.

This marriage was the last great festival in Vienna for a very long
time and, as is so often the case, the last was the most splendid of all.
But there was already signs and rumours that the end of an epoch
was approaching, and that nothing would ever be quite the same
again. The face of Europe was changing—indeed, had already
changed, for Frederick of Prussia, who had dominated the European
scene for half a century, was dead. Only eighteen months after the
marriage of Francis and Elizabeth the new epoch was born—with
the storming of the Bastille.

From 1788 onwards da Ponte's patron, the Emperor, had less and
less time to spare for such luxuries as opera. He was a sick man
himself, but it was rather the sickness of the Austro-Hungarian
Empire which preoccupied him. In 1787 the Low Countries had
rebelled; order had been restored by force, but the unrest and discontent remained. On 8th February, 1788, Joseph declared war
against the Turks, thus carrying out his agreement with Catharine
of Russia, and from that time until his death, two years later, he was
overwhelmed by problems of state both at home and abroad. Ill as
he was, Joseph did not spare himself or anyone else; he aggravated
his illness by interminable work, by difficult and tiring journeys to
visit his troops and, above all, by ceaseless worry. As he saw all his
life's work disintegrate, most of his theories rejected, and many of his
reforms proved injudicious, as his ears rang with the 'I told you
so's' of his critics, as he battled against lung-trouble, malaria and
exhaustion, as he read with alarm the latest reports from France and
heard of the difficulties and indiscretions of his favourite sister,
Marie-Antoinette, Joseph found himself forced to neglect the opera
almost entirely.

Almost, but not quite; he continued, even in these last, difficult
years, to send directives to Rosenberg, directives which were still

detailed and to the point. Occasionally these directives, usually written in bad French, contained a certain wry humour, as for instance when he told Rosenberg, 'Le mariage de Mombelli avec la Laschi peut s'exécuter sans attendre mon retour, et je vous cède a ce sujet le droit de Seigneur'—a remark no doubt inspired by *Figaro*, and one which, according to Casanova, Rosenberg was quite capable of interpreting literally. On 7th December, 1787, shortly after the first performance of *Don Giovanni* in Prague, Joseph appointed Mozart as his *Kammerkomponist* in succession to Gluck, who had died on 15th November.

On 28th February, 1788, the Emperor left Vienna for his military headquarters, and did not return to the capital until the following December. He was not, therefore, present at the first performance in Vienna of *Don Giovanni* on 7th May. The opera was not a success. The Viennese public, which was familiar with the old Don Juan legend as a farce, had gone to the opera to laugh; but probably, from the first sinister notes of the overture, it felt out of its depth. People had gone to laugh, but when they found that they were made to think and feel as well, they were baffled and disappointed. Mozart is said to have remarked that he had written the opera 'not at all for Vienna, a little for Prague, but mostly for myself and my friends', and the Viennese seemed to feel that the opera was not for them. Various changes were made, new arias were added, but it was all to no avail. Joseph's verdict, presumably delivered after the performance of 15th December, 1788, was: 'the opera is divine; perhaps even more beautiful than *Figaro*, but it's not food for the teeth of my Viennese'; to which Mozart replied: 'We'll give them time to chew it.' But in spite of praising the opera to its authors, Joseph was critical of Mozart's work; on 16th May, for instance, he had written to Rosenberg and expressed the opinion that 'la musique de Mozard (sic) est bien trop difficile pour le chant'.

Not all the singers who had taken part in the first performance of *Figaro* sang in the first performance in Vienna of *Don Giovanni*. Nancy Storace and Michael Kelly had left Vienna in February 1787 in company with Mozart's pupil, Stephen Storace, Thomas Attwood, Nancy's mother, and her lap-dog. On their way home to England they had passed through Salzburg and had called on

Mozart's father—'a pleasing, intelligent little man', Kelly remarked. The travellers were invited to attend a party given by Mozart's old employer and enemy, the Archbishop of Salzburg 'a very fine-looking man, particularly gallant and attentive to the ladies'.

In the original cast of *Don Giovanni* in Vienna the title-rôle was taken by Francesco Albertarelli, and Donna Anna was played by Mozart's sister-in-law, Aloysia Lange. Caterina Cavalieri, who played Donna Elvira, was a very notable singer; in spite of her Italianised name she was Austrian by birth, and was the pupil and protégée of Salieri—da Ponte says she was his mistress. When Mozart had written the part of Constanze for her in *Die Entführung aus dem Serail* he had been forced to 'sacrifice an aria a little to her flexible throat'. The part of Zerlina was taken by Luisa Mombelli, and that of Don Ottavio by Francesco Morella. Francesco Bassani, who had played Don Bartolo and Antonio in *Figaro*, once more played two parts—Masetto and the Commendatore. Leporello was played by Benucci, who had created the part of Figaro.

The cast was a strong one, but it was of no avail; *Don Giovanni* did not please in Vienna. On Mozart's advice da Ponte had the opera performed several times in quick succession so that the audience could get accustomed to it, and altogether fifteen performances were given in 1788. After that it dropped out of the repertoire altogether until 1792 when, after Mozart's death, it was revived in Vienna in a German translation.

The subsequent history of *Don Giovanni* is well known—too well known to be repeated here. The judgment of Prague, and not that of Vienna, has been endorsed by subsequent generations, and the 'opera of all operas' has been performed in all the great opera houses of the world and in almost every European language. Mozart and da Ponte's work has had an enormous influence, not only on music, but on literature too, and each new generation has interpreted the work in its own way. Volumes have been written about the Romantic interpretation of the opera in general, and about Hoffmann's interpretation in particular. It is not proposed to discuss this influence here, for so much has been written about it that further comment would be superfluous. It may, however, be of interest to mention one great work of art which was directly inspired by

Mozart and da Ponte, which is comparatively little known in Western Europe.

Don Giovanni was first performed in Russia in 1797 in St Petersburg, in a German translation; the opera was an immediate success, and made a great sensation both there and in Moscow. Alexander Pushkin, the great Russian poet, may have seen the opera in German at St Petersburg, where it was revived in the seasons of 1817-1819, or he may have seen it in Odessa, where an Italian troupe performed it a year or two later. It seems probable, however, that Pushkin heard the opera for the first time in Italian in Moscow during the season of 1826-7. It made a great impression on him—so great an impression, in fact, that three years later he himself wrote a new version of the Don Juan legend, which he called *The Stone Guest* (*Kamennyi Gost'*). At that time—the autumn of 1830—Pushkin was much interested in Mozart, probably because of his friendship with Alexander Oulibicheff, who was then planning his three-volume biography of the composer which was published in 1842, after Pushkin's death. Only a week before he wrote *The Stone Guest* Pushkin had written his *Mozart and Salieri*, a magnificent piece of poetry which had a most unfortunate influence, for it helped to spread the rumour that Salieri had poisoned Mozart—a rumour which had absolutely no foundation in fact. When Pushkin wrote his poem Salieri had only been dead five years; nowadays his family would have brought an action against Pushkin, but the poem probably took some time to reach Vienna in Russian, let alone in translation.

The Stone Guest is prefaced with a quotation—or rather, a misquotation—from da Ponte, and there are several other quotations from *Don Giovanni* in the poem; but Pushkin's version of the story differs very considerably from its predecessor. Donna Anna is the wife, not the daughter, of the Commendatore, for example, and Pushkin introduces two new characters, Don Carlos, the Commendatore's brother, and Laura, an actress who had been Don Juan's mistress, and who was in love with him. Don Juan, who has been exiled from Madrid, returns there secretly and goes to visit Laura; he finds Don Carlos there, they fight, and Don Carlos is killed. Don Juan does not invite the statue to dinner, but to Donna Anna's house where, in disguise, he has a rendezvous with her.

When the statue comes to fetch him Don Juan's last words are: 'Oh, Donna Anna!'—for he is in love with her. Dramatically, these alterations to the plot are no improvement—on the contrary; but poetically Pushkin's poem is a masterpiece, a masterpiece in the Russian manner. Although directly inspired by Mozart and da Ponte's work, this Russian version is imbued with a different spirit. There is something of the spirit of nineteenth-century romanticism in it, but the nineteenth-century romanticism of Russia, not of Western Europe. Russian literature has always taken Western literary movements as models, but it has always transformed them into something quite different and often scarcely recognisable. Romanticism, realism, symbolism, surrealism, and all the other -isms become, in the hands of Russian artists, something so different to their Western models that when they return to Western Europe like a boomerang, they are sometimes not even recognised by their parents, but are taken for something absolutely new.

Unfortunately, no adequate English translation of Pushkin's *The Stone Guest* exists, and it is doubtful if one will ever be made, so there is little chance of the work becoming better-known in Western Europe. Pushkin's version of the Don Juan legend is the last to be made by a great poet in the old tradition, the tradition that originated with Tirso de Molina, that was spread by Molière and Goldoni, and that has been immortalised by Mozart and da Ponte. Almost all the versions written after *The Stone Guest* have been influenced by Mozart and da Ponte, but diverge from the direct line of succession from Tirso de Molina. As Professor Dent has said, 'Ever since Goethe the Germans have perpetually tended to translate Don Juan in terms of Faust', and not only the Germans, but the Russians too—Alexei Konstantinovich Tolstoy's version is an example. Don Juan has become a different person as a result.

CHAPTER VIII

THE LIBRETTIST

Così Fan Tutte

AT the end of the 1788 season, the Emperor decided to close the Italian opera. It was a costly luxury, and Joseph felt that when the country was at war it was a luxury which was not justified. Even in peace time, in spite of his genuine if rather limited love of music, Joseph had always considered his opera singers—'ces frédonneurs' as he was wont to call them—as inferior to any private in his army. On 29th July, 1788, therefore, the Emperor wrote to Rosenberg, informing him of his decision: 'Je crois que c'est le moment de renoncer entièrement à l'Opéra pour l'année prochaine', he wrote, 'et de dénoncer par conséquence tout engagement ultérieur à ceux de la trouppe qui sont à Vienne et de point en faire venir du dehors.'

The news was broken to the singers at rehearsal one day by Thorwart, the deputy director of the theatre, and it caused consternation. Not only the singers, but the musicians, scene-shifters, workmen, and all the other innumerable people who are needed behind the scenes to produce an opera, were faced with unemployment. Da Ponte, of course, was horrified. He depended entirely on the opera for his livelihood, and the prospect of it being closed at the very moment when, after years of struggle, he had at last achieved success, was very galling. He resolved to try to save the opera at all costs, and evolved a scheme to that end.

Da Ponte's scheme had the merits of simplicity and practicability. He asked the many rich opera enthusiasts in Vienna to subscribe to an opera fund which was to be reserved for the payment of all expenses, and calculated that the nightly takings from the sale of tickets would therefore constitute a clear profit. Being all too well acquainted with the intrigues and gossip of the theatrical world, he decided that it would be prudent to have someone not directly connected with the theatre to administer the fund; he therefore asked Baron Gondar, a rich Viennese, to become director, while he himself modestly chose to be assistant director.

When Joseph, who had been with his military commanders in the field, returned to Vienna, da Ponte went to see him in order to explain his plan. After saying a few well-chosen words about the grief he felt at losing his royal patron, da Ponte got down to brass tacks. He asked the Emperor to let him have the use of the theatre, promising in exchange to provide the same performances as before, with the same performers. When he had fully explained his plan and shown the Emperor a list of subscribers, Joseph agreed.

Da Ponte was triumphant; the opera had been saved, and everyone should be grateful to him, da Ponte, for saving it! But when he went to tell Rosenberg and Thorwart of his success, they were less than enthusiastic. There would be endless disputes between the Italian singers and the German actors who would have to share the theatre, they argued; the scenery and costumes available were inadequate, and so on. 'It can't be done', they repeated in unison. 'It can't be done!' The directors of the theatre had never liked da Ponte, and were probably not at all keen that he should gain any more power in the theatre; his considerable influence with the Emperor made him a great nuisance as it was. But their protests were of no avail. Da Ponte as usual appealed to Joseph who, when he had heard of the directors' attitude, asked the poet to give him a copy of his project for running the opera; on it he wrote the following note to Rosenberg:

'Count: Tell Thorwart that it can be done, and that I will keep the theatre personally, according to the plan of da Ponte, whose salary is to be doubled.

JOSEPH.'

That clinched the matter, and da Ponte was the hero of the hour, for he had saved not only himself, but the whole opera company from dismissal and probable unemployment. But a sense of obligation rarely engenders affection, and da Ponte, who had never been very popular in Vienna, soon became very unpopular indeed.

The reasons for his unpopularity were numerous and complex; one of them was undoubtedly his own personality, for he was always his own worst enemy. He was an adventurer and an *arriviste*, and as such had few scruples in dealing with his colleagues and rivals. The fact that he was the Emperor's *protégé* did not endear him to those who were not so fortunate, and he must have been an intolerable nuisance to the directors of the theatre, for he was continually invoking the Emperor's assistance and scheming against them behind their backs. There were, too, more concrete accusations levelled against him. There was a good deal of criticism, for instance, about some of his work; it was suggested that, even in an age when copyright was non-existent, his 'borrowing' from other writers sometimes went a bit too far, and other poets had good reason to dislike him.

However, the main source of da Ponte's troubles, as he himself admitted, was his mistress, or rather, one of his mistresses. Adriana del Bene, usually known as La Ferrarese, whose voice had so much impressed Dr Burney years before in Venice, probably arrived in Vienna either just before or just after the first performance of *Don Giovanni* in that city. She made her début in Martin and da Ponte's *L'Arbore di Diana* on 13th October, 1788, taking the part of Diana. The fact that she first appeared in Vienna as the chaste goddess had a certain irony, and no doubt aroused comment, for her reputation was dubious, to say the least. Those who heard her sing agree that she was a very mediocre artist, and not a particularly attractive woman. 'Madame Allegranti is far better than Madame Ferrarese', Mozart told his wife; 'which, I admit, is not saying much.' Joseph said of her: 'She has a rather weak contralto voice; understands music very well, but has an ugly face', but he was wrong about her voice, for she was a soprano, and the part of Fiordiligi in *Così fan Tutte*, which Mozart wrote for her, is a very exacting one. She had also sung in England, where she was considered 'but a very moderate performer'. Da Ponte himself admitted that she was not beautiful and was a poor actress, but maintained that she was a very fine singer; he was deeply in love with her, and his musical judgment was not particularly sound at the best of times, so his opinion has not much value.

This liaison was no secret; da Ponte was, with her husband's consent, La Ferrarese's official lover. It was a love affair which was to cost him a great deal, for La Ferrarese was not popular with the Viennese public or with the other singers, and it was mainly due to her that he ultimately fell from favour.

Da Ponte wrote several libretti for his mistress; most of them, like *Il Pastor Fido* and *La Cifra*, both with music by Salieri, are now forgotten, but one of them was his last—and most disputed—libretto for Mozart: *Così fan Tutte*, or *La Scuola degli Amanti*.

Così fan Tutte was commissioned by the Emperor; in fact, it was the only Italian opera Mozart was ever commissioned to write for Vienna. On 29th August, 1789, *Figaro* had been revived, after three years; La Ferrarese took the part of Susanna, and Mozart wrote two new arias for her. Writing of one of these arias, he said it 'ought, I think, to be a success, provided she is able to sing it in an artless manner, which, however, I very much doubt'. This production of *Figaro* was enthusiastically received, and its success probably reminded Joseph of Mozart's existence and prompted him to commission a new opera from him. It is said that the Emperor himself suggested the plot to da Ponte, and that it was based on incidents which had actually occurred in or near Vienna; the fact that the scene of the opera was originally laid in Trieste, and not Naples, seems to support this theory. In any case, for once the plot was an original one, and not 'borrowed' from some other poet.

Very little is known about how the opera was written. Da Ponte had apparently no great pride in his share of the work; he scarcely mentions *Così fan Tutte* in his *Memoirs*, and in his old age, when he was only too ready to boast about his association with Mozart, he referred only to *Figaro* and *Don Giovanni*, never to *Così fan Tutte*. Indeed, his reticence on the subject was so marked that in 1922, at the time of the first production of the opera in New York, a certain Mr Littlefield wrote a letter to the *New York Times* in which he expressed the opinion that the libretto was not by da Ponte at all. A very acrimonious correspondence ensued in the American press in which da Ponte was defended by Joseph Russo and H. E. Krehbiel, the music critic; Mr Littlefield was ignominiously routed. Although da Ponte would have considered the tone of the correspondence far too gentlemanly, he would undoubtedly have much enjoyed it all the same; he was himself greatly addicted to battles in the press during his lifetime, and would have been delighted had he known that he would occupy so much space in American newspapers almost a century after his death.

Così fan Tutte went into rehearsal during the last weeks of 1789; on 29th December Mozart invited his friend and benefactor, Michael Puchberg, to one of the rehearsals, Joseph Haydn being also present. The first performance of the opera took place on 26th January, 1790, and it was enthusiastically received. La Ferrarese took the part of Fiordiligi, and her sister, Louise Villeneuve, played her stage sister, Dorabella. The fact that the two sisters in the opera are described as 'Ladies from Ferrara' was probably appreciated by the audience; everyone knew that La Ferrarese, who of course was so called because she came from Ferrara, was da Ponte's mistress. Mozart also had several laughs at La Ferrarese's expense; she had an extremely flexible voice with a very wide range, and in some of Fiordiligi's arias the music underlines the singer's capacity for vocal gymnastics and parodies that type of singing in a most amusing way. Whether La Ferrarese realised that Mozart was poking fun at her one cannot tell; probably not, for she was inordinately pleased with herself and proud of her accomplishments. The sisters' lovers were played by Benucci (Guglielmo) and Vincenzo Calvesi (Ferrando), while the parts of Don Alfonso and Despina were taken by the Bussanis, husband and wife—she had been the first Cherubino in *Figaro*. It was, therefore, quite a family affair; one can imagine da Ponte anxiously watching his mistress as, for the first time, she interpreted the part he had written for her. Would the opera please? Would she be a success? Fiordiligi's part was an exacting one, and demanded qualities which, it seems, La Ferrarese did not possess; da Ponte no doubt knew that if anything went wrong, he would be blamed, and his life would be made a misery. But all went well, the opera was applauded, and no doubt da Ponte and his mistress celebrated their triumph that evening. Had they been able to see into the future they would not have felt much like celebrating, for *Così fan Tutte* marked the end of the most successful and the most agreeable period of da Ponte's life.

Da Ponte's libretto for *Così fan Tutte* has always been the subject of controversy. It has been extravagantly condemned and equally extravagantly praised, and for over a century there was scarcely a critic who could discuss it objectively. The main criticisms against da Ponte's text were that it was absurd, frivolous, and immoral; those who admired Mozart's music while condemning the words tried to prove that Mozart had used the libretto against his will and had disliked working on it. Stendhal, for example, considered that the libretto would have been ideal for Cimarosa, but not for Mozart, 'who could not trifle with love'.

George Hogarth, an English critic writing in 1838, was of the opinion that that was precisely what Mozart had done. 'Treated seriously', he said of *Così fan Tutte*, 'it is a gross and injurious libel against the female character; and Mozart, by making his personages perfectly in earnest, and inspiring them with sentiment, feeling, and occasionally an almost tragic depth of passion, has only rendered a matter of mere *badinage* disagreeable and revolting.'

There is no evidence at all that Mozart disliked the libretto—on the contrary, the sparkling music could never have been written *à contre coeur*. That the plot is absurd is true, it is as absurd and as artificial as the convention of opera itself. Nor can it be denied that the plot is frivolous; it is as frivolous as the eighteenth century, and as witty. As to whether it is moral or immoral, that depends entirely on the outlook of the age. In the eighteenth century it was certainly not regarded as immoral; in the nineteenth century it shocked Europe; and in the twentieth century it shocks no one. Perhaps the most valid criticism that can be made of *Così fan Tutte* is that it was written too late; in 1790 it was already a wonderful relic from a vanished age, it was the eighteenth century distilled in music. But on 14th July of the preceding year the eighteenth century and all it stood for had been extinguished; the nineteenth century did not understand or feel any sympathy with its predecessor, and it could not understand this last, artificial, frivolous and perfect flower of eighteenth-century art. In a century which produced such men and women as Tolstoy, Queen Victoria, Beethoven, Florence Nightingale, Wagner and Karl Marx—who have only one thing in common, their sense of purpose—*Così fan Tutte* was quite incomprehensible.

It is as purposeless as a piece of Dresden china—and as pleasing.

As a libretto, *Così fan Tutte* is particularly interesting, for it shows what da Ponte could do in the way of original work when he tried; he usually preferred to take someone else's play and to polish it and adapt it. In spite of all the adverse criticism it has received, the libretto is a first-class piece of craftsmanship. The plot has the outstanding virtues of simplicity and economy; there are only six characters, or rather, three pairs of characters, and the action of the drama unfolds with the stylised smoothness of a ballet. In this libretto, more than in any other, Mozart's condition, that 'the poetry must be altogether the obedient daughter of the music', was fulfilled. In *Così fan Tutte* the libretto has found its proper place; it gives the musician unlimited scope yet at the same time it acts as a frame, as a kind of corset which prevents the opera from becoming a shapeless and amorphous mass. Not every creative genius needs or can work within the limits of such a corset, but Mozart was stimulated by it; in his work he always kept to the rules and the conventions of his day, he never repudiated the established order and became a law unto himself, like Beethoven or Wagner; his achievement is all the more astounding in that restrictions and limitations were, to him, not a hindrance, but a challenge. He believed in evolution, not revolution. *Così fan Tutte*, that artificial, stylised work, with its economy of action, of emotions, and of characters, was a challenge which Mozart was fortunate enough to meet when he was at the summit of his creative powers. The result is an opera as perfect in form as Flaubert's *Madame Bovary* or Madame de Lafayette's *La Princesse de Clèves*—there is nothing superfluous in it, it is complete, polished, and sophisticated.

Present-day audiences are inclined to forget that, when it was first produced, *Così fan Tutte* was a modern opera in modern dress. Opera is, in itself, such an artificial convention—'an exotic and irrational entertainment', Dr Johnson called it—that it is easier for an audience to accept an opera set in some remote and foreign past than one dealing with contemporary life. Metastasio fully realised this, and almost all his operas had a classical or mythological setting; his successors, too, avoided contemporary themes. It is all very well, for example, to watch Aïda singing as she is buried alive in Ancient

Egypt; nothing about the plot or the costumes seems real anyway, and the audience is so hypnotised by the unreality of the scene that it scarcely questions whether Aïda would have felt like singing under such circumstances or not. Even those operas which have a modern setting are usually made more palatable by situating them in a remote country—*Madame Butterfly*, with its exotic Japanese setting, is less of a strain on the audience's credulity than contemporary operas set nearer home. One of the reasons why *La Traviata* was a failure when it was first performed was just this—the audience, seeing the actors on the stage dressed in modern dress, found the whole thing ridiculous, but as the years passed and the opera became a period piece, people ceased to notice how ridiculous it was. In the case of *Così fan Tutte* this question did not really arise; it was clear that however the singers might be dressed and wherever the action might be supposed to take place, the opera in fact belonged to no time and no place that ever existed.

Although *Così fan Tutte* was a success when it was first performed in Vienna, its subsequent career was less fortunate. The libretto was always severely criticised—even as early as 1792 the serious-minded German press began to attack it—and several attempts were made to replace da Ponte's text by entirely new words. Mozart, who took such infinite care to compose music not only in keeping with the dramatic spirit of his libretti, but also for the very words of the poet, would have been horrified and probably, at the same time, amused by these attempts. Some of them were, in fact, very odd. An entirely new text based on a play by Calderon was made in 1909 by K. Scheidemantel, and performed in Dresden as *Die Dame Kobold*, for example. In 1813 a new libretto with the title *Le Laboureur Chinois* was made; for this one-act *pasticcio* music was taken from other works of Mozart besides *Così fan Tutte*, and also from other composers. In 1863 a new French libretto, based on Shakespeare's *Love's Labour's Lost*, was made by J. Barbier and M. Carré, and the opera was rechristened *Peines d'Amour Perdues*. None of these operatic curiosities held the stage for long.

It seems very unlikely that the Emperor Joseph II ever saw *Così fan Tutte*, the opera he had at long last commissioned from Mozart. At the time of the first performance, 26th January, 1790, Joseph was

G

already dying—slowly, painfully, and with the added misfortune of retaining all his mental faculties until the end. His passion for organisation never left him, and his own death, which he stage-managed personally, was a model of its kind. During his last weeks Joseph methodically dictated letters of farewell to his allies, such as Catharine of Russia, to his ministers and marshals; he made his doctor, who had had the courage and honesty to tell him he was dying, a baron: next he summoned his few close friends and rela-tives to his bedside in order to take leave of them personally. His favourite niece, the young Archduchess Elizabeth, was so overcome when he said farewell to her that she fainted; she was expecting to be confined in a few days' time.

Before he died, fate had one more bitter blow in store for Joseph, whose personal life had been so sterile and unhappy. On 17th February Count Rosenberg had the sad duty of informing the Emperor that Elizabeth had given birth to a still-born child the day before, and had herself died some hours afterwards. When he heard the news Joseph showed no emotion; he only asked where her body would be placed for the lying-in-state. Rosenberg replied: 'In the Court Chapel'. 'No', said Joseph, 'that is impossible. That is my place. I don't want to disturb her. Put her somewhere else where she can rest in peace.'

Two days later, on the evening of the 19th of February, Joseph became delirious. His faithful friend, Count Rosenberg, and his confessor, a monk, remained with him throughout the long hours of suffering, which he bore most courageously; outside in an ante-room da Ponte and a few other people waited in silence. Early the next morning their vigil was at an end. 'Il n'est plus, Madame', his life-long friend, the Prince de Ligne, wrote to Catherine of Russia, 'il n'est plus, le prince qui faisait honneur a l'homme, l'homme qui faisait le plus d'honneur aux princes. Ce génie ardent s'est éteint comme une lumière dont l'enveloppe était consumée; et ce corps actif est entre quatre planches qui l'empechent de se remuer.'

Joseph had been neither a great prince nor a great man; he had almost been both. As a ruler he had been a visionary and an idealist; he had not realised that just as Rome was not built in a day, so the vast, reactionary, retarded and immensely diverse Austro-Hungarian

Empire could not be transformed into a modern state by one man and in one man's lifetime. As a person he had had immense qualities, but he had lacked the principle ones of humanity and love. He had lived as a lonely, embittered and misunderstood man; he died an unpopular monarch. At his death, few people mourned him sincerely; amongst those few who did were two men who hated each other, but who had had real affection for Joseph—Count Rosenberg, his chamberlain, and Lorenzo da Ponte, his poet.

CHAPTER IX

THE HUSBAND

LEOPOLD, who succeeded Joseph, was quite a different type of man. He had not approved of his brother, or of his brother's reforms and ideals, and all his life he had suffered from being an ambitious man condemned to take second place. He was scheming and intelligent; twenty-five years in Tuscany, from where he had been forced to witness what he considered Joseph's mad reforms in Vienna with furious impotence, had given him ample time for reflexion. When he finally succeeded to the throne he knew precisely what he wanted to do. Like most new monarchs, one of his first actions was to get rid of the favourites of the previous reign. It was quite natural that Leopold should do so; apart from the fact that he had never seen eye to eye with Joseph, he had his own favourites from his court in Tuscany, and he brought them with him to Vienna. There was a good deal of jockeying for position, and on the whole those who had been Joseph's men went to the wall. All Joseph's closest friends, Rosenberg and the Prince de Ligne amongst them, were snubbed or ignored by Leopold.

The only immediate effect of Joseph's death, so far as Mozart and da Ponte were concerned, was the closing of the opera for a period of two months' court mourning. *Così fan Tutte*, which had had four performances between 26th January and 11th February, was revived when the theatre reopened again in April, and had five more performances during the next few months; it then fell out of the repertoire.

On the occasion of Joseph's death da Ponte had felt it his duty to compose an ode in memory of his royal patron. He was not the only person to write something in memory of Joseph: Beethoven, then a youth of not quite twenty, wrote a *Cantata on the Death of the Emperor Joseph II*; it was his first large-scale choral work, and he later used some of the music he had written for it in *Fidelio*. Like da

Ponte, he had found Joseph II a kind and sympathetic man; he once told a friend that when he had visited Vienna for the first time as a boy of sixteen, only two people had shown any interest in him—Joseph II and Mozart.

Having written his ode, da Ponte felt that it might be tactful also to write some lines in praise of the new Emperor who, he hoped, would become his new patron. His admiration and affection for Joseph were sincere—perhaps too sincere for Leopold's taste—and he no doubt realised that, with Joseph's death, his position in Vienna had become precarious. It was extremely important for him to gain the new Emperor's favour; but at the beginning of his reign Leopold was too busy to pay much attention to da Ponte and his odes. For some months the poet's life remained unchanged.

In 1791 the King of Naples visited Vienna, and Prince Adam Auersperg commissioned da Ponte to write a cantata for this occasion. The music to this work—*Il Tempio di Flora*—was by Joseph Weigl. The cantata, which was performed in the garden of the prince's palace, was a pretty, typically eighteenth-century trifle about Venus and Apollo, of which da Ponte was inordinately proud —he was much prouder of it than he was of *Così fan Tutte*. It was apparently a great success, for the prince rewarded him handsomely for it.

The Neapolitan Ambassador, the Marquis del Gallo, had also commissioned a cantata for the same occasion, but he had chosen Piticchio as the composer, and the words were to be written by the Abbé Serafini, a learned scholar who held a minor diplomatic post in Vienna. Unfortunately when it came to the point, the Abbé's inspiration failed him, and the Ambassador appealed to da Ponte, whose cantata had been such a success, for help. Da Ponte undertook to do the work, but was indiscreet enough to give the sum which the Ambassador had sent him in payment—a sum which da Ponte considered quite inadequate—to the servant who had brought it to him. To make matters worse, when the Ambassador tried to make amends for his meanness by giving da Ponte a gold watch, the poet gave that away to his mistress of the moment, who had 'inspired' his verses. It is scarcely surprising that the Marquis was mortally offended, and became one of da Ponte's enemies for life.

In fact, the number of the poet's friends was steadily diminishing, mainly because of La Ferrarese. She had not had much success in Vienna as a singer, and much to everyone's delight her contract was due to expire shortly. But her lover was far from delighted, and was tactless enough to do everything he could to have her contract renewed. He became a perfect pest, importuning everyone on behalf of his mistress, until things reached such a pitch that even the Emperor and the Empress came to hear about it. Leopold, who was concerned with more important things than opera tittle-tattle, and who was none too favourably impressed by the Poet to the Imperial Theatres anyway, is said to have remarked: 'To the devil with this disturber of the peace!' Rumour in Vienna had it that da Ponte had even gone so far as to write anonymous letters to the new singers who had been engaged for the coming opera season, painting a black picture of Vienna in general and of the opera in particular, in order to discourage them from taking up their new appointments.

After nearly two hundred years it would be almost impossible to unravel the complicated tangle of theatrical intrigues and the mixture of truth and fiction which da Ponte himself wrote about this period of his life. Two facts do, however, emerge: that da Ponte had suddenly become very unpopular in Vienna, principally because of his championship of La Ferrarese; and that the new Emperor, Leopold, was ill-disposed towards him. With the death of Joseph, da Ponte had lost his only true and powerful ally; he had never been on good terms with the directors of the theatre, and would certainly never have been able to keep his job for so long without the Emperor's protection.

Da Ponte had overstayed his welcome in Vienna, and he knew it; he began to look for new openings and possibilities elsewhere. Martin, who had gone to Russia in 1788 as Director of the Italian Opera in St Petersburg, wrote and suggested that his librettist should join him there. Da Ponte jumped at the idea, and gave in his resignation to the Directors of the Imperial Theatre in Vienna. His contract had not quite expired and his resignation was not immediately accepted; by the time he had obtained his release from Vienna the vacancy in St Petersburg had been filled.

He next suggested to Mozart that they should go to London

together; their old friends Stephen Storace and Kelly were managing the opera there, and would be sure to welcome them. But Mozart was then working on *Die Zauberflöte*, and asked da Ponte to give him six months in which to think his project over. Six months later Mozart was dead.

Whether da Ponte did, in fact, resign from his position as Poet to the Imperial Theatres is not clear. It seems unlikely that the directors would have been reluctant to release him; probably he was dismissed, and given five months' salary in lieu of notice. In any case, whether voluntarily or involuntarily, he gave up his job, and remained in Vienna for some time, doing nothing. One day he decided to go and see his opera *Axur*, which was being performed with a new cast. To his amazement, when he arrived at the theatre he, da Ponte, the author of the play, the ex-Imperial Theatres Poet, was refused admission. When he enquired on whose authority he was forbidden to enter the theatre he was told that the order had come from Thorwart, the Deputy-Director. It was a bitter blow; although some of his influential friends, Prince Adam Auersperg amongst them, offered to intervene on his behalf, he decided not to avail himself of their offer. He probably realised that things had gone too far, and that any attempt to rehabilitate himself in Vienna would be useless. In this he was quite right, for on the day on which the theatre opened for the new season he received orders to leave the Austrian capital. For once he acknowledged his defeat, and retired to the village of Moedling, just outside Vienna.

What had happened? Why was he banished? Da Ponte himself was at great pains to explain, and the reasons which he gave for his banishment all seem plausible enough. He alleged, for example, that his rivals and more especially his compatriots had begun to intrigue against him as soon as his royal protector was dead, which was more than likely. He affirmed that the new director of the theatre—Count Ugarte, who had replaced Joseph's friend, Count Rosenberg, in March, 1791—was ill-disposed towards him, which was also very probable; the old director had been, too. He stated that the singers feared that he might try to intrigue against them, and that one of them had even said that she would not dare to appear in public while da Ponte was in Vienna. This, too, was very probably true;

his campaign on behalf of La Ferrarese was notorious, and he was quite capable of resorting to the basest methods in order to defend her. Yet he made no mention whatsoever of what was, in fact, the principal reason for his fall and his banishment.

Some weeks before he was ordered to leave the city, and very probably after he had been forbidden to enter the theatre, da Ponte had written a letter in blank verse to Leopold. This letter, although couched in flowery language, was all the same sufficiently insolent to annoy Leopold very considerably. (Curiously enough, Casanova considered these lines of enough interest to translate them into French; a copy of his translation was found amongst his papers in Dux.) Not content with this poem, which was indiscreet, to say the least, da Ponte also wrote something far more indiscreet about the Emperor, something very scurrilous indeed, which he circulated privately. The text of this libel, for such it apparently was, has been lost, which is probably just as well. Those who saw it were not impressed. 'I have read those verses by da Ponte', Zaguri wrote to Casanova on 11th June, 1791, and added a comment which sums up da Ponte better than any other. 'He carries within him, and will always carry, a canker which eats away all the roots of his good fortune. I had hardly read the verses when I exclaimed: it's too bad! it's too much! He deserves only one thing—contempt. Il y a des choses qui ne piquent point a force d'être extrêmes.'

Although da Ponte later denied that he had ever written anything against Leopold, and informed everyone that he was the victim of wicked intrigues, there is little doubt that his downfall in Vienna was entirely due to his own indiscretions, to that destructive canker within him which, as Zaguri rightly observed, always sooner or later prompted this strange, gifted man to destroy his own success.

Da Ponte spent about four months, March-June 1791, at Moedling. He employed his time in trying to prove his innocence—no easy matter—and in trying to enlist the help of all his friends and acquaintances in clearing his name. He made several attempts to see the Emperor, but in vain. At this time he also tried to obtain permission to return to Venice; his term of banishment had another three years to run, but he hoped, through the influence of Memmo,

Zaguri, and other influential Venetians, to have the term reduced. Zaguri did make some efforts on da Ponte's behalf, but with no success.

Da Ponte's next appeal was to Casanova. 'I could not follow your advice to go to Rome or Madrid', he wrote to his old friend on 18th June, 1791, 'because on the very day when I received your letter I also received an order to return to Vienna to present my defence in writing.' He went on to tell Casanova of his efforts to obtain permission to return to Venice. Apparently his half-brother had presented a petition to the Council of Ten, a petition which Memmo, Zaguri and others had supported, but which had failed for want of two votes. With his usual lack of tact da Ponte had also enlisted the help of La Ferrarese, who had gone to Venice with her husband; but, as Zaguri told Casanova, no sooner had da Ponte fallen from favour than his mistress dropped him completely, and referred to him as a 'madman'. In any case, any intervention La Ferrarese might have made on his behalf would probably have done more harm than good. 'But I believe all these efforts will be insufficient', da Ponte continued in his letter to Casanova, 'if my prayers and the steps I have taken are not also supported by my dear Casanova. If you would be so good as to take the matter up strongly with the noble gentlemen who are my protectors, if you would write to each of them, the difficulties would be smoothed out. Be so good as to do so immediately', da Ponte wrote and added, no doubt tongue in cheek, 'with the ardour which is so characteristic of you.' In a postscript to this letter, he informed Casanova that he would be leaving for Trieste in a few days' time.

Da Ponte had heard that the Emperor would shortly be visiting Trieste, and he had made up his mind to go there and to make one last attempt to have an audience with him. Leopold was not nearly so accessible to his subjects as Joseph had been, and all da Ponte's attempts to see him in Vienna failed. The fact that he wished to see the Emperor at all is curious; he cannot really have expected to be pardoned and reinstated at the theatre after all that he had written against Leopold, who scarcely knew him and had never liked him anyway. What could he expect to gain from such an interview? It seems probable that he was so used to hoodwinking other people

GX

that he sometimes even hoodwinked himself, and that he really believed that he had been unjustly treated.

When da Ponte arrived in Trieste he found that the Emperor was not yet there, so he resolved to wait for him, and in fact had to wait for almost a month. The time passed pleasantly enough; he made friends with Count Brigido, Governor of Trieste, who was not only an agreeable companion, but an influential one as well, and with one or two other people.

On 11th July Leopold arrived in Trieste. That same evening he went to the theatre, and was very disagreeably surprised when he caught sight of da Ponte in the crowd. The Emperor summoned the Chief of Police, Baron Pittoni, and informed him that da Ponte could on no account be allowed to remain in Trieste. Count Brigido pointed out to the Emperor that the poet had come there with the express purpose of obtaining an audience with him. At first Leopold remained adamant, and gave orders for da Ponte to be expelled from the city, but the next morning, thanks to Brigido's efforts, he relented, and ordered da Ponte to appear before him at 11 o'clock. An interview which lasted over an hour and a half ensued.

What happened during that interview? Unfortunately, we shall never know, for there were no witnesses, and even Pittoni, the Chief of Police, did not know precisely what passed between the Emperor and the poet. However, as Pittoni wrote to his friend Casanova, although he did not know what actually took place, he had a pretty shrewd suspicion: 'It's very likely that he spoke about intrigues, as it is very much his style. I have reason to believe that the subject of his conversation bore on the unmasking of rogues. That's about all you can tell the fair ladies who asked you for news of him. . . .'

Da Ponte's own account of the interview, though in other respects it is probably fictitious, confirms Pittoni's theory. It would seem that, in an attempt to ingratiate himself with Leopold, he had done his best to get everyone else connected with the theatre into trouble. There was known to be a great deal of corruption in the Imperial Theatres, and da Ponte had no scruples about implicating his numerous enemies, Thorwart in particular. In other words, he turned informer in an attempt to save his skin. The attempt was partially successful; as a result of his interview with the Emperor some of the police regulations against him were relaxed, and he obtained permission to remain in Trieste, though not to return to Vienna.

So da Ponte stayed on in Trieste; the society there was agreeable, and if only he had had some money, or some means of making it, he might have quite enjoyed his stay there. His friends Count Brigido, the Governor, and Pittoni, the Chief of Police, were friends of Casanova, and probably, therefore, congenial companions. Casanova, who had made Pittoni's acquaintance in 1773, said of him: 'Being in favour of bachelorhood on principle, he was most attentive to pretty women and championed the cause of all libertines.'

Da Ponte's financial situation was truly desperate; as in the old days in Venice and Padua, he was once more reduced to selling his clothes in order to buy food, not only for himself, but also for two of his half-brothers, whom he was supporting, and for a lady whom he had known for ten years, and who had followed him into exile in Trieste. Who the lady was is not known, but she certainly was not La Ferrarese, who had shown no desire to share her lover's misfortunes, in spite of the fact that they were, at least in part, due to his intrigues on her behalf. La Ferrarese was at that time in Venice, where da Ponte had hoped to join her, but the two petitions which he addressed to the Magistrato della Bestemmia, in May 1791 and April 1792, had both been refused, and he therefore did not dare to revisit the Republic. La Ferrarese was probably not very sorry; now that he was no longer Poet to the Imperial Theatres, rich and famous, but only a down-at-heel abbé with a bad reputation and no income, she had lost all interest in him. She had already found a new lover, who had duly been approved by her husband.

The months which he spent in Trieste must have been some of the bitterest in da Ponte's whole life. His fall from favour had been sudden and complete, and it had, after all, been a fall from a great height. He had been in Vienna for almost ten years, and in that time had succeeded, through his very real ability, in becoming a celebrity. He had arrived in Austria a penniless, unknown fugitive from ustice, and he had risen to be Court Poet, the Emperor's protégé

and friend, the collaborator of Salieri, Mozart, Martin and all the
foremost composers of his day. His operas, more especially those
which he had written with Martin, had had an unprecedented
success, and were being performed not only in Austria, but all over
Europe. His private life, too, had been far from unsatisfactory; he
was attractive, amusing, full of charm, and while he was rich and
famous women had been more than kind to him. Now everything
was changed; he had lost his patron, his job, his mistress, and most of
his friends; he was once more under police supervision and, perhaps
worse than anything else, he was exiled from the capital. Da Ponte
was, in spite of, or perhaps because of, his childhood in the country,
an essentially urban individual; he was only happy in capital cities,
where he was at the centre of everything, where the tempo of life
was heightened, where intrigues of every kind flourished, where
society was rich, cosmopolitan, and sophisticated, and where his two
sources of livelihood—the theatre and literature—had their roots.
In the provinces, in small towns, he wilted; he felt bored and stifled
by the slow, bourgeois pace of life, by the dullness and narrow-
mindedness of the inhabitants. In his youth, Treviso had suffocated
him; now, in his early middle age, Trieste numbed him. He longed
for the big cities, for Venice and Vienna, where he could not go;
he dreamed of visiting new countries, of conquering new capitals,
Paris, Madrid, St Petersburg. . . .

Meanwhile, the monotony of life in Trieste was temporarily
broken by the arrival of a company of singers and a company of
actors. Da Ponte's flagging spirits revived a little, more especially
when he was asked to write or provide something for both companies. He did not feel it was worth while to write anything new for
Trieste, so for the opera he chose *L'Ape Musicale* which, under the
title of *Il Pasticcio*, he had written in Vienna in 1789 for La Ferrarese.
It was not really an opera, but rather what would nowadays be
called a revue; the lyrics were for the most part satires or comments
on well-known personalities in the theatrical world, and the music
was taken from popular operas by several different composers. Such
entertainments, with their rather esoteric humour, have always been
popular, especially with those who pride themselves on being 'in the
know' about theatrical gossip; *Il Pasticcio* was no exception, and had

gone down very well in Vienna. The Emperor Joseph had been particularly pleased with it, but some of the singers and musicians, notably Salieri, had been less enthusiastic; perhaps da Ponte's arrows had struck home.

The play which da Ponte provided for the company of actors was probably *Il Mezenzio*, a tragedy which his brother Luigi had left unfinished at his death, and which Lorenzo later completed. When the play was published in New York in 1834 Luigi da Ponte's name did not appear on it. An old acquaintance of da Ponte's, Coletti, who had organised the Arcadian Academy in Gorizia and whom da Ponte particularly disliked, was now editing a newspaper in Trieste. He reviewed da Ponte's play with his customary exaggerated enthusiasm, but this review, far from earning him any gratitude, only increased the poet's animosity to him. Some little time later da Ponte vented his spleen in a satirical ode, of which the first two lines were:

> Mio caro Coletti,
> Non far più sonetti ...

It was at about this time, in the autumn of 1791, that another old acquaintance passed through Trieste on his way to Vienna. Since he had left the Austrian capital in 1786 Casti had visited Constantinople, and had also travelled a good deal in Italy. The news of the Emperor's death had reached him in Florence, where he still nominally held the position of Court Poet to Leopold, although he was only very rarely in the Tuscan capital. Casti, it seems, had had a sincere affection for Joseph as a man, but the news of his death probably caused him very little grief. On the contrary, now that his own master, Leopold, was Emperor, there was no reason why he should not achieve his ambition and become Caesarean Poet. Joseph had always refused to appoint anyone as Metastasio's successor, and had maintained that da Ponte was the only poet he needed. Casti was on his way to rejoin his master in Vienna when he met da Ponte in Trieste.

When the two poets had last met, four years previously, da Ponte had been in favour and had held an official position, and Casti, as a result of his satire on Catharine of Russia, had been in disgrace. Now that the rôles were reversed Casti, who had formerly let no opportunity for baiting da Ponte escape him, felt that he could afford to be more gracious. In Trieste he did all he could to make himself agreeable to his fallen rival, from whom he now had nothing to fear. Da Ponte, delighted to meet someone of his own sort—even Casti—in his dull retreat, poured out the story of his troubles with a wealth of picturesque and inaccurate detail. Casti listened kindly—he was interested to hear all the latest gossip from Vienna, advance knowledge of which would probably be very useful to him on his arrival there—and then he offered da Ponte some good advice. 'Go to Russia, or to England, or to France', he said. When da Ponte replied that Leopold had promised to recall him to Vienna one day, Casti merely laughed, and told him that Leopold had promised to make him, Casti, Court Poet, and had also already commissioned four libretti from him in advance. Although this news cannot have come as a great surprise to da Ponte, it was a bitter blow for him all the same; the Leopold-Casti combination was too strong for him, and he knew it.

Leopold did not, however, make Casti Court Poet, for on 1st March, 1792, before he had had time to do so, he died. When the news of the Emperor's death reached Trieste da Ponte set out immediately for Vienna, in order to make one last attempt to regain his position there. He must have known the new Emperor, Francis II, well, for Francis had spent much time at Joseph's court, and had been more or less trained for the throne by his uncle who had found him a disappointing pupil. 'If only I could get a word in before Casti . . .' da Ponte thought. 'Perhaps, who knows . . .' But Casti was in Vienna already, on the spot, and had no doubt already taken steps to make his position under the new Emperor as secure as it had been under Leopold.

Count Brigido gave da Ponte enough money to enable him to make the journey to Vienna. When he arrived there he went straight to Casti, who had suddenly and unaccountably become his only friend. Casti was as affable as ever, and could not do too much to help him; he gave him advice, encouragement, sympathy, and so on, which cost him very little and won him da Ponte's lasting gratitude. He did more—through his friend Count Saur he even tried to obtain an interview for da Ponte with the Emperor. After all, he, Casti, was sure of his position and had nothing to lose by trying to help an old friend.

Francis refused to see da Ponte, but he did give him permission to remain in Vienna, and may have given him some money. Casanova, who was kept informed of all the gossip by his friends, heard from Count Collalto that rumour had it da Ponte had asked the Emperor to reinstate him in his former position, and had also told him that Leopold had promised him some money; no one knew what had passed between da Ponte and Leopold, and it is very likely that after Leopold's death the poet made all sorts of claims of this kind.

Now that da Ponte had at last received permission to return to Vienna, it was not of much use to him. La Ferrarese happened to be there at that time, on her way to take up an appointment in Warsaw, but she had refused to see him—or rather, her husband, who was usually so tolerant about her lovers, had forbidden him to come to their house. Da Ponte's old position of Poet to the Imperial Theatres had already been filled—not by Casti, but by none other than Bertati—that same Bertati whose *Don Giovanni Tenorio* da Ponte had so largely appropriated and adapted in his own *Don Giovanni*. Da Ponte paid him a visit, but was coldly received. He noted with satisfaction that Bertati was surrounded with rhyming dictionaries and so on, and was obviously finding his new appointment a strain.

Casti, who had waited so long for the title of Caesarean Poet, had not waited in vain. Some six months later Francis II appointed him to the position which Metastasio had held for half a century. Casanova's comments on his appointment were not unjustified: 'I heard that this shameless libertine, this ignorant and lewd rhymer had just been nominated poet to the Emperor', he wrote. 'What a dishonourable succession to the memory of the great Metastasio!'

Casti did not dishonour the memory of his predecessor for very long. Like da Ponte, he could not refrain from intrigue; in 1796 he was suspected of Jacobinism and had to leave Vienna. When he fell from favour he went, like da Ponte, to Trieste, 'le refuge des êtres disgraciés', as Zaguri called it. After eighteen months there he went to Paris, where he seemed to grow younger in spirit as he grew older in years. He produced some of his best work at the very end of his life, and remained gay and sprightly in spite of his advanced age. He still had so many ideas and was so mentally active that when he was working—which he invariably did in bed—he was often obliged to stop writing and play a game of cards with himself, in order to allow his brain to cool down. In 1803, when he was seventy-nine, he returned home late one night after an excellent dinner with some friends, and died of indigestion.

There was no longer any place for da Ponte in Vienna. His libretti, it is true, were still popular and were performed frequently, but new stars were rising in the operatic firmament—such as Cimarosa, whose *Il Matrimonio Segreto*, with a libretto by Bertati, made a sensation at its first performance on 7th February, 1792— and the brightest star of all was already burnt out. On 5th December, 1791, Mozart had died at the age of thirty-five, and had been buried in a pauper's grave. Da Ponte had been in Trieste at the time of his friend's death, an event to which he made no reference whatsoever, either in his *Memoirs* or, so far as can be ascertained, in his letters. Egocentric to the core, he had always been too preoccupied with his own minor misfortunes to pay much attention to the real tragedies of others.

It may be, however, that in his last, bitter months on earth, Mozart's thoughts turned occasionally to the strange, gifted adventurer who had provided him with the framework for his three great Italian comic operas. A letter written by him in Italian in September, 1791, to an unknown friend—a letter which is not, incidentally, accepted by all experts as authentic—was probably addressed to da Ponte, and seems to indicate that the poet's suggestion that Mozart should accompany him to London had prompted this reply. It is a most moving letter, the expression of the strange premonitions which haunted Mozart in his last months, and which had been increased by the commission he had received from an unknown person to write a requiem—a requiem which he soon became convinced was to be for his own death. It was of these most intimate thoughts that Mozart wrote in this letter:

My Dear Sir,
    I would like to take your advice, but how can I succeed? My head is distracted, I feel stunned and I cannot banish the vision of

that stranger from my eyes. I see him continually; he entreats me, he begs me, and impatiently asks me for the work. I go on working, because composing fatigues me less than rest. Moreover, I have nothing more to fear. I know from what I feel that the hour is striking; I am on the point of death; I am finished before I have had time to enjoy my talent. And yet, life was so beautiful, and my career opened under such happy auspices—but one cannot change one's own destiny. None can measure his own days. We must be resigned, for it will all be as Providence pleases. I thus conclude my funeral song, which I must not leave unfinished.

MOZART

Did da Ponte, in exile in Trieste, ever receive this letter? As he busied himself with the production of his play in the provincial theatre, as he bickered with Coletti, flirted with the ladies, gambled with Pittoni and quarrelled with his mistress, did he sometimes spare a thought for Mozart, dying in Vienna? Let us, after all these years, give him the benefit of the doubt.

Mozart was dead, the Emperor Joseph II was dead, Leopold II was dead. An epoch had ended, a great epoch; those who had not lived through it, so Talleyrand said, had not known 'la douceur de vivre'. But what of those who, like da Ponte, outlived that epoch, who had not the fortune, like Mozart, to die with their age, but who survived into the nineteenth century, pale forgotten ghosts from a lost world? A few of them, like Talleyrand himself, were able to adapt themselves to the new circumstances, to the new rulers of Europe, to the new spirit of Europe; but they were in the minority. Da Ponte was not among them. In 1792 he was forty-three years old; Fate decreed that he was to live for another forty-six years, that more than half his life was to be spent in that new age with which he had nothing in common, and in which there was no place for him. From henceforward he was to be a spiritual refugee.

There was no point in da Ponte remaining in Vienna any longer, and he decided not to do so. He took leave of the few friends he had left there—ironically enough his most touching farewell came from his old enemy and rival, Casti—and made preparations to leave the Austrian capital, the scene of his triumphs, and his second home.

Where should he go? He could not return to Venice; there was no place for him in St Petersburg, the refuge of so many Italian artists and musicians at that time; he had no friends or prospects in Madrid. Finally he decided to go to Paris. Before his death Joseph had given him a letter of introduction to Marie-Antionette, who had greatly admired *Una Cosa Rara*. Da Ponte had apparently been far too pre-occupied with his own affairs to pay much attention to events in France, for he decided—and it was in the summer of 1792 that he took the decision—that a letter of introduction to the Queen of France was of value. He would go to Paris and try his fortunes there; but before doing so he had to return to Trieste, where he had already half-committed himself to embarking on an extraordinary under-taking. This undertaking, which was to change the whole course of his life, was no more nor less than marriage.

II

Perhaps the most remarkable thing about da Ponte's marriage was not the fact that he contemplated it—he had often done so—but the fact that he found someone willing to become his wife. As a husband he had very little to recommend him, especially at that particular juncture in his life. He was a Catholic priest, a fact which was well-known to everyone, for he had never troubled to conceal it; he had been banished from his own country, and had just left another country under a cloud of suspicion; he was unemployed—although he did have, it is true, an imposing record of theatrical successes to his credit; he had only just concluded a scandalous and much-publicised liaison with a singer whose reputation was almost as unsavoury as his own; and he had been keeping and most likely living with another woman in the small town of Trieste where he met and courted his future wife. By no standards could he be con-sidered an eligible husband or son-in-law, and yet he found a well-to-do and, so far as can be ascertained, respectable merchant who was not only willing to entrust his beautiful and virtuous daughter to da Ponte, but who actually asked him to marry her.

During his stay in Trieste da Ponte had become acquainted with a man whom he described as a 'rich English merchant'. John Krahl or Grahl was, in fact, neither very rich nor very English. He was almost certainly of Jewish origin, had been born in Dresden, but had lived for many years in England. As to his wealth, shortly after da Ponte met him he went bankrupt, and had to leave Trieste in a hurry.

Grahl was reputed to have a beautiful and accomplished daughter, and da Ponte was anxious to make her acquaintance; but when she was introduced to him for the first time he was disappointed to see that she was wearing a black veil, so that he could not see her face.

'Mademoiselle,' he said jokingly, 'the way you wear your veil is not at all fashionable!'

'Why, what is the present fashion?' asked Miss Grahl, mystified and no doubt a little annoyed by da Ponte's remark.

'Like this, Signorina,' he replied, and he raised the veil. The face he uncovered was indeed attractive, but Miss Grahl was not at all amused by his joke, and she left the room in a huff.

In this way da Ponte first met the woman who eventually became his wife. It was not, however, a case of love at first sight, for his immediate reaction after their first meeting was to try to arrange a marriage between her and an Italian friend of his in Vienna who had expressed the desire to marry an Englishwoman. Ann Celestine Grahl—Nancy, as she was generally called—always maintained that she was English, and she was probably born in England.

While negotiations for this marriage, with da Ponte playing the part of match-maker, went ahead, while letters and portraits were exchanged and so on, da Ponte whiled away the time by giving Nancy Italian lessons in exchange for the French lessons which she gave him. It was not long before he realised that he had made a great mistake in offering this charming young girl to his friend in Vienna, but the marriage was already more or less a foregone conclusion, and Nancy's parents were only waiting for the young man's arrival in Trieste to give their formal consent. It seemed that, yet once more, da Ponte had destroyed his own happiness, for he was really in love, and in love with a girl some twenty years younger than himself. It was, perhaps, the first time in his life that he had ever been in love with innocence and inexperience. Most of his mistresses—Angiola Tiepolo, Angioletta Bellaudi, La Ferrarese—

had been of quite a different type to Nancy Grahl; they had been as free and easy in their morals, as experienced in the art of love, and as cynical in their approach to it as da Ponte himself. But now he was forty-three, an age at which respectable married men take mistresses and disreputable adventurers think about marriage. Like his father had been at the same age, he was captivated by youth, inexperience, and virtue as never before.

Nancy, too, was attracted by da Ponte, probably for precisely opposite reasons. He was, to her, a fascinating man of the world, old enough to be her father, yet handsome, charming and clever enough to win her heart. No doubt, instead of teaching her Italian grammar, da Ponte told her stories about his life at the Viennese court, about his friend the Emperor, about his successes in the theatre and in society. No doubt he gave her glowing descriptions of his youth in Venice, of his patrician friends there, and of his success as a poet. No doubt, too, there was a great deal which he omitted to tell her—his trial and banishment, his children taken to the Foundling Hospital, his humiliation in Vienna after Joseph's death, and so on. Nancy was dazzled by da Ponte's wit and charm, by his fame as a librettist, by his exalted friends; she was also attracted to him as a man. As they gave each other lessons and waited for the arrival of her future husband from Vienna, da Ponte and Nancy suffered the joys and agonies of nascent and undeclared love.

After a few weeks a letter came from Nancy's fiancé; da Ponte opened it with a sinking heart, fearing that it announced his friend's arrival in Trieste. But the young man had only written to enquire what dowry Nancy would receive on her marriage—a reasonable enough request under the circumstances, it would have seemed; after all, it was an arranged marriage. John Grahl, however, took quite a different view of the matter; he snatched the letter from da Ponte, and tore it into shreds, crying: 'Ah, so he'd marry my money, not my daughter, would he?' Then, so da Ponte says, Grahl turned to him and impulsively offered him his daughter's hand in marriage. Without hesitation, da Ponte accepted.

Where and when the actual marriage ceremony took place—if, indeed there ever was a marriage ceremony—is not clear. Da Ponte himself states that on 12th August, 1792, at about two o'clock in the afternoon, Nancy's parents entrusted her to his care 'after the usual social ceremonies and formalities'. What precisely he meant by this phrase no one knows; rumour had it that he had been married according to the Jewish rites, but Pittoni, who was Chief of Police in Trieste and therefore in a position to know, denied this. In any case, it is unlikely that a Rabbi would have agreed to marry a man known to be a Catholic priest. Patient research by scholars has failed to reveal any trace of his marriage having taken place in Trieste, and it seems improbable that it did. If da Ponte did ever go through a marriage ceremony with Nancy it was probably in England where his past was not so well-known and where he might have been married according to the Anglican rites; later on, in America, the da Pontes were described on official documents as 'Anglicans', and a child of theirs born in the United States was baptised by an Anglican priest.

In any case, whatever the ceremonies may or may not have been, da Ponte took his marriage seriously. Indeed, it was a most serious step, and one which made life even more difficult for him than it had been before. The marriage was, so far as can be ascertained, a happy one; it lasted for forty years, and then was only broken by Nancy's death. Nancy proved to be a good wife, energetic, hardworking and capable, though she was not, to judge from her handwriting, highly-educated; and extraordinary though it may seem, da Ponte was not a bad husband. As Walter Bagehot once said in another connection, he 'infinitely preferred a marriage to a ministry'.

After the 'social ceremonies' da Ponte and Nancy set off for Paris. Financially, their situation was precarious, but da Ponte had not dared tell his new father-in-law that he was practically penniless in case he too should be suspected of being more interested in Grahl's money than his daughter. Nancy's mother—'ottima donna e vera gemma famiglia' da Ponte called her—gave her daughter some money before she left, which later on proved very useful. The first night of the honeymoon was spent at Ljubljana, and then they continued their journey towards Prague.

On his arrival in Prague da Ponte found that all three operas which he had written with Mozart were being performed, and with as much success as ever; he therefore had an opportunity of proving to his bride that at least some of the stories he had told her about his past glory were true. After a few days in Prague the couple left for Dresden, but remembering that Casanova owed him a small sum of money, da Ponte decided to break his journey at Dux, and to pay a visit to his old friend.

Casanova had been installed at Dux as librarian to Count Waldstein since 1785; he had met the Count—a nephew of the Prince de Ligne—in Paris in 1784, and they had liked each other immediately. The Count was interested in the occult sciences and the Cabal—subjects in which Casanova had dabbled all his life; Casanova, who was then fifty-nine years old and penniless, was interested in finding a comfortable retreat in which to spend his old age. When Waldstein invited him to accompany him to Bohemia and to become his librarian and secretary, Casanova accepted with alacrity.

It was time for Casanova to retire, to leave the scenes of his triumphs, the courts and capitals of Europe, while he could still do so gracefully and before he became too ridiculous; he was lucky to find so kind a patron as Waldstein and so comfortable a retreat as Dux, instead of having to spend his last years in penury in the slums of some city where, in his youth, he had conquered everyone and everything. He realised he was lucky; he was perhaps even grateful to Waldstein for giving him a peaceful, quiet and secure old age; but he did not enjoy it. To Casanova old age was insupportable; peace and quiet were not his elements, he could not reconcile himself to exile from the great world, even though he knew that his powers were failing and that he was too old to enjoy the great world any more. At Dux he was irritated by everyone and everything, more especially by the Count's servants who, when their master was away, which was fairly often, laughed at the old Italian adventurer, treated him with scant respect, played tricks on him, and reduced him to a state of wild, impotent rage.

Nothing was right: the plate of macaroni—which he insisted on having every day, even in Bohemia—was cold; the soup, on the other hand, was too hot; dogs barked and kept him awake at night; a servant did not raise his hat to him as he passed; everyone else was given strawberries before him, and when his turn came there were none left; the Count's steward, or the other servants, had put his portrait on the door of the lavatory, where no one could fail to see it or to read the rude inscription which they had written on it. It was not only the servants at Dux who exasperated Casanova. The village priest annoyed and bored him with pious talk and attempts to reform him; the Count did not say good-morning to him before greeting everyone else, or lent someone a book from the library without warning him, Casanova, the librarian. Worst of all, everyone laughed at him; the servants laughed at him, the Count laughed at him, visitors laughed at him—or Casanova imagined that they did. They laughed at his old-fashioned, polished manners, of which he was so proud; they laughed at the out-moded clothes which he put on for the benefit of grand visitors, and which he still considered to be the height of elegance; they laughed at his verses, they laughed at his stories; worst of all, they laughed at him. Casanova, the great, the dashing, the amorous Casanova, the friend of kings and princes, every woman's dream and every man's envy, had become a dyspeptic, irritable, senile old man, weeping and talking about magic and macaroni.

Casanova was to remain at Dux altogether for fourteen years—that is, until his death. Apart from quarrelling with everyone, he spent his time conducting a voluminous correspondence with his many friends all over Europe, lamenting the fall of the Republic of Venice, teaching the village girls all manner of '*sottises*' so that their mothers made complaints about him, and accusing all his enemies of being Jacobins; he also spent much time reliving his happier days in his memory and in his *Mémoires* which he was then writing.

Casanova was delighted whenever visitors arrived to break the monotony of life at Dux, more especially when they gave him an opportunity to retell some of his famous stories, such as his escape from the Leads in Venice. He was pleased to see da Ponte again, even though he had often criticised him behind his back; they had many interests and many friends in common, and it was a delight to talk to a fellow-Venetian instead of having to spend his time with semi-literate German and Bohemian servants and boors. Nancy was young and, as Casanova was quick to note, she was pretty; the old adventurer was gallant to the end, and the mere sight of a pretty woman was still enough to make him forget his indigestion and the insults he had suffered, and to encourage him to turn on all the remnants of his charm for her benefit.

Nancy was fascinated by Casanova, amazed by his sprightliness, entranced by his stories, and completely captivated by his charm. Later, whenever her husband wrote to him, she would add a post-script to the letter, postscripts such as women only write to men they find attractive. Even at the age of almost seventy, the world's greatest charmer had not quite lost his touch.

The time passed agreeably enough at Dux, but it was quite apparent that Casanova had even less money than da Ponte, and was in no position to repay the sum he owed him. After two or three days' stay the honeymoon couple decided to go on to Dresden, and Casanova accompanied them as far as Toeplitz, a town a few miles away from Dux. On the way there the carriage overturned, and the travellers were obliged to wait for some hours while it was repaired; when they finally reached Toeplitz da Ponte found that the carriage was still unsafe, and that he would be forced to sell it. Casanova transacted the deal for him, pocketed a commission, and in exchange gave da Ponte three pieces of advice. 'If you want to make your fortune', he said, 'don't go to Paris—go to London; but when you are there be careful never to go to the Italian Café, and never sign your name to anything.' Then they parted—Casanova to return to Dux, and the da Pontes to continue their journey to Dresden. They never met again.

As they drove along in the carriage, Nancy plied her husband with questions about the extraordinary man they had just left, and da Ponte did his best to satisfy her curiosity. He told her what he knew of Casanova's past, of his fabulous escape from the Leads in Venice, of his travels all over Europe from Spain to St Petersburg, of his fantastic adventures, of his dabblings in the occult, and perhaps something about some of his love-affairs. She listened enthralled to the story of his grand hoax on the Marquise d'Urfé, the fabulously rich, credulous and gullible old lady whom Casanova had persuaded that he could give back her youth; and although da Ponte got some of the details of this elaborate and cruel jest a little muddled, the main ingredients of it—such as the beautiful courtesan whom Casanova disguised as an old woman and then 'transformed' into a young woman before the eyes of the Marquise—were all there.

Another story which da Ponte told his wife about Casanova was probably more interesting to her, for, unlike the episode of Madame d'Urfé which had taken place long before da Ponte had met Casanova, her husband had been an eye-witness of part of this adventure himself. In his youth Casanova had had an Italian servant called Costa, who was not unlike Don Giovanni's Leporello; he looked after his master's interests, helped him in his intrigues, and Casanova was particularly fond of him. In the winter of 1761 Casanova, who was then engaged on his elaborate plan to dupe Madame d'Urfé and to extract from her as much of her fortune as possible, decided to leave Paris for a while and temporarily to transfer his operations to Strasbourg and Munich. Madame d'Urfé had promised him not only some money for his journey, but also some valuable jewels, snuff-boxes and other presents. Casanova was in a hurry to reach his destination, there was some delay over the Marquise's presents, and so he set out for Strasbourg without them, leaving Costa in Paris with instructions to collect the jewels and also some fine clothes which Casanova had ordered from the tailor, and to take them all to Strasbourg. Costa, who had apparently learned a good deal from his master, collected the jewels and the clothes, but instead of rejoining his master in Strasbourg with them, he went to Italy. Both Costa and the valuables disappeared without a trace.

Some twenty-three years later, in 1784, Casanova went to Vienna where, for just over a year, he acted as secretary to the Venetian Ambassador. Da Ponte, while walking in the Graben one day with Salieri, met Casanova by chance. He had not seen him since he had left Venice, and had no idea that he was in Vienna, but by a strange coincidence he had dreamed the night before that he had met Casanova in precisely similar circumstances. While Casanova remained in Vienna the two Venetians saw a good deal of each other—indeed, it is probably during this period that what had been little more than an acquaintanceship in Venice developed into a close friendship.

One day, when they were walking together—once more in the Graben—da Ponte was amazed to see Casanova suddenly rush up to a man who was passing them, shake him violently, and shout in rage: 'I've caught you at last, you robber!' The man was none other than Costa, Casanova's old servant who, after a very varied and colourful career, was now in the service of Count Hardegg in Vienna. Casanova was beside himself with rage at the sight of his dishonest ex-valet, and started to abuse him; as a crowd was beginning to assemble da Ponte thought it prudent to drag his friend away before there was trouble. They continued their walk, and Casanova told da Ponte the story of how Costa had absconded with the jewels many years ago. Meanwhile, they noticed that Costa had gone into a café; after a short while a boy came to Casanova with a note from his old servant.

Among his other accomplishments Costa was something of a poet —he had once, apparently, attacked da Ponte in verse—and he had written the following lines to his old master:

> Casanova, non far strepito:
> tu rubasti e anch'io rubai:
> tu maestro ed io discepolo,
> l'arte tua bene imparai:
> desti pan, ti do focaccia;
> sarà meglio che tu taccia.'[1]

Casanova read these lines, thought for a moment, and then laughed. 'The rogue is right,' he said to da Ponte, and went into the café to find Costa. Da Ponte watched them walk off together, apparently on the best of terms, and later on Casanova showed him a ring—all that remained of the stolen jewels—which Costa had given him. It was a cameo ring, and appropriately enough bore a picture of Mercury, the protector of thieves.

Da Ponte's stories about Casanova made the journey pass quickly and agreeably, and no doubt were only interrupted, but not concluded, by the couple's arrival in Dresden. In the Saxon capital da Ponte found old friends, such as Mazzolà and Father Huber, who gave him a pleasant welcome. Mazzolà, in particular, was very friendly, and da Ponte spent much time in his house. How the saintly Father Huber reacted to da Ponte's marriage is not known,

[1] 'Casanova, don't make a row, you have stolen, so have I; you're the master, I'm the pupil, you taught well: it's six of one and half-dozen of the other; the best thing you can do is to keep quiet.'

but can well be imagined; it seems unlikely that da Ponte could have concealed Nancy or his relationship with her during his stay in Dresden, but he may not have told people that she was his wife.

In fact, da Ponte was only now beginning to realise the full significance of his marriage himself. Writing to Casanova from Dresden, on 24th September, 1792, he said: 'Today I am no longer my own master. Providence orders all my movements, I am nothing but a kind of machine which accurately obeys any given impulse. I force myself to behave blindly, like a man who has fallen into the sea and who moves his hands and feet in order not to drown, and so as to reach the shore. Really, I am staking all for all. If the risk is great, the reward which I have received in advance makes it worth while. I can no longer say: 'nocet empta dolore voluptas': I am giving myself up entirely to the search for happiness, and only misfortune is possible. Misfortune may come, perhaps, but I don't want to make myself unhappy by anticipating it.'

After about ten days in Dresden, the da Pontes regretfully took leave of their friends, and continued their journey towards Paris. They set off on the road to Cassel, and made their first halt at Spires. When da Ponte arrived at the inn there he was surprised to see a young nobleman of his acquaintance standing at the door; when the young man saw him he ran to welcome him with open arms, and almost dragged him from the carriage in his excitement. 'Heaven must have sent you here today to help me,' he said. 'You must write me a sonnet!'

If da Ponte was surprised at being greeted with such a request, he was even more surprised when he heard the reason for it. The young man was deeply in love with a girl who, unfortunately, was quite indifferent to him. The girl's father, who liked the young man and wished to help him, had proposed that they should all make a journey together in the hope that his daughter might grow to love the young man when she knew him better. But it was no use; the girl remained unmoved by all the young man's efforts to please her. On the very day of da Ponte's arrival in Spires she had jokingly said at dinner that she would promise to love the young man if he would write her a sonnet—a feat which, as she very well knew, he was quite incapable of performing.

Da Ponte had arrived in the nick of time. In less than half an hour he had written a sonnet with which the young man successfully wooed and won his girl. Da Ponte received a handsome gold watch in payment for his verses.

It was while he was at Spires that da Ponte heard the news of Marie-Antoinette's imprisonment and the advance of the French forces on Mainz. It seemed hardly the moment to continue his journey to Paris with his letter of introduction to the French queen, and so, remembering Casanova's advice, he changed his plans and decided to go to London instead.

After leaving Spires, therefore, da Ponte and his bride set off in the direction of Holland. Their journey was uneventful, apart from a narrow escape from bandits, and in due course they arrived safely in London. All da Ponte possessed on his arrival in England was six louis, a gold watch, a ring which he soon sold for six guineas, and a young and attractive companion who may, or may not, have been his lawful wedded wife.

Part III

LONDON

'On arriving in England, a foreigner needs
to be fortified with resignation . . .'

CASANOVA.

CHAPTER X

THE EXILE

'THE air of London has qualities similar to those of the Waters of Lethe,' da Ponte wrote to Casanova soon after his arrival in England, and he did not subsequently change his opinion. London is not an easy city to conquer at the best of times, and da Ponte lacked the three most important things—a knowledge of English, influential friends, and money. Nancy, it is true, spoke English well and knew London; her sister Louisa, who was married to a certain Niccolini, was living there, and on their arrival the da Pontes stayed with the Niccolinis for a few days; they found them neither rich nor hospitable.

The only friends da Ponte had in England were the Storaces, brother and sister, and Michael Kelly. On his arrival he went to call on them, no doubt expecting to receive a warm welcome and possibly some employment. Kelly was one of the principal singers at Drury Lane Theatre and stage-manager of the Italian Opera in the Haymarket; Storace was one of the most popular and successful operatic composers of the day—and had not da Ponte written an excellent libretto for him in Vienna?—and Nancy was still one of the most successful singers not only in England, but in the whole of Europe. Da Ponte found his friends changed; they were older, more sure of themselves, and more important than they had been in Vienna. They were now at home, on their native soil, and they had forgotten the far-off days when both they and da Ponte had been foreigners in the service of the Hapsburgs. Storace was now writing English, not Italian operas—his *Siege of Belgrade* (1791) with a libretto by Cobb had incorporated some of the music from Martin's *Una Cosa Rara*. Kelly was still singing, also mostly in English opera, and his managerial activities at Drury Lane and the Haymarket kept him very busy. His singing had apparently deteriorated on his return from Italy, and one critic said he had 'retained or regained so much

of the English vulgarity of manner' that he was not popular as a
serious singer, although his Irish charm and wit and his gifts as an
actor made him very popular in light opera. At this time he had
already fallen in love with Mrs Crouch, the singer, and was living
with her quite officially. During the season before da Ponte's arrival
they had given a series of brilliant receptions at their house in Pall
Mall which had been attended by the fashionable and artistic society
of the day; Sheridan, a close friend of Kelly's, was a frequent visitor,
as were the Storaces, Madame Mara, Mrs Billington, and also the
Prince of Wales who, it was rumoured, shared the favours of Mrs
Crouch with Kelly.

Da Ponte found that he was greeted rather coolly by his old
friends; they were all busy, successful, and popular in London
society, and had not much time to spare for a down-and-out Italian
poet, whose reputation was none too good. Antonioli, the poet to
the Italian Opera, had just died, and da Ponte thought he might
succeed him; but although for two months he was given vague hopes
and even vaguer promises, in the end Badini, who had been living
and working in London for many years, was given the job. All that
da Ponte achieved was an introduction to the celebrated singer,
Madame Mara; she asked him to write a play, and he adapted his
tragedy *Mezenzio* for her. Although it seems never to have been
performed, Mara paid him thirty guineas for it.

Mara's commission arrived just in time. 'I have sold or pawned
everything I possess rather than let people see my plight,' da Ponte
wrote to Casanova, with whom he had begun an intimate correspondence after his visit to Dux. It was not the first time that da
Ponte had found himself penniless in a strange city and had been
forced to pawn his clothes, but now he was no longer alone; in the
room which he had taken at 16 Sherard Street, Golden Square, he
and Nancy spent many sad and hungry evenings.

However, he had lost none of his old initiative, energy, and tact-
lessness, in spite of his complaints about the soporific effect on him
of the London air; he went on making plans, pulling strings, cadging
introductions to influential people and writing odes in the hope of
finding some work or income. He described one of his bright ideas
in a letter which he wrote to Casanova in January 1793: 'As the

John Bull at the Italian Opera
by T. Rowlandson

Ticket for the Benefit of Brigida Banti

Italian Opera House, Leonard and Church Streets, New York

directors (Storace and Kelly) have deceived me so bitterly, I have decided to avenge myself in a noble way. I am thinking of publishing a periodical news-sheet entitled *La Bilancia Teatrale*, in which I hope to make these gentlemen understand what a mistake they have made in treating me like that. This news-sheet will appear on the day after each performance at the Opera; I have only sixty subscribers so far, but I hope to collect two hundred, which would be sufficient for me.' The scheme came to nothing for want of subscribers—it is surprising that he interested so many as sixty people in his plan—and it was really just as well. Da Ponte would have gained nothing from such a publication, except some notoriety and the enmity of Kelly and Storace who were not, so far, hostile, but merely indifferent to him. His other ventures into journalism give some idea of the type of scurrilous abuse and obscene invective he would have published about his former friends.

His next plan was more promising; he would publish some poetry in order to attract Londoners' attention to the presence in their midst of the ex-poet to the Austrian Emperor. He chose as his theme the recent execution of Louis XVI, and called his collection of poems *Il Tributo del Core*. This work was dedicated to the Duc de Choiseul, but the results were not as satisfactory as the author had hoped. Indeed, the immediate result was that his rival and enemy, Badini, published a satire on da Ponte which must have made him the laughing-stock of Italian-speaking London; it was entitled *Il Tributo della Coglionatura*, and the less said about it the better. Like Badini, Casanova did not think highly of da Ponte's poem; he covered the pages of the copy the author had sent him with adverse comments.

At this time Casanova's patron, Count Waldstein, happened to be in London; he had just arrived from revolutionary Paris where he had passed through adventures worthy of one of Baroness Orczy's heroes. Da Ponte saw a good deal of him in London, no doubt in the hope that he would become his patron, but Waldstein was too much preoccupied with horses during his stay in England to take much interest in poets, and in any case he was probably not keen to support another Venetian adventurer, having one already permanently installed at Dux. He was amiable to da Ponte, but did not part with any money.

H

What could an Italian poet do to earn a living in London? Casanova wisely suggested that he should teach languages, but da Ponte affirmed that in England only 'valets, shoemakers, bandits and *sbirri*' exercised that profession. However, he did contemplate giving Italian readings, if only he could procure enough money to furnish his room 'decently' beforehand. But this was just another plan, and like so many he made it came to nothing. Da Ponte's attempts to gain rich and influential patrons were not very successful either. Although he affirmed that he was 'on good terms' with Lord Salisbury, and had been promised an introduction to the Duke of Bedford who, he wrote, 'is as rich as God the Father, but twice as mean', nothing much came of it. Lord Salisbury and the Duke of Bedford were patrons and governors of the opera, which is why da Ponte was particularly keen to obtain their favour.

For he had by no means lost hope of becoming poet to the Italian Opera, in spite of the fact that Badini was firmly installed in that position. Da Ponte wrote to Casanova with his usual self-assurance that he did not want to be merely poet to the opera, but director of it as well. It was the same self-assurance and effrontery which had made him, when young and unknown in Vienna, aspire to succeed the great Metastasio as Caesarean Poet, and then he had almost been successful; but London was a very different place to Vienna. For one thing, the Italian influence was not so strong in England as it was in Austria, nor was it held in such high esteem. Da Ponte had made a bad start in London; Badini's satires against him had had a certain success, da Ponte had naturally replied, and in language quite as inelegant as that employed by Badini if not more so, and only a few months after his arrival in England he had already become almost as notorious as he had been in Vienna. It was the same old 'destructive canker' which Zaguri had noted in him, that strange twist in his character which always made him destroy his own good fortune—after all, when he had arrived in London scarcely anyone had known anything about him or his past, and he really could have made a new start. It was, of course, mainly thanks to Badini that the whole of London knew about most of the unsavoury incidents in his career, including a few which had never taken place, for Badini had a fertile imagination. He even accused da Ponte of sodomy, and da Ponte was advised by his friends to sue him for libel; but he had scarcely enough money to live on, let alone to go to law. He did, however, reply to Badini's attacks. His replies did him no credit, either as a man or as a poet, but he was inordinately proud of them all the same, and considered that he had painted his enemy's portrait in one poem 'with a brush worthy of Titian'. The few specimens of this mud-slinging competition which have been preserved show both Badini and da Ponte in a most regrettable light.

The only thing that went well at this period of da Ponte's life was his marriage. The letters which he wrote to Casanova from London which were, in the main, catalogues of misfortunes, poverty and injustices, all contained touching references to Nancy and to his new-found domestic bliss, which must have made the old cynic at Dux smile when he read them. 'Nancy is well,' her husband wrote; 'she loves me, I love her, and if only God would improve our situation we should be very happy together. . . .' Casanova, however, thought that Nancy, and not God, could improve the family finances, and he apparently sent a cynical suggestion to that effect. Nancy thanked the old man for his advice and replied as follows:

'Vous n'avez jamais été marié, voilà pourquoi vous voudriez me donner le petit conseil que votre Italien Santo Ambrogio n'a pas manqué donner à sa nation. Mais vous savez que les Anglais ont proscrit les Saints, et voilà pourquoi la morale ne serait pas bonne pour moi. . . .'

Her husband replied to the suggestion more briefly: 'Anything you like, except horns.'

In May 1793, da Ponte announced to Casanova: 'My dear Nancy, my official wife, will soon become a mother.' Did he use the rather strange adjective 'official' to indicate to this friend that he had at last been through some marriage ceremony with Nancy in London? It seems very probable that if there ever was any ceremony at all, it took place in England, and that Casanova, at any rate, knew that there had been no proper marriage in Trieste before da Ponte and Nancy visited him at Dux. Perhaps the fact that Nancy was expecting a child had made da Ponte decide to try to make their relationship legal in England for his child's sake.

At any rate, the expected child made da Ponte even more desperate

to find work, and was perhaps the cause of his decision to go to
Holland. He had heard that the French theatre there had been closed
as a result of the war, and he thought that it might therefore be
possible to open an Italian theatre in The Hague or in Amsterdam.
Nancy had lived in Holland, and had friends and connections there
who might prove useful, and Madame Mara had just sent him the
thirty guineas which she owed him for his play, so he was able to
pay for the journey. Nancy remained behind in London, with the
intention of joining him later if he was successful.

II

On 18th July, 1793, da Ponte was in Brussels, from where he sent
an urgent request for funds to Count Waldstein, through the intermediary of Casanova. He had some scheme for promoting Italian
opera in Brussels, but it fell through because, according to da Ponte,
Nancy Storace failed him. She had apparently offered to sing for
him in Brussels; but when he arrived there her demands—£400 for
twelve performances and one evening as her Benefit—were so
exorbitant that da Ponte could not agree to them. He tried to find
another *prima donna* to replace Storace, and even made an attempt
to get in touch with his ex-mistress, La Ferrarese, who was then in
Venice, but with no success.

From Brussels da Ponte went to Rotterdam, from whence he sent
another desperate appeal for funds to Casanova. Nancy had by then
rejoined him, for he had written—a little prematurely—to tell her
that the prospects in the Low Countries seemed very favourable and
had suggested she should come at once. From Rotterdam the da
Pontes went to Amsterdam, and thence to The Hague—'a town full
of cheese and savages' Lorenzo called it, for he did not find the
Dutch either attractive or helpful.

Everywhere da Ponte went in Holland it was the same story; he
always *almost* succeeded in organising an Italian opera company,
but at the last moment his plans always fell through for one reason
or another. In Brussels Nancy Storace's 'perfidy' had been responsible for his failure; at The Hague and in Amsterdam everything was
almost settled, and da Ponte was jubilant—then news came that the

French had defeated English and Dutch forces at Hondschoote, the Prince of Orange had been wounded, and the Dutch, as da Ponte said, from then on thought only of closing their theatres and opening their churches instead.

The da Pontes were desperate; they had no money left and were already in debt at the inn where they were staying. Lorenzo cudgelled his brains to find some way out of their predicament. Desperate letters were sent to Casanova, who only replied: 'When Caesar wrote to friends, he never discussed business.' If prose did not move Count Waldstein to pity, da Ponte thought, perhaps verse might; no less than a hundred and twelve lines were despatched to Dux, but with no result. Someone suggested that da Ponte should open a hat-shop—Nancy would make artificial flowers, and they could sell fashion accessories—but how should one set about such an enterprise? Da Ponte was a poet, unpractical in the extreme, and he had absolutely no idea. He would arrange a series of concerts, he would write to La Ferrarese, he would get in touch with Guardassoni, the manager of the Prague theatre, he would write an ode, he did write a cantata, he would do anything. . . . But the results of all this frenzied mental activity were merely that Nancy and her husband were reduced to a diet of dry bread, and had to pass their time playing chess for kisses.

'Why have I so many enemies, even here in Holland?' da Ponte asked Casanova, convinced that everyone was against him, whereas in fact it was really only the circumstances that were unfavourable—with Revolutionary France alarming all Europe with her aggressive intentions it was hardly surprising that no one was very interested in Italian opera at that time. But da Ponte's conscience was troubling him a little: 'I have never done anything of which I could be ashamed,' he wrote. 'If it wasn't for the fact that *my head was tonsured* . . .' It seems that he was now desperately trying, for the first time in his life, to conceal the fact that he was a priest. He sent a letter to Casanova by a young man who, he warned his friend, 'has seen my Nancy, *but knows nothing about the tonsure and cassock* . . .', and he warned Casanova to be careful what he said about him in Vienna. Casanova told him that he would be wise in future to avoid Italy in general and Rome in particular; da Ponte replied that he did not think he had anything to fear—unless, of course, Casanova himself were to reveal 'The Great Secret'. But most of his insistence on secrecy was in vain; Badini had seen to it that the whole of London knew he had been a priest, and no doubt the news had by now reached the Low Countries too.

For economy, the da Pontes moved from the inn where they had been staying, and took a room in the house of a kindly German. Although they had sold most of their possessions, they still could not pay the rent. After a week the landlord, who saw that he would not get any money out of them, was forced to give them notice. What could they do? Where could they go? Nancy, whose child was due to be born very shortly, had eaten nothing all that day as it was. Fortunately, while they were discussing the problem, a friend came to visit them; he was almost as poor as they were, but had brought them a little food, and also the cheering news that he had had a dream that the da Ponte fortunes were about to change for the better. Da Ponte was a great believer in the significance of dreams, but as they sat down to eat what would probably be their last meal for some time, he found it hard to be optimistic. The next day they would be literally in the street.

Da Ponte woke the next morning to the sound of the landlord knocking on his door, and got up gloomily. He took the paper which the landlord handed him, presuming it to be the bill, which he could not pay. It was not the bill, but a letter, for which he was obliged to pay a shilling before it could be handed over to him. He had no money at all, and the only object which he had not yet sold or pawned was his handkerchief; the landlord was kind-hearted enough to buy that for a shilling, so that da Ponte could read his letter.

The letter was from Nancy's sister in London; it ran as follows: 'My Dear da Ponte,

Badini has behaved so badly that the impresario of the opera has been forced to dismiss him from the theatre. As he wants a poet, and has heard of you, he sent for me and asked me to write to offer you the post. Badini has cheated him out of sixty guineas on account of his salary, and he would therefore like to get this sum back by deducting it from the two hundred guineas a year which he is offering to pay you. I am sure you will agree to this proposal, as you should be tempted less by the money than by this excellent opportunity for making yourself known in London. With this in view, I took the liberty of assuring him that you would come. He gave me twenty guineas for your travelling expenses. Make haste and come at once. All your friends, including Ferrari, Rovedino, Kelly and Nancy Storace, are eagerly expecting you; and I am dying to embrace my Nancy again.'

When he had finished reading this letter, da Ponte broke down completely, and burst into tears of joy and relief. 'I knelt down,' he said, 'and repeated with deep religious gratitude four lines from my *Axur*:

> Dio protettor de'miseri,
> tu non defraudi mai
> quelli che in te confidano,
> che speran solo in te.'

He received this letter, and the news of his appointment as Poet to the King's Theatre in the Haymarket, London, at the end of 1793. It was exactly a year since he had arrived in England for the first time, penniless and unknown; it had taken him almost precisely the same time in England to rise from nothing to the highest appointment in his profession as it had taken him to perform the same feat in Austria ten years earlier.

III

'For twenty-five years the wretched London theatre has been in the hands of brigands,' da Ponte wrote to Casanova. 'Absolute idiots are in charge of it, and when they can't pay, they go bankrupt. Unfortunately, if one takes the management away from them, they burn the theatre down.' There was a good deal of truth in the first part of this statement, at any rate, and although the fires were more often due to carelessness than arson, London theatres certainly did burn down remarkably often at that epoch. The King's Theatre in the Haymarket, the home of Italian opera, had been destroyed by fire in 1789, and performances of opera were given instead first at

Covent Garden, then at the Little Theatre in the Haymarket, and finally at the Pantheon in Oxford Street. The King's Theatre was rebuilt in 1790, but could not obtain a licence for the performance of opera until the Pantheon, in its turn, was burnt down in 1792. Covent Garden (burnt down in 1808 and 1856) did not become the Opera House until 1847, and Drury Lane, which had been pulled down in 1791, was re-opened in 1794—one need hardly add that it, too, was burnt down—in 1809. In 1793, therefore, the Italian opera opened in the rebuilt King's Theatre in the Haymarket, under the management of a certain William Taylor; it was Taylor who had engaged da Ponte as poet to the theatre.

On his return to London da Ponte immediately went to see Taylor in order to make his acquaintance and to find out something about his new work. When he entered Taylor's room the manager was sitting at a desk, with his back to the door. 'Here is da Ponte,' said Federici, the conductor of the orchestra, who had come to effect the introduction. Taylor went on writing, and appeared not to have heard this remark. 'Mr Taylor, here is the poet!' Federici repeated, louder this time. The impresario turned round, nodded his head, and then went on writing again. After waiting a few minutes longer, Federici indicated to da Ponte that the interview was at an end. Da Ponte, who had been used to having long intimate chats about his work with the Emperor of Austria, was surprised and insulted. He did not see Taylor again for three months, during which time the manager made no attempt whatever to communicate with his new poet.

Indeed, da Ponte's new employer very little resembled his old one. As da Ponte discovered when he got to know him better, Taylor was a most eccentric character, not unlikeable, but in no way fitted to run a theatre. He had started life as a bank clerk at Messrs. Snow and Company in the City but, according to John Ebers, 'the climate of Snow and Co. was, as he expressed it, too cold for his complexion. He got rid of this complaint admirably well, by becoming proprietor of the King's Theatre, which was hot water for life for him.' Although clever and astute, he was completely devoid of any business sense, and his principal pleasure was playing elaborate practical jokes on people without ever considering the consequences.

After three months' silence Taylor at last sent for da Ponte. A production of Gazzaniga's *Don Giovanni Tenorio* was being prepared, in spite of the fact that da Ponte had apparently brought a copy of Mozart's *Don Giovanni* with him from Vienna, and had suggested it for production at the King's Theatre. Da Ponte revised Bertati's libretto for *Don Giovanni Tenorio* for the London production—the libretto which had, in fact, been the basis for his own libretto for Mozart; he made it into a one-act 'tragi-comic opera', and introduced Leporello's 'catalogue' aria into it; this version was produced at the King's Theatre on 1st March, 1794; Mozart's opera was not publically performed in England for another twenty-three years. At the beginning of the same season Cimarosa's *Il Matrimonio Segreto*, also with a libretto by Bertati, had been performed; on the libretto printed in London there was no mention of Bertati's name, but the words: 'Poete, Mr L. Da Ponte. The translation, By Mr John Mazzinghi' no doubt gave the impression to the uninitiated that da Ponte was the author. In this way he got his own back on Bertati, whom he had always disliked, and who was now occupying his old position in Vienna.

Things were not going too well with the King's Theatre at that time, and Taylor, thinking that some new talent might improve matters, asked da Ponte to write to his old friend, the composer Martin, to invite him to come to London. Kelly had made the same request the year before, and da Ponte had written off to St Petersburg, but with no success. Martin was at that time bound by contract in Russia, and was writing operas in conjunction with a very eminent librettist indeed—no less a person than Catharine the Great herself. He had, however, promised to come to England as soon as he was freed from his obligations in Russia, and when Taylor sent for him in 1794 he was able to accept the invitation.

In acquiring both Martin and da Ponte Taylor no doubt considered that he had brought off a remarkable *coup*. In Vienna their collaboration had been one of the most successful in recent years, and their best-known opera—*Una Cosa Rara*—had already been performed in London before da Ponte's arrival in England, and had been acclaimed by the British public. Da Ponte, too, was delighted to see Martin again; they had always worked well together and had

HX

been close friends. There is no doubt that at this period, when it was only apparent to the most discerning that Mozart was one of the greatest geniuses of all time, da Ponte considered Martin's operas superior to those of Mozart. Who shall blame him? He was not a musician, and was not even particularly interested in music, and he gauged the value of operas by the reception they received from the public. Martin's operas had completely eclipsed those of Mozart in Vienna, and the opinion of the Viennese public was good enough for da Ponte. Later on, in his old age, when Mozart was beginning to be more appreciated and estimated at his true worth, da Ponte made more of his connection with him, but even then he remained convinced that Weigl, Martin and Salieri were in the same category as the composer of *Don Giovanni*.

When Martin arrived in England da Ponte invited him to stay in his house. Martin was as gay and light-hearted as ever; his success in St Petersburg had been remarkable, but he was probably not sorry to see da Ponte again. As a librettist, Catharine the Great had her limitations—she admitted as much herself in a letter to Voltaire— and the strain of collaborating with that remarkable woman must have been considerable. One of Catharine's operas, *Gorye Bogatyr Kosometovich*, for which Martin wrote the music, was supposed to be a satire on Gustavus III of Sweden; but there is reason to believe that Catharine's satire was, in fact, directed against her lover, Potemkin. This opera was performed in the Ermitage in the presence of the Imperial family and specially-invited guests, but Catharine herself wrote on the manuscript: 'Not to be performed in public theatres, on account of Foreign Emissaries.'

Having secured his poet and his musician, Taylor next thought of his singers. Gertrude Mara, who had commissioned da Ponte to write a play for her, was no longer very young; she had virtually retired from the stage, although she still sang in oratorio and at concerts. In any case, at about this period she abandoned her husband, an elderly 'cellist, and eloped to Russia with a young flautist named Florio. Taylor therefore decided to engage two very well-known and accomplished ladies, Brigida Banti for *opera seria*, and Anna Morichelli for *opera buffa*, and no doubt felt that, with such talent in his company, he had every chance of organising a brilliant and profitable season.

Taylor was perfectly right about the success of Banti, at any rate. She was one of the outstanding singers of the day, and her rise to fame had been sensational. She had started life as a street singer, and had attracted attention by her truly remarkable voice; she was eventually given a musical training, and made her operatic début in Paris. She was lazy, and never took the trouble to become an accomplished musician, but nevertheless had that inborn musicality which is so much more important than anything else. Her voice had an unusually wide compass, and she excelled equally in the *bravura* and *cantabile* styles; but it was apparently above all the pathos, feeling and refinement which she put into her singing which were responsible for her popularity and success. Banti's refinement, however, was restricted entirely to her singing; as a woman she was and remained a product of the streets, with all that that implied at that period. She was coarse, licentious, addicted to drink, and very capricious, and her private life completely belied the impression of tragic nobility which she produced on the stage.

Anna Morichelli was a different type of singer, and also a different type of woman. Although her voice was not in the same category as Banti's, she had a far greater knowledge of music; but by the time she came to England she was past her prime, was inclined to sing out of tune, and her taste had been 'spoilt by long residence in Paris'. Morichelli's arrival in England was preceded by a good deal of advance publicity on her behalf, which tried to make out that she was equal, if not superior, to Banti; the British public did not endorse this opinion. As a woman, Morichelli was much more subtle than Banti. Da Ponte, in fact, described her quite simply as an old vixen. She was intelligent, cautious, far-sighted and scheming, and although her morals were little better than those of her rival, she managed to disguise the fact by such a modest and reserved manner that, also according to da Ponte, those who did not know her well might easily have mistaken her for a virgin of fifteen.

It need hardly be said that Banti and Morichelli were deadly enemies and rivals; Taylor should have had the foresight to realise that by engaging them both at the same time he was letting himself in for a good deal of trouble. The ladies arrived by the same boat early in April 1794, and no doubt were at each other's throats before they had even stepped off the gangway at Plymouth. On their arrival in London their first contest was for the possession of Taylor's affections—a contest which was speedily decided in favour of Banti, who was the younger of the two, and whose forceful frontal attack won Taylor more quickly than Morichelli's more subtle diplomacy.

Da Ponte had had a good deal of experience of Italian opera singers by that time, and he viewed the arrival of Banti and Morichelli with misgiving. It was clearly important for him to keep on good terms with both, but it was not going to be an easy business. He soon received a commission to write two operas—an *opera seria* for Banti, and an *opera buffa* for Morichelli—and both ladies made it quite clear to him in their different ways that if one opera was more successful than the other, the poet would be in trouble. Da Ponte himself was inclined to favour Morichelli, probably because he realised that his own talent, like hers, lay in comedy rather than tragedy, and because Martin was to compose the music for the *opera buffa*. The music for the *opera seria* was being written by Francesco Bianchi.

The comic opera was finished first—it was called *La Scola de Maritati*, but was later sometimes performed as *Gli Sposi in Contrasto* or *La Capricciosa Corretta*. This was da Ponte's first completely new work to be written in England, although he had made several translations and adaptations of other libretti, and written one or two short poems. In May, 1794, for example, Martin and da Ponte's *Il Burbero di Buon Core* had been given at the King's Theatre, and da Ponte had written a new duet for the occasion; the music for this duet was probably composed by Haydn, who was in London at the time. Da Ponte had also written, under his old Arcadian name of Lesbonico Pegasio, a *Sonetto* for Banti's benefit, and had tactfully and rapidly followed it with a similar work for Morichelli's benefit a week later. He had written a cantata, *La Vittoria*, which was performed in honour of Lord Howe's victory, 'The Glorious First of June', and which was received with much patriotic acclamation.

La Scola de Maritati was first performed on 27th January, 1795, and as it was da Ponte's first work for the London stage, it aroused a certain amount of curiosity. The first night was not without mishaps:

'The unlucky fall of the toilet might have proved the downfall of a less-deserving burletta,' one critic remarked. 'Morichelli passed over the accident with great good humour—perhaps she had studied the character of Pope's fine lady who

"Keeps her temper e'en tho' the China fall . . ." '

What can have happened? All the other critics ignored the incident. Whatever did occur did not, apparently, detract from the success of the opera. 'More rapturous applause we never heard on any occasion,' another critic wrote, while a third was so overwhelmed that he could only say: 'It is not easy to speak in adequate praise of this composition.' At that time music critics were far more indulgent than they are today. Da Ponte had every reason to be pleased with the reception of his opera, and although it did not hold the stage for very long in England, it had a considerable success on the continent.

Taylor, who was by now so completely enslaved by Banti that he had lost what little business sense he had once possessed, had done his best to make the comic opera for Morichelli a failure, and had even paid Badini to write a satire against it; but the old recipe of Martin's pretty, catching tunes, and da Ponte's elegant witty verses, still held good, and Taylor was not successful in wrecking his own enterprise. The *opera seria* for Banti was not so well received; as da Ponte's new libretto, *Merope*, was not yet ready, it had been decided to put on Bianchi's *Aci e Galatea*, which was advertised as 'an entirely new work'. It had, in fact, been produced in Venice in 1792, as da Ponte quickly pointed out to Taylor. He may even have indulged in some mild blackmail, for he had a copy of the Venetian libretto in his possession, which Taylor finally persuaded him to burn. *Aci e Galatea* was duly produced as a new work 'composed here', but it was not a great success for all that.

Meanwhile, da Ponte was at work on another libretto for Martin, *L'Isola del Piacere*. It was to be the last product of their long and successful partnership, and it was also their least successful work, for it was written in an atmosphere which was, to say the least, cool. What had happened? The two friends who, a year earlier, had been so delighted to see each other again, who had so many successes to their credit, and who had always been such kindred spirits, had suddenly fallen out, quarrelled, and separated.

Probably much of the trouble was caused by da Ponte's marriage. Martin and da Ponte had been bachelor friends, and as such had had a great deal in common. When Martin arrived in London he found his old friend sadly changed; far from being gay and amusing, da Ponte was now dull, bourgeois, and almost respectable, weighed down with financial and domestic cares and ties, and already the father of one—perhaps two—more or less legitimate children. Martin had accepted da Ponte's invitation to stay in his house, but it had been a mistake. It was no longer like the good old days in Vienna, when the authors of *Una Cosa Rara* had been fêted and pampered and invited everywhere; nor was it like St Petersburg, where Martin had been received with all the lavish extravagance of which the Empress of All the Russias was capable. Now da Ponte was ruled, not by an Emperor, but by Nancy, and as Martin was staying in her house she probably ordered him about too. Instead of being surrounded by beautiful women, as he had been in the past, da Ponte was now surrounded by crying babies. Martin was bored by the da Pontes' domestic life, and consoled himself as best he could. He started an affair with Morichelli, who was old enough to be his mother, but this was more of a business connection than anything else, and did not satisfy Martin's ardent temperament. He therefore seduced the da Pontes' servant girl, and when Morichelli discovered his infidelity and made a scene of jealousy, Martin blithely told her that not he, but da Ponte, was the father of the girl's expected child, and that he was merely covering up his friend's indiscretion for him. When da Ponte taxed Martin with this, the Spaniard treated the whole affair as a joke—had they not had hundreds of similar jokes together in Vienna? Martin sent the girl some money, and leaving the da Pontes, with their babies and their newly-acquired respectability, he went to live with Morichelli. It was the end of a very long, sincere, and profitable friendship; Martin soon returned to St Petersburg, where he was decorated for his services by Paul I, and where he died in 1806.

Da Ponte felt the estrangement with Martin very deeply. He finished the libretto for *L'Isola del Piacere*, but with no enthusiasm. 'I felt as if I was writing for Righini', he said regretfully, 'not for Martin, the author of *Una Cosa Rara*. . . .' Morichelli did nothing to improve the play by insisting on having a mad scene in it—she had had great success in a similar scene in Paris, but a mad scene was, as da Ponte remarked, about as suitable in the new opera as Pilate in the Creed. *L'Isola del Piacere* was not a success; the poet and the composer were no longer working together, and the public felt it. The mad scene was not a success either, and at the end of the season Morichelli left London for Venice.

Da Ponte had lost Mozart, and now he had lost Martin, the composer who had brought him most fame and success, and who had been one of his closest friends. It was a great blow, and he poured out his troubles in a long letter to Casanova. Musicians' jealousies, women's intrigues, directors' ignorance and local prejudices had been responsible for the rift, he said, and Martin, his dearest Martin, the composer of *Una Cosa Rara*, had joined the ranks of his enemies, the bastard! Of course, everyone had always known that Martin was false and deceitful, wrote da Ponte who, not so long before, had called him his dearest friend and implored him to join him in London. Martin was perfidious, a cowardly flatterer, an incorrigible miser, incapable of honesty, of gratitude, of friendship, or of any other decent sentiment. . . . What was worse, Martin's gossip had made da Ponte new and influential enemies who supported Badini, and Badini was just waiting for an opportunity to step into da Ponte's shoes. . . . It was all very distressing. Would Casanova put in a good word for him with Count Waldstein, just in case. . .?

So ended the season of 1795. Da Ponte was finding his salary inadequate for his needs, and for those of his growing family. A daughter, Louisa, had been born in 1793, and a second child was born in 1795; before its birth da Ponte had asked Casanova if this child might be called Giacomo after him, but it turned out to be a girl, and was given the name of Frances instead. In order to augment the family finances da Ponte leased the theatre café from Taylor, and Nancy ran it—apparently with some success, for eighteen months later, after the announcement of a Grand Masked Ball, the following notice appeared in the press:

'Madame Daponte, who has the honour to serve the ordinary refreshments at the Masquerades as well as the opera, begs leave most respectfully to acquaint the Nobility, Gentry, and the Public, that in consequence of the very great success with which the Masquerades, upon the plan adopted abroad without suppers, have lately been given at the Opera-House, she will, upon the present occasion, provide and serve in the Great Concert-Room extra refreshments of the first quality for those who may require them; consisting of Sandwiches of all kinds, Fruit, Ice, Lemonade, etc. etc. upon the most reasonable terms; and humbly hopes in her endeavours to please that she shall experience the encouragement and protection of the public.'

During the season of 1796 da Ponte translated or adapted various old operas—notably Gluck's *Ifigenia in Tauride* and Grétry's *Zemira e Azore*—and wrote two new ones—*Antigona*, with music by Bianchi, and *Il Tesoro*, with music by Mazzinghi.

In 1797 da Ponte's old friend Nancy Storace reappeared on the London stage after a long absence; she was at this time living with John Braham, a young man of German-Jewish extraction who had a most remarkable tenor voice. Braham made his début in this season, and it was probably at the end of 1797 that he and Nancy Storace went abroad, first to Paris, where they gave concerts under the patronage of Josephine de Beauharnais, and then to Italy. They returned to England in 1801. Nancy Storace was considerably older than her lover—by whom she had a son who eventually became an Anglican priest—and in 1808 she retired from the stage. The end of Mozart's first Susanna was sad; in 1816 Braham married someone else, and Nancy died shortly afterwards, it is said of a broken heart. 'In later years,' one critic wrote, 'the signora increased in bulk, and her features, always strong, became coarse. She persisted to the last in playing parts for which she was unsuited.'

At about this time da Ponte set up as a publisher; his first publication was a translation from the French which he had made himself— *Evelina*, or *The Triumph of the English over the Romans*. This opera pleased the critics: 'The correct elegance with which it has been brought forward, and the faithfulness of the translation from the French by Mr Du Ponte, the poet of the theatre, are equally praiseworthy . . .' one of them remarked.

Amongst other works by da Ponte which were performed during the season of 1797 the first performance in England of *L'Arbore di Diana*, with music by Martin—the opera da Ponte had originally written for La Ferrarese's début in Vienna—is worthy of note; Nancy Storace and Braham were both in the cast. A cantata with words by da Ponte and music by Bianchi was also performed in honour of the victory of British naval forces at Cape St Vincent; da Ponte had originally written the words for the marriage of the Prince of Wales with Caroline of Brunswick, and had to adapt them hastily and none too successfully to suit a naval victory. In June 1797 a new opera by da Ponte and Bianchi was performed—*Merope*. 'The story is from Voltaire,' one of the critics noted, 'and has been most admirably dramatised.'

Now that Morichelli had left London, Banti was the unchallenged queen of the opera, and of Taylor's heart. Da Ponte had gradually become fond of the wayward impresario, and was by now very friendly with him; he was not, however, so fond of Banti. Taylor was always short of money, and was constantly trying to persuade his friends to raise it for him; most of them knew him too well to have anything to do with his finances, but da Ponte was not as yet disillusioned about his employer, and was still very ignorant about English customs and laws. He did all he could to obtain money for Taylor and, completely forgetting Casanova's warning that he should never sign his name to any document in London, he was unwise enough to back Taylor's bills. Taylor was an indolent individual, and little by little he handed over what he considered to be the boring business of theatrical administration—more especially the detail of paying his staff—to da Ponte, who soon became the theatre's general factotum, Figaro to Taylor's Count Almaviva. This suited Taylor perfectly; some years later, when da Ponte had left London and when Taylor lived more or less permanently within the rules of King's Bench for debt, a friend said to him one day: 'Mr Taylor, how can you conduct the management of the King's Theatre, perpetually in durance as you are?'

'My dear fellow', Taylor replied, 'how could I possibly conduct it if I were at liberty? I should be eaten up, Sir, devoured. Here comes a dancer: "Mr Taylor, I want such-and-such a dress!"

Another: "I want such-and-such ornaments". One singer demands to sing in a part not allotted to him, another to have an addition to his appointments. No—let *me* be shut up,' Taylor continued, 'and they go to Masterson.' (Masterson had, by this time, replaced da Ponte as Taylor's assistant.) 'He, they are aware, cannot go beyond his line, but if they do get at me—pshaw! no man at large can manage that theatre; and in fact,' he added, 'no man that undertakes it ought to go at large!'

Banti was, needless to say, not particularly faithful to Taylor, although she managed to conceal her other love-affairs from him. After having had an affair with Federici, the conductor of the orchestra, she next turned her attentions to da Ponte. It was an awkward situation; whatever he did, da Ponte was bound to offend someone—either his employer Taylor, or Banti herself, the most influential person in the opera, or Nancy. Da Ponte was still very much in love with Nancy, and anyway the prima-donna's rather more mature charms did not appeal to him, so the only question was how to evade Banti's advances as tactfully as possible. His diplomacy was soon put to the test. Taylor had decided to spend some time in the country together with his family and Banti, no doubt in order to get some fishing, a sport of which he was very fond. No sooner had he decided to leave London than Banti sent for da Ponte and 'with glances which were enough to frighten a chaste Joseph' she implored the poet to accompany her to the country too. As she was doing so, Taylor himself came into the room, and he also invited da Ponte to stay with them at Holywell. It was a most embarrassing situation, and da Ponte did not know what to do; if he refused to go with them he might well lose his job, but if he did go. . . . In the end he decided to go, but to take Nancy with him. When the da Pontes arrived at Taylor's country house, Banti gave Lorenzo a look of fury and then, controlling her rage, gave Nancy a charming if insincere welcome. When she remained alone with da Ponte she said: 'So your wife has come too! So much the worse for you!' Da Ponte pretended not to understand what she meant, but he knew that he had made a dangerous enemy. The da Pontes' visit, which cannot have been very agreeable for anyone, only lasted three days.

It would be pointless to mention in detail the various libretti which da Ponte wrote or translated or adapted for the London stage between 1794-1798. Although most of his work was well received in London when it was first produced, none of it has endured, for it was all written for inferior composers. After Martin's departure da Ponte worked principally with Francesco Bianchi. Bianchi, who was born in Cremona in 1752, had joined the Paris Opera in 1775 as deputy to Piccini; in 1790 Joseph II had offered him a post in Vienna, but the Emperor had died before Bianchi reached the Austrian capital. Bianchi remained in London for some years, and finally committed suicide in Hammersmith in 1810. Da Ponte wrote or adapted altogether six libretti for him.

In the autumn of 1798 da Ponte's activities in London were interrupted, for Taylor asked him if he would like to go to Italy in order to engage some new singers for the opera. He had not visited the country of his birth or seen his family for some twenty years; one can imagine with what alacrity and delight he accepted Taylor's proposal.

CHAPTER XI

THE PRODIGAL SON

O N 2nd October, 1798, da Ponte and Nancy left London for the continent. They had bought a small carriage, and also took with them the very considerable sum of a thousand pounds. They reached Hamburg a week later, and from there made a pleasant and uneventful journey across Europe to Italy. On the 2nd November they arrived at Castelfranco: here they parted, for da Ponte had decided to go on to visit his family at Ceneda alone, and it was arranged that Nancy should meet him again at Treviso two days later. On the evening of the same day da Ponte reached Conegliano, which was only a few miles from his home.

It was almost twenty years since he had last visited Ceneda; the sight of his birthplace and the thought of seeing his family again filled him with deep emotion. He had not announced his arrival; for a few minutes he stood outside his father's house listening to the voices within, and then he knocked on the door.

'Who is there?' someone shouted through the window.

'Open the door!' he answered, trying to disguise his voice as much as possible; he was not successful, one of his step-sisters recognised him immediately.

'It is Lorenzo! It is Lorenzo!' she cried, and in a few seconds the door was open, and Lorenzo was surrounded by his step-brothers and sisters, all embracing him and asking questions at the same time. Hearing the commotion, his father came out of his room to see what was happening; when he saw his eldest son he was so amazed that for a few moments he could neither move nor speak. Gaspare da Ponte was in his seventy-seventh year.

It was All Souls' Day. As was the custom, the whole family had assembled in the old man's house, and a few minutes earlier he had asked them to drink a toast: 'To Lorenzo!' he had said, 'and may God grant that I see him again before I die!' Such a rapid and unexpected fulfilment of his wish completely overwhelmed him, and he could only embrace his son in silence.

Ceneda was such a small place that it was not long before the news of Lorenzo's arrival had spread throughout the village. Hearing his name called in the street, he looked out of the window and saw, in the moonlight, the friends of his childhood and youth gathered outside the house and waiting to greet him. He went to welcome them, wine was brought, and they all sat up till the small hours of the morning exchanging news, talking about the past, the present and the future. When the party finally broke up Gaspare da Ponte led his eldest son to his own room, and asked him to sleep there with him. Before he retired for the night the old man knelt down before the crucifix and said his prayers, ending with the *Nunc Dimittis*. When he finally rose from his knees he embraced Lorenzo, saying: 'Now that I have seen you again, my son, I shall die happy.'

When Lorenzo awoke the next morning his father had already dressed and gone to the market to buy the choicest food to celebrate the prodigal's return; but as soon as they heard that Lorenzo was awake, his brothers and sisters and their children all came into his room and sat on his bed while he ate his breakfast. Nothing spoilt the happy reunion except the thought of Girolamo and Luigi, his two brothers who had died long ago in their youth. Da Ponte tried to console his father for their absence by promising him that he would soon introduce him to a charming and beautiful companion whom he had brought with him from England; he had not yet announced his marriage to his family, and wished it to come as a surprise when Nancy arrived in Ceneda. It probably came as a not altogether pleasant surprise to his devout father. Meanwhile, taking advantage of Nancy's absence, Lorenzo went to visit all his old sweethearts in the village.

Da Ponte had so much news to tell his relatives, and they had so much to tell him, that the whole of the day and most of the night was spent in conversation. The recent fighting in Italy had been very near Ceneda, and da Ponte's father had some exciting stories to tell him about the war. French troops had passed through the village, and had been billeted on the local inhabitants. Gaspare da Ponte, having two married and five unmarried daughters, and knowing the

reputation of the French troops, had barred and shuttered his house
on their arrival. He decided to make an appeal to the French
general's better nature and to try to obtain exemption from the
billeting order, so he stationed himself at the window of his house,
which overlooked the main square of Ceneda, in the hope of inter-
cepting the commanding officer. It was not long before he saw a
group of French officers come along the street and sit down at the
café next door to his house. Leaning out of his window, the old man
addressed the French general in respectful but definite terms. If no
French troops were allowed to enter his house, he said, he would
pray God for the success of the general and his armies; if, however,
the general would not grant his request, he was ready to defend his
daughters' chastity and would ignite a barrel of gunpowder which
he had ready should the soldiers attempt to force his door. The
general listened to the old man's impassioned plea and, touched by
his courage and his outspokenness, granted his request. As a result,
the da Pontes' house was the only one in Ceneda which escaped the
attentions of the victorious and licentious French. So far as he could
remember, Gaspare da Ponte continued, the French general's name
was Napoleon Bonaparte.

On 4th November da Ponte left Ceneda for Treviso, where he
had arranged to meet Nancy. He was accompanied by his youngest
sister, Faustina, a beautiful young girl still in her 'teens, and by his
favourite half-brother, Paolo, who had been with him in Trieste.
When they reached Treviso they found that Nancy had not yet
arrived. Da Ponte had been teasing his young sister by telling her
that he had brought a ballet-girl with him from London, but had
not yet told her that she was his wife. Paolo, who had known Nancy
in Trieste before da Ponte had married her, also had no idea of the
identity of his brother's companion. When Nancy did at last arrive,
late in the evening, she stepped out of the carriage with her face
covered by a veil. Paolo, remembering the veil incident at Trieste,
played the same trick that his brother had used at his first meeting
with Nancy, lifted the veil, and was amazed to see a face which he
knew. He was even more amazed to learn than Nancy was now
married to Lorenzo.

In Treviso da Ponte met several old friends—including Giulio

Trento—and heard news of others. His one-time pupils from the seminary greeted him affectionately, and flattered him by addressing him as 'nostro caro Maestro'—they had presumably forgotten the circumstances which had led to their 'caro Maestro's' dismissal from Treviso and his banishment from Venice. Da Ponte found his old patron, Bernardo Memmo, was also now in Treviso, still living with Teresa, and still completely dominated by her. The years had not been kind to the girl who had once flirted with da Ponte behind Memmo's back—she had become old, fat and ugly.

Treviso was only a few miles from Venice, and da Ponte could not resist the temptation to visit the scenes of his youth again. Indeed, there was now nothing to stop him doing so, for the Republic had fallen to Napoleon, and had been ignominiously handed over to the Austrians in 1797; in any case, the term of da Ponte's banishment had ended four years earlier. He decided that it might be prudent to visit Venice without his wife, and so Nancy went back to Ceneda with Paolo and Faustina, and da Ponte continued his journey alone.

On his arrival in Venice the first thing that he went to see was, of course, the Piazza San Marco; he approached it from behind the clock-tower, knowing that if he did so he would be able to take in one of the most beautiful man-made views in Europe—the Piazza San Marco and the Piazzetta—in one glance. Full of emotion, he hurried through the dark, narrow streets, and finally stepped out into the brilliant sunlight of the square. An extraordinary sight met his eyes—the vast space, which formerly had been so crowded with people that it had resembled some enormous and brilliant *salon*—was empty; the cafés were empty; there was scarcely a soul to be seen in the whole Piazza, which had always been the social centre of the city. For the first time in her long and glorious history Venice was tasting the bitterness of occupation, and her citizens hardly dared show their faces in public.

Everywhere that da Ponte went he heard the same story—a story which has become familiar in almost every country in Europe in recent years: food was scarce, prices were rising, the aristocracy had lost all its power and wealth, and its members, who had never before been faced with the problem of earning—literally—their daily bread and who usually had no training to enable them to do so, were reduced to performing the most menial tasks or to selling their property to the occupying forces in order to keep their families alive. Austrian soldiers were everywhere, treating the proud Venetians as an inferior race; spies and fifth-columnists were in every café, ready to denounce anyone who said a word that could be construed as criticism; old men were dying of hunger and cold, and young men were conscripted by the Austrians and sent far away from their country. As usual, the latest conqueror was the worst, and the Venetians thought with nostalgia of the relatively happy times they had spent under the French occupation; after all, they said, one could feel some sort of kinship with the French; they were at least a Latin race, and one could almost understand what they said, whereas the Austrians . . . Da Ponte found the plight of his country-men heartbreaking; what had once been the gayest city in Europe had now become one of the saddest.

The first familiar object which da Ponte saw in the Piazza San Marco was a nose of quite extraordinary proportions; it belonged to Gabriele Doria, who was married to the sister-in-law of that Angioletta Bellaudi on whose account da Ponte had been banished from Venice. Da Ponte can hardly have been pleased to see Doria, whom he had always suspected of having denounced him to the Inquisitors of State, but his chance meeting at least enabled him to find out what had happened to Angioletta. Doria informed him that she had become reconciled with her husband, and he gave him her address. Da Ponte went to visit her and was received, so he said, with joy such as that with which 'a loving sister would receive her brother'.

What can da Ponte's emotions have been when, after almost twenty years, he saw his old mistress again, the companion of his most turbulent, his most disgraceful youth, and the mother of at least two, and probably three, of his children? What can Angioletta have felt when, after years of humdrum marriage with her insignifi-cant and ill-educated husband, she went to answer a knock on her door to find, standing outside, unannounced and unexpected, the lover with whom she had earned the nickname of 'the priest's tart', the man who had been banished from his country because he had seduced her? She had certainly heard rumours of his fame, of his glorious career in Vienna, and may have seen some of his operas in Venice, but she can scarcely have dreamed that she would ever see da Ponte again. What passed between them when they did meet, she a fairly respectable middle-aged woman, perhaps even a grand-mother, and he newly-married and desperately trying to be respect-able? Although it was so many years since they had seen each other, although so much had happened to them in the interval, although, as the saying goes, *la soupe rechauffée n'est jamais bonne*, it seems that something of their old passion remained, and that Angioletta wel-comed Lorenzo in a less sisterly fashion than he tried to make out.

He had done well not to bring Nancy with him to Venice, for Angioletta was not the only old love whom he sought out in that city. He made enquiries about the other Angiola, Angiola Tiepolo, who had been his mistress when he came to Venice for the first time as a very young man, and who had stripped him of his illusions about women. He was told that she had died, but he met her brother by chance in the fish-market, where the once-proud and haughty young patrician who had gambled with da Ponte at the Ridotto was now living like a pauper and selling fish. Da Ponte did what he could to help Tiepolo, whose character had been changed very much for the better by adversity, and then made enquiries about La Ferrarese, who was also said to be in Venice at that time.

The singer who had dropped him so quickly when he had fallen from favour in Vienna was now delighted to see him again; she had already heard that he had been sent to Italy to engage singers for the London opera. She gave da Ponte a great welcome, informed him that she had no *cavaliere servente* at the moment, and suggested that he should take her to the theatre that evening. Da Ponte had nothing better to do, and willingly agreed. They were a little early for the performance, and so da Ponte asked their gondolier to stop at a café and to bring them ices.

La Ferrarese set herself out to re-ensnare her old lover, in the hope of procuring an appointment at the London theatre. 'You know, da Ponte,' she said dramatically as she took his hand, 'you are hand-somer than ever!' But da Ponte was not to be taken in by her flattery, and was still smarting from the way she had treated him

when he had fallen on evil days. 'I wish I could say the same of you!'
he replied tartly, and then immediately regretted his unkindness.
To make up for it he told her about his marriage, and explained that
as a result of it he did not feel that he had the right to talk about love,
particularly to her. The word 'particularly' in this connection seemed
to please La Ferrarese. She laughed, and they finished their ices
amicably and set out for the opera.

It so happened that *Il Re Teodoro* was being given that evening;
what memories Casti's libretto and Paisiello's music must have
evoked for da Ponte, as he watched it in Venice, La Ferrarese at his
side! So much water had flowed under the bridges since the first
performance. Casti had been made Caesarean Poet after all, but he
had already lost his title, and was now in Paris. Paisiello, whose
political opinions had always been extremely flexible, to say the
least, was about to land very much on the right side of the fence; he
became a great favourite of Napoleon, who ultimately invited him
to Paris and showered every imaginable favour on him. Count
Rosenberg, who had done so much to encourage Casti and Paisiello
and to discourage da Ponte, had died in 1796. After the opera da
Ponte and La Ferrarese dined with some of the singers; he then
conducted her home, and returned alone to his inn, his head awhirl
with confused impressions and memories.

The next day he received a visit from Angioletta and her husband,
Carlo Bellaudi. He invited them to stay to dinner with him; they
accepted, and during the course of conversation da Ponte learned
that Doria, the owner of the enormous nose and Angioletta's
brother-in-law, had become her *cavaliere servente*, that he tyrannised
her, her husband, and the whole family, and that he was now furious
at da Ponte's presence in the city, jealous of him, and quite capable
of taking some kind of action against him. Da Ponte thanked
Angioletta for her warning, and made up his mind to leave Venice
again as soon as possible—after all, Nancy was waiting for him at
Ceneda.

In the evening he again went to the opera, where he met another
old friend whom he invited back to his inn for supper. When they
arrived at the inn two figures were waiting for them in the dusk;
as they approached one of the men moved off down the street, but

as he did so da Ponte thought he caught sight of an enormous nose.... The other man approached da Ponte, and told him that he was a messenger from the Chief of the Austrian Police; he came to inform him that, on Imperial orders, he was to leave Venice within twenty-four hours.

Had Doria really denounced da Ponte? If so, had he done so from jealousy, as da Ponte insisted, or from some other motive? Or had the authorities heard of the poet's presence in the city, looked up his police-record, and simply come to the conclusion that he was a trouble-maker and a very undesirable character, and expelled him as a result? Or had the Austrian police such a long memory that da Ponte's Viennese misdemeanours still told against him? It is difficult to say; but it seems more likely that it was da Ponte's past history that worried the authorities rather than his present activities, for he had scarcely spent long enough in Venice this time to get involved in any very complicated intrigues—he had only been in the city for a few days.

Da Ponte had nothing but memories to keep him in Venice and had no desire to get into trouble with the police. Very early the next morning he took a gondola to Fusina, and from there he went to Padua. He decided not to return to Ceneda to fetch Nancy, partly because a battle between French and Austrian troops massed near Verona seemed imminent, and also probably because he had been ordered to leave not only Venice, but all Venetian territory, within twenty-four hours. When Nancy arrived in Padua they set out together for Bologna. Now that he could no longer remain in Venice and spend his time picking up the threads of his old romances, da Ponte had suddenly remembered that his journey to Italy had not originally been conceived purely as a pleasure trip; Taylor, who had helped to finance his journey had, after all, asked him to engage singers for the London theatre, although so far, apart from going to the opera with La Ferrarese, da Ponte had done nothing whatsoever about it. Bologna was one of the most musical cities in Italy, and he decided to go there in the hope of being able to find singers there for Taylor.

The journey from Padua to Bologna was not without incident. Before they had even left Padua the da Pontes were stopped by

Austrian passport officials, who suspected Nancy of being a spy; she spoke too many languages too well, they considered, to be a harmless traveller during wartime. Fortunately, while she was being questioned, a general who had known da Ponte and his operas well in Vienna came into the room, and gave orders that the travellers should be allowed to continue their journey.

Their first stop was at Ferrara, where they spent a few days in the company of Giorgio Pisani, da Ponte's old friend and employer. Since they had last met twenty years ago in Venice, when da Ponte had been tutor to Pisani's sons and had defended his employer's political views in indiscreet verse, Pisani's fortunes had fluctuated considerably. He had spent a good many years in prison for his revolutionary sympathies, and although he had now regained his freedom and was well treated by the French, da Ponte found him very much changed for the worse. In his middle age da Ponte, who had once been considered a dangerous advanced thinker himself, had become a staunch conservative, and he now strongly disapproved of Pisani's revolutionary activities which he had once shared with such enthusiasm.

At Bologna da Ponte met Ugo Foscolo for the first time, and conceived a great admiration both for the man and for his work. Foscolo praised da Ponte's poems, and da Ponte gave Foscolo some fine cambric shirts which had taken his fancy. Life in Bologna was very agreeable, the society there was pleasant and cultivated, and da Ponte considered it a delightful place.

His pleasant stay was, however, suddenly and unpleasantly interrupted by a letter from Taylor. Da Ponte had once more quite forgotten the object of his journey, and instead of looking for opera singers had spent his time in pleasant company discussing literature, or showing Nancy the sights of the town. But from Taylor's letter it was clear that unless he took steps to engage some singers very quickly, he would not receive a warm welcome on his return to London, and might even lose his job. As he could find no suitable singers in Bologna, he resolved to go on to Florence. He had never been in Tuscany, and his decision to go there was probably influenced more by his desire to see a new place than by business considerations. As it was intensely cold at the time, and also perhaps because, as in Venice, he longed for a few days' freedom, it was decided that Nancy should remain in Bologna.

When he went to the post to enquire if there was any possibility of reaching Florence, da Ponte was told that he could leave at once, if he did not mind travelling with a lady; the postmaster pointed out to him a young and attractive woman who was about to leave for Florence, alone. Da Ponte replied that he had no objection at all to travelling with her, and at four o'clock in the afternoon they set off. For about two hours they travelled in silence; then da Ponte's companion said tentatively:

'I feel very sleepy!'

'Indeed, so do I!' da Ponte replied. There was another long silence.

Some time later the lady said: 'I can't sleep!'

'Neither can I!' da Ponte replied politely.

'Then do you mind if we talk a little?' she asked.

'With great pleasure, Madam,' said da Ponte, and the following conversation ensued.

'Where do you come from, sir?'

'I'm a Venetian, at your service.'

'And I am a Florentine.'

'Two beautiful places.'

'The most beautiful in all Italy. I have been in Venice many times. It is beautiful. But Florence! Florence takes some beating! Do you know Florence?'

'No, Madam, I've never been there.'

'Ah, you'll see, you'll see, it's divine! And the women! . . . They are absolute angels. Do you like beautiful women?'

'As much as is permissible for a married man of my age,' replied da Ponte cautiously.

'You have a wife?'

'Yes, I have a wife; it was she whom you saw at the door of my inn when we got into the coach.'

'What! That young girl? That was your wife?'

'Yes, that was my wife.'

'Forgive me, but I thought that was your daughter. Congratulations, you have excellent taste! But is she really your wife?'

'What! Are there some who are wives really, and others who are not really?'

'Oh! She might have been your lady-friend, and you her *cavaliere servente*.'

'I beg your pardon, Madam. My wife is not Italian, she was born in England.'

'Don't English women have *cavalieri serventi*?'

'No.'

'Then how much I pity them!'

'For what reason?'

'Because a *cavaliere servente* is the most amiable creature in the world.'

'I think a husband who puts up with one is even more amiable. Are you married, Madam?'

'I was, but thank heaven! I am not any longer. Death set me free after six months.'

'A lady like you will soon find another husband.'

'I, find another husband? Sir, a woman with a grain of sense can swallow a pill like that once, but certainly not twice.'

'So you'll have *cavalieri serventi*?'

'I have had them, and I hope to have them again; but at the moment, to tell the truth, I'm without one. Will you be my *servente* until we reach Florence?'

Da Ponte pretended to be non-plussed. 'Madame, I wouldn't be up to it . . .' he stuttered.

'Don't worry, I'll teach you,' she replied confidently. 'And I assure you that once you start you'll find it very agreeable.'

'Madam, I have no desire to become that "amiable creature" . . . that pleases you so much . . .'

How the situation might have developed we shall never know, for at that moment two young men stopped the coach and asked for a lift to Pietramala. The gay young widow turned her attentions to the newcomers, who were not only nearer to her own age, but also more forthcoming than da Ponte. That evening, when they reached Pietramala, they all dined together; but next day da Ponte continued his journey to Florence alone. The young widow had remained behind with her new friends.

Da Ponte found Florence came up to all his expectations. He was charmed by the beauty of the city, and found the Florentines pleasant, hospitable, and cultured. He was asked to read some of his verses aloud at a literary *salon* which he attended, and he would very much have liked to prolong his stay in the city, had it not been for the thought of an irate Taylor awaiting him on his eventual return to England. He could find no suitable singers in Florence, and so was reluctantly forced to go back to Bologna.

It was not a pleasant journey. The road was covered with deep snow, and rumours about troop movements and impending battles made speed essential. On the way to Pietramala da Ponte fell asleep; some time later he was rudely awoken, and found that he was lying in the snow, with the overturned carriage on top of him. He was not badly injured, but it took some time to free him from under the carriage, and he was more dead than alive from cold as a result. The carriage was useless, but the next morning after a rest at an inn and some glasses of Chianti, he was able to set out on horseback with a guide, and he arrived safely in Bologna that evening.

Da Ponte decided that the time had come to go back to England. The tension between Austria and France was growing daily, and he had no desire to be caught by the war on the Continent and prevented from returning to London. He went to a theatrical agent in Bologna and casually engaged two singers for the London theatre— the only two singers in Italy, he alleged, who were free at that time. They were Maddalena Allegranti and Natale Damiani. Although da Ponte maintained that they were 'first-class 'singers, Allegranti had a sweet but rather weak voice and was now well past her prime, and Damiani had never sung in anything except secondary parts.

Da Ponte may have had personal reasons for engaging Allegranti; they had a mutual friend—Casanova—who had apparently tried, unsuccessfully, to put da Ponte in touch with the *prima donna* when he had passed through Dresden on his journey to England. When Casanova had visited Florence in 1771 he had stayed in the house of Allegranti's uncle; he had been very comfortable there, but had nevertheless decided to change his lodging. Maddalena, who was then little more than a child, caused him 'des distractions incessantes'; she was beautiful and full of innocent charm, and would often come into Casanova's room to wish him good-morning, ask him if he had slept well and if there was anything he needed. . . . Casanova felt that he would not be able to resist her charms for long, and that it was better to leave her uncle's house before it was too late. In after-years he corresponded with Maddalena, and it is not impossible that he asked da Ponte if he could do anything to help her. When da Ponte met her in Bologna she was married to a Mr Harrison, and had one child.

Towards the end of December da Ponte left Bologna, accompanied by his wife; Allegranti, her husband and child; Damiani; and Banti's son, a little boy of eleven, whom he was escorting back to England. They travelled through Augsburg, where Banti's son, who was as high-spirited as his mother, ran away from them and hid in a peasant's house, but was eventually safely recovered by a military search-party. Their journey from Augsburg to Hamburg was not a comfortable one; inn-keepers were inhospitable, and it was intensely cold. In fact, it was so cold that they travelled from Arburg to Hamburg on the frozen Elbe, and their spirits were not improved when, soon after they set out, they passed the wreckage of a coach-and-six sticking out of the ice. However, they reached Hamburg safely, and although Harrison, who was Irish and excitable, challenged da Ponte to a duel because he had taken the best room in the inn, nothing came of it. Harrison said that he refused to fight with a man who was not of noble blood, and da Ponte did the only thing possible under the circumstances, and laughed heartily. Within a day or two he and Harrison were good friends again.

It was just as well, for Hamburg was ice-bound, and so da Ponte and his party were forced to stay there for over a month. This unexpected and prolonged stay cost da Ponte a great deal of money, and when he finally arrived in England, on 1st March, 1799, he only had fifty guineas left out of the thousand he had taken with him from London. However, he had no regrets; his journey to Italy had given him so much pleasure and enjoyment that it had been worth every penny he had spent—it was even worth facing Taylor's displeasure on his return.

Da Ponte was never to see Italy or, indeed, the Continent, again; he left his heart behind in Venice, but he brought away with him that deep love for Italy and for everything Italian which he had always had, and which he was soon to carry half across the world.

Proposals for establishing a College of young Gentlemen in the Town of Sunbury under the immediate direction of Lorenzo da Ponte

There are to be three different departments, each having its respective Teacher, the first consisting of the English language, arithmetic, Algebra, book keeping, the study of the Globes and Geography.

The Sec. of the Greek, and French languages, logic, metaphysic, Natural philosophy, Mathematics, Astronomy, and chemistry.

And the third to consist of Latin and Italian, History, Mythology, belles lettres and Ethic.

Conditions

1. 200 Doll' per annum to be paid quarterly in advance for boarding, lodging and education. (Bed, bedding, and washing to be provided by the parents.)

2. None to be admitted under the age of 11 years, or above that of 18.

3. After the first year the parents of the Students to form an agreement for 3 others, or to withdraw their children.

4. The Students shall not absent themselves from the college except in vacation time, which will be from the first of July to the first of Sep', but with a note from the parents and a permission of the Director.

5. Day Scholars will be admitted at proportionate pay.

6. Young Ladies may receive instruction half the day in a private room —

7. Besides the said Director there will be two Trustees to inspect the capacity and conduct of the Professors, and to overlook the progress of the Scholars.

8. A public examination shall be held twice a year and a premium distributed to the most diligent Students. No other study permitted but music.

Method of the College.

First year. The English teacher will teach also writing, arithmetic, and Geography
The French — — — — — logic, and metaphysic
The Latin — — — — — History, and mythology
Sec. year d° d°		algebra, and Geography
d° d° d°		Mathematic and Astronomy
d° d° d°		History and belles lettres
3. year the English d°		Algebra and the globes
Greek and french d°		Mathematic and natural
Latin and Italian		Belles lettres & Poetry
The English d°		Arith. and Algebra and
the Greek and Fr.		Chemistry and nat.
Latin & Italian —		Belles lettres and Ethic

Proposals for establishing a College of Young Gentlemen:
facsimile in da Ponte's handwriting

Lorenzo da Ponte
in old age

CHAPTER XII

THE PUBLISHER

ON his return from his travels da Ponte received a very cool welcome from Taylor, and the singers he had engaged in Italy received an even cooler welcome from the British public. Damiani, in point of fact, never appeared at all; without asking Taylor's permission, da Ponte had inserted a clause in his contract allowing him to choose the opera in which he was to make his début—a heated dispute with Taylor ensued, and Damiani left London shortly afterwards. Allegranti appeared in Cimarosa's *Il Matrimonio Segreto* in April 1799, but, as an eye-witness who had formerly very much admired her said: 'Never was there a more pitiable attempt: she had scarcely a thread of voice remaining, nor the power to sing a note in tune: her figure and acting were equally altered for the worse, and after a few nights she was obliged to retire, and quit the stage altogether. Of course again our climate, not her age, was blamed for the total loss of her voice; but she was at least remembered to have had one, and was looked upon only with compassion.'

Qui va à la chasse perde sa place—during da Ponte's absence several Italian poets had been scheming to get his job, and the lamentable way in which he had carried out Taylor's commission to find new singers had done nothing to improve his reputation or his popularity. Sometime after his return from Italy, probably in the autumn of 1799, he was dismissed, and Serafino Buonaiuti—whose verses, da Ponte said, were 'even rougher and harder than his head, with which he could very well have butted a goat'—was appointed in his place. Da Ponte did not entirely sever his connections with Taylor, for whom he continued to raise large sums of money by very dubious means. Taylor was extravagant and improvident by nature, and he found that Banti was a most expensive luxury; she was a luxury which in the end proved to be both his—and da Ponte's—undoing.

Early on 10th March, 1800, da Ponte was peacefully lying in bed receiving Nancy's congratulations on the occasion of his fifty-first birthday. Suddenly, without a word of warning, a total stranger burst in upon this happy domestic scnee, and announced that he had a warrant for da Ponte's arrest for debt. Da Ponte was taken away, cursing Taylor and his own stupidity at forgetting Casanova's advice that he should never back a bill. The next day he found someone to go bail for him, and he was released—only to be arrested twice more within twenty-four hours for Taylor's debts. Taylor himself had been elected Member of Parliament for Leominster in 1797, and as a result enjoyed immunity from arrest for debt.

From then on Da Ponte's life became a nightmare; he was hunted by money-lenders and lawyers, badgered by Taylor and Banti, and no doubt reproached for his lack of foresight by his wife. He was, so he says, arrested for debt no less than thirty times in three months. His furniture was sold, his printing press was mortgaged by Taylor, and his salary ceased. How far all these misfortunes were due to his own fecklessness and stupidity, and how much they were due, as da Ponte himself believed, to the jealousy and intrigues of his enemies, it is not possible to say—in any case, the results were the same: he had heavy debts, no source of income, and a young family to support. It was by no means the first time that he found himself in such a position and, also not for the first time, his own energy, intelligence and imagination saved the situation.

One day, when his fortunes were at their lowest ebb, da Ponte happened to be walking along the Strand when an escaped bull came charging along the street towards him; in order to avoid the animal he hurriedly entered a near-by shop. It turned out to be a bookseller's; da Ponte enquired of the owner if he had any Italian books, and was told that he had—only too many, in fact, and the bookseller would be very pleased to get rid of them at a purely nominal price. This gave da Ponte an idea; he decided to set up an Italian bookshop in London. Somehow he managed to scrape together a little money, he returned to the bookseller, and bought up his entire stock of Italian books—five or six hundred volumes—for thirty guineas; some of the books he thus acquired were very fine and rare editions, and he later sold them at a great profit. He acquired other books at auctions and so on, and ordered new books from Italy and France. His bookshop, No 5 Pall Mall, at that time had no competitors, and was extremely successful; at the end of a year it contained over eight thousand choice volumes, and da Ponte did a brisk and profitable trade.

Now that his finances were on a firmer footing once more he was able to pay off the mortgage on his printing press, and when he had done so the first thing he published was a small volume of his own works. He modestly gave it out that he only decided to do so in order to test the abilities of two young printers he had engaged; if this was so they must have lamentably failed the test, for the *Saggi Poetici*, printed and published in 1801, are riddled with printers' errors. Although this volume probably brought its author very little financial gain, it made him a new and influential friend.

One day a distinguished-looking gentleman came into da Ponte's shop and, seeing a volume of poems on the counter, he began to read it. He liked the poems, and enquired who was the author. Da Ponte modestly admitted that the poems were his, and as a result was invited to visit the gentleman's house. His host was Thomas Mathias, a man of letters and a fine Italian scholar, who later held the post of Librarian at Buckingham Palace. He had at least two things in common with da Ponte: a deep love for, and understanding of, Italian literature, and a taste for writing satires against other literary men and politicians—satires which, according to de Quincey, were marred by 'much licence of tongue, much mean and impotent spite, and by a systemmatic pedantry without parallel in literature'. Naturally da Ponte and Mathias got on splendidly together; they discussed the beauties of Petrarch and Tasso, and chortled over each other's obscenities in the satires which they were both so fond of publishing against their enemies. Mathias had written a particularly coarse attack on Sheridan in 1795, and da Ponte, of course, had a host of such works to his credit. But it was a profitable friendship too; in spite of his literary lapses, Mathias was a fine scholar, and his knowledge of Italian literature was profound; he did much to encourage a taste for Italian letters in the England of his day, and as a result he indirectly helped da Ponte's bookselling business; he also published a number of fine editions of the Italian classics, with his own commentaries, amongst them an edition of da Ponte's *Ode on the Death of Joseph II*. Mathias' later ventures into publishing were disastrous; he was a great admirer of the poet Gray, and in 1814 published a magnificent edition of his works which was offered to the public at the fantastic price—for those days—of seven guineas; hardly any copies of the book were sold, and Mathias lost enormous sums of money as a result, He eventually went to live in Italy, from whence he corresponded with da Ponte, and died there in 1835.

At the end of 1801 da Ponte was officially reinstated as poet to the Italian Opera. He had never quite lost touch with the theatre, for many of his operas had been revived while he was in the wilderness —one in 1800, and eight of his libretti or adaptations of libretti in 1801. The 1802 season opened with *Angelina*, with music by Salieri; da Ponte adapted the libretto for the London stage and also published it.

As a publisher da Ponte had a rival in Michael Kelly, who at that time also set up as a publisher, of his own music chiefly—Sheridan unkindly dubbed him 'Composer of wines and importer of music'. Kelly was not so successful as a bookseller as da Ponte, although he had an excellent pitch in Pall Mall and, at Taylor's suggestion, had constructed a private passage which connected his shop with the King's Theatre. For the sum of two guineas a year ladies and gentlemen who visited the opera and who wished to have speedy and easy access to their carriages and sedan-chairs in Pall Mall were entitled to use Kelly's passage. Kelly bemoaned that 'most of them immediately put down their *names*, but very few of them ever put down their *money*', and the venture was not a financial success. Unlike da Ponte, Kelly was not a well-educated man; da Ponte's Italian bookshop succeeded because it supplied a real need, and because da Ponte himself knew the value of his wares and appreciated the literary merits of the books he sold.

Kelly was really far too busy to attend to his shop. Apart from being stage manager of the Italian opera, he also appeared in English opera at Drury Lane, made constant tours all over England and Ireland, still very occasionally appeared in Italian opera if no other tenor could be found, composed a good deal of mediocre music, and spent much time drinking wine with his friends—a habit which caused him great pain in later years, for he suffered very badly from gout. He was amusing, quick-witted, and very Irish, and had a good many rich and aristocratic patrons who enjoyed his company and stood by him in his old age which, in spite of his long and successful career and his popularity as a man, was clouded by deep personal sorrow. For years Kelly had been living *maritalement* with Mrs Crouch, the English singer with whom he almost always appeared on the stage; in 1805 she died, at the age of forty-two, and Kelly was broken-hearted. He lived on for another twenty-one years, retired from the stage in 1808, and published his very amusing *Reminiscences* in 1826, but he never really recovered from the loss of his beloved Anna Maria, who was, he said 'beautiful almost beyond parallel in her person, and equally distinguished by the Powers of her Mind'. Her portrait, by Romney, now hangs in Kenwood House in Hampstead.

Kelly also lost his two friends, the Storaces, while they were both still young. Nancy died in 1816, and Stephen, who was perhaps Kelly's closest friend, had died in 1796 at the age of thirty-two. Storace had been engaged in composing a song for Kelly when he fell ill; he sent for his friend just before his death and said: 'My dear Mic, I have tried to finish your song, but find myself unable to accomplish it; I must be ill indeed when I can't write for you, who have given so much energy to my compositions. I leave you the subject of your song, and beg you will finish it yourself; no one can do it better, and my last request is that you will let no one else meddle with it.' So ended the friendship which had begun, so many years ago, on the quay at Leghorn.

On June 1st, 1802, a new opera, *Armida*, was produced at the King's Theatre; the music was by Bianchi, and the libretto by da Ponte—the first original work he had written for some time. This was the last of Bianchi's many operas, and it was also the last opera in which Banti appeared in London. Taylor had probably already fled to France before this production, for in June of that year Parliament was dissolved, and when he ceased to be an M.P. he lost his immunity from imprisonment for debt. Although da Ponte was not at all sorry to see the last of Banti—she had never forgiven him for rejecting her advances—he was really sorry to say good-bye to

Taylor, in spite of the fact that the impresario's finances had caused
him so much trouble. Taylor, but not Banti, returned to London
later on.

In place of Banti two first-class singers were engaged—Mrs
Billington, then at the height of her powers as a singer, although her
personal charms had been impaired, so one critic said, by 'a degree of
embonpoint which deprived her action of the elegance and grace
which ·had formerly distinguished them'. She had a fine voice,
sound musical knowledge and judgment, a handsome, good-
humoured, though rather expressionless face, and she was no actress.
On the other hand, Grassini, who was engaged a year later, was an
excellent actress, and her gifts were admired by no less a critic than
Mrs Siddons; she was a beautiful woman, full of grace and charm,
and with a fine contralto voice. A new composer was also imported
from abroad—this was Peter von Winter, who was born in Mann-
heim in 1755 and at a very early age became Kapellmeister to the
Elector of Bavaria. It was for Winter that da Ponte wrote his last
three works for the stage.

If da Ponte had been able to stick to writing libretti and avoid
business, all would have been well. His first work for Winter, *La
Grotta di Calipso*, was received on 31st May, 1803, with great enthusiasm, and it seemed that a new and highly successful collaboration
had been inaugurated. Their second work, *Il Trionfo dell' Amor
Fraterno*, was produced on 22nd March, 1804, and did nothing to
dispel this impression; Mrs Billington took the leading part, and
was supported by Viganoni and Braham. The third opera by da
Ponte and Winter, *Il Ratto di Proserpina*, followed two months later,
on 31st May, 1804, for Grassini's benefit—she sang the part of
Proserpina, and Mrs Billington appeared as Ceres. This was one of
those great operatic occasions which leave an indelible impression
on the audience, and which become legendary. Grassini, who had
not been very favourably received as a singer when she first
appeared in England, was made by her performance in this opera—
the only one in which she and Mrs Billington ever appeared together
—and became the favourite of the English public as a result of it.
Il Ratto di Proserpina was the last libretto which da Ponte ever wrote
—although it was by no means his last connection with the opera—

and the fact that its *première* was such a memorable occasion must, in after years, have been a source of great satisfaction to him.

Away from the theatre, however, his life was less satisfactory. Although he possessed all the qualities which should go to make a good business-man—vision, unbounded energy, intelligence, charm, a good appearance, the capacity for making friends—da Ponte lacked something; perhaps it was that he had no luck. In any case, although many of his business enterprises, such as his bookshop, started well, they always ended in disaster. His first big mistake was when he entered into an association with Corri and Dussek, music publishers. The only thing he acquired from this partnership was a substantial debt; Dussek went abroad, Corri went to Newgate, and da Ponte was left to account for their affairs.

His next business venture, with Dulau and Nardini, printers and publishers, went quite well at first. It was in association with this firm that he published, in 1803, an edition of Casti's *Gli Animali Parlanti*—a publication which led to an exchange of correspondence between the two poets, who had not seen each other for ten years. Da Ponte considered that some of Casti's lines would be strong meat for the English public, and that it might be more prudent to publish *Gli Animali Parlanti* in an expurgated edition—he had recently dealt with *Orlando Furioso* in the same way, with great success. Casti, then living in Paris, got wind of his intentions, and wrote him a long letter of protest. How could such an honest, upright and talented man as his dear friend da Ponte contemplate such barbarous treatment of his poems? he asked. Besides, an expurgated edition of the poems was quite unnecessary. Casti enumerated a number of obscene words used by Arisoto and Dante, some of which, he protested, he would never have dreamed of using himself, and in any case, if he did use them he did so in a much less indecent way than Dante, for example. Dante and Ariosto were sold in England unexpurgated—how could da Ponte even think of toning down his—Casti's—lines? As to the suggestion that his satire was often aimed at specific personages, who were easily recognisable in the poems, that was a fantastic idea! As if he would ever stoop so low as to write malign and libellous satires! Surely da Ponte knew him better than that!

Da Ponte knew Casti only too well. He wrote him a long and

respectful letter, assured him in the most fulsome terms of his admiration and affection, and maintained that the alterations which he had made in the poems were very unimportant, and that in any case he would have dealt with Tasso and Dante in precisely the same way if he had undertaken to publish *them* in England. By telling Casti that he had quite forgotten the bitter war which he and Rosenberg had waged against him in Vienna and now only remembered his kind acts, da Ponte made it perfectly clear that he had neither forgotten, nor forgiven. As to Casti's suggestion that he might publish some of his *Novelle*—he thanked him for the kind thought, but was afraid that a publication of that kind would not be good for his reputation. He did not want to become known as a publisher of obscene literature.

Casti never replied to this letter, and died shortly after he received it. In spite of their long-standing feud, da Ponte mourned him sincerely, and in his *Memoirs* wrote a handsome tribute to his powers as a poet. Da Ponte had sometimes hated Casti and often feared him, but at the same time he had always admired him. He felt, in his heart of hearts, that Casti had a stronger personality than he had, and more power and originality as a poet. Perhaps he was right, for Casti's poetical works are still to be found in libraries—often, it is true, amongst the 'special' books—whereas da Ponte's poems, as opposed to his libretti, are unobtainable. It can, of course, be argued that smut never dates.

In 1803 Taylor had sold a third of his share in the theatre to Francis Gould, and during his absence in France Gould managed the opera. Taylor was eventually obliged to sell out altogether, and Gould became sole manager. He was an Irishman, with a private income and with good social connections; when he took over the opera it was in a lamentable state owing to Taylor's extravagance and incompetence, but by engaging some first-class artists Gould managed to organise the opera on a sounder and more business-like footing.

After some months in France Taylor was unwise enough to decide to return to England; he did so secretly, as he feared arrest, and indeed no sooner had he arrived in England than he was promptly put in prison for debt. When da Ponte heard of his arrival

from abroad and his arrest, he immediately exerted himself to get
Taylor released, and his efforts were successful—temporarily, at any
rate. But Taylor was incorrigible; his debts had reached quite overwhelming proportions, and he was soon back in prison again. He
spent most of the rest of his life within King's Bench rules—which
meant that, having paid a certain sum of money, he was not actually
sent to a debtor's prison, but was kept under surveillance and confined to a certain area. This did not particularly worry Taylor; he
found many congenial people living under similar conditions, 'a
coterie being thus formed which, in point of vivacity and zest of
enjoyment, could not be excelled by the freest of the free', as one of
his friends said. Indeed, Taylor considered that he *was* more or less
free; he would frequently steal off to the country for a day's fishing,
and at one point he even succeeded in raising enough money to buy
himself a country house. 'There he went and lived and ate and drank
and fished, till at the end of two or three months the officers of the
law hooked him, and reconveyed him to his accustomed habitation',
the same friend remarked. Back in London with his fellow debtors,
Taylor 'would not infrequently become exceedingly elevated with
wine, and be guilty of the greatest extravagances. One evening he so
broke through all restraint that Lady Ladd found it expedient to
empty the boiling contents of the kettle on him—an operation which
had the somewhat paradoxical effect of completely cooling him.' At
another time this eccentric but not unlovable character managed to
slip away to Hull, where he stood for election as M.P. for the
borough, but was not returned. For many years Taylor was involved
in litigation with his successors at the King's Theatre, and lawyers of
the day must have been genuinely sorry when he eventually died.

So far as da Ponte was concerned, Taylor's return to England was
a disaster. Their finances had become so inextricably mixed that da
Ponte could no more disentangle himself than Taylor could. Little
by little he was forced to sell his truly magnificent stock of books at
a loss in order to pay his debts or to pay for litigation about them,
and he was also forced to move into a smaller house. By this time
his family consisted of four children: two daughters—Louisa, aged
eleven, and Frances (usually called Fanny) aged five; and two sons
—Joseph, aged four, and Lorenzo, who was only a few months old.
JX

In addition, his step-brother Paolo, who had obtained a job in a piano factory in London in about 1800, was also living with him.

In the summer of 1804 da Ponte was forced to take a very grave decision. Nancy's parents and her brother and his wife had been living in America since at least 1794; they had managed to establish themselves there on a fairly sound footing, and they wrote and suggested that Nancy should pay them a visit. In those days crossing the Atlantic was no simple matter, and no one undertook it lightly, especially with four small children. When da Ponte agreed to let Nancy and the children go it was probably because his financial situation was so desperate that he already envisaged the possibility of escaping to America himself. In addition, Nancy had acquired a certain amount of money of her own—she may have made it when she was in charge of the catering at the opera—and it is not impossible that da Ponte was anxious for this money to be transferred to a safe place, out of reach of his creditors. He had still not quite lost all hope of making good in London—he had his finger in so many different pies that it was quite possible that one, at least, of his ventures might turn out successfully—and so he decided to let Nancy go to the States with the children, and to remain behind in London himself, together with his brother Paolo, who was in business with him.

At the beginning of August 1804 he accompanied his family to Gravesend and saw them embark on the *Pigou*, which was bound for Philadelphia. It was a tragic parting; da Ponte had become a true family man, he adored his wife and was deeply attached to his children, and as he saw the ship moving off, taking his family on a long and dangerous voyage into the unknown, he must have wondered if he would ever see them again. Even if they did arrive at their destination safely, it would be several months before he could hear that they had done so. He returned sadly to London with Paolo, bitterly regretting that he had ever agreed to his family leaving him. How Nancy fared on the voyage has not been recorded; the *Pigou* arrived in Philadelphia after a voyage lasting fifty days which, with three children under twelve and a baby in arms, cannot have been a pleasant experience.

On his return to London da Ponte was not able to indulge in grief for long; he was kept so busy trying to make both ends meet, staving off creditors, parleying with lawyers and trying to raise money by every imaginable means, that he had no time either to miss his family or to write anything for the theatre. The idea of going to America himself occurred to him more and more frequently; one day he mentioned it to his friend Mathias. Now that da Ponte was alone they saw even more of each other; Mathias had given da Ponte some financial help, and he would occasionally invite him to breakfast, during which they would discuss da Ponte's enemies and read Petrarch aloud. Mathias considered his friend's idea of emigrating to the States, and after a moment or two asked him: 'But Lorenzo, what would you *do* in America?' It was a very pertinent question, and one which da Ponte had not considered himself; it seemed unlikely that there would be much demand for Italian poets in America at that time, but as usual he did not worry much about what he would do—he would trust to his lucky star; something would turn up. Something always had turned up so far whenever he had gone to a new country, to Austria or to London, for instance. He had always landed on his feet in the Old World; why should he not do so in the New World too? Mathias pointed out that conditions in America might be very different to those in Europe, but his friend was not discouraged; apart from anything else, his wife's family appeared to be quite well off, they would be sure to help him . . .

In spite of his debts and in spite of his dreams of joining his family in America, da Ponte stayed on in London for another nine months, during which he says he 'endured hell on earth'. One day, at the beginning of March 1805, a meeting was arranged between his own lawyer and his creditors in a last attempt to get his business straightened out. Although a great deal of wine was drunk at his expense at the meeting, nothing was decided, and after it was over da Ponte went home and went to bed early. He had just fallen asleep when he was woken by the sound of knocking on the door and someone calling his name. Although he recognised the voice as that belonging to one of the officers of the courts, he went to let him in, for he knew that the man was well-disposed towards him and honest and straightforward. Indeed, he had come not to arrest da Ponte, but to warn him that he would be obliged to do so early the next morning, and to advise him to leave London. Da Ponte thanked the man for his kindness, tried to tip him. He refused and da Ponte gratefully accepted a few guineas from him instead. When his visitor had left da Ponte took stock of the situation.

Obviously, the time had once more come for him to move on; but he had no money with which the pay his fare to America. Taylor had already suggested that he should go to America for a time until his—Taylor's—affairs took a turn for the better, and had promised to pay him his salary while he was away if he would send him libretti from time to time. Da Ponte decided to go to Gould, tell him the whole story, and to try to borrow some money from him. It was not yet midnight, so he dressed hurriedly and went to see the manager of the theatre. Gould received him kindly, listened to his troubles, and readily agreed to give him a hundred guineas on account. After a few hours' sleep da Ponte rose again at daybreak and went to the city to try to book a passage. He was lucky; at the first place where he enquired he was told that the *Columbia* was sailing for Philadelphia on 7th April.

There was no time to lose: da Ponte rushed to the Aliens' Office to obtain a passport, managed to persuade the officials there not to mention his departure to anyone, and then took a postchaise to Gravesend. He was accompanied only by his brother Paolo, who was very fond of him, and who was broken-hearted at his departure. Da Ponte managed to console him by promising that he would either come back to London in six months' time, or send for his brother to join him in America. They never met again—Paolo remained in London, and carried on da Ponte's publishing business for him until his death which, according to Lorenzo, was in 1807; but the name of Da Ponte, Foreign Booksellers, is to be found in the London directories until 1810. Lorenzo never returned to Europe again.

Part IV

NEW YORK

'New York, the nation's thyroid
gland . . .'
Christopher Morley

CHAPTER XIII

THE GROCER

IN after years, when da Ponte looked back on his voyage to America, he remembered it as one of the most disagreeable experiences of his life. He sailed from Gravesend on 7th April 1805 in the *Columbia*, and did not reach Philadelphia until 4th June, fifty-seven days later. On board the *Columbia* the food was scarcely edible, the sleeping accommodation for passengers was nothing but hard wooden bunks with no mattresses, and the company was extremely boring. Da Ponte spent his time gambling with another passenger, Richard Edwards, whom he referred to as 'Odoardo', and by the time he reached America he had lost every penny he possessed to him. Edwards was obliged to pay duty on the few possessions da Ponte had brought with him—a fiddle, a tea-urn and a carpet; a trunk full of books and 'one box of fiddle-strings and suspenders' were admitted free of duty. This long and uncomfortable voyage cost forty-four guineas and seemed, in retrospect, even longer than it had been in fact; by the time he wrote his *Memoirs* da Ponte remembered it as having lasted eighty-six days.

When he arrived in America da Ponte did not apparently know exactly where his family was living. He made enquiries in Philadelphia, and having learned that his wife and children had settled in New York, he set off immediately for that city. After a touching reunion with Nancy and the children, he began to consider the serious problem of how he should earn a living.

There was no question of working for the opera, for there was none. Italian opera did not come to the States for another twenty years, and at the time of da Ponte's arrival in New York even the theatre was still in a relatively primitive state; the first play to be acted by professional actors in New York—Farquhar's *The Recruiting Officer*—had been produced less than a century earlier, in 1732; and although by the beginning of the nineteenth century the theatre was well-established, the puritan attitude towards it was still by no means dead. As to Italian literature, it was little known and less appreciated in America at that time, and da Ponte realised that it would be impossible for him to make a living by writing poetry or, indeed, by any other intellectual work. He therefore decided, on the advice of his father-in-law, to set up as a grocer; he did so first in New York, and then in Elizabethtown, New Jersey, where he remained until 1807.

Da Ponte was not a good business man, and his natural element was not a grocer's shop in a small provincial town in America, but the great theatres and salons of the capitals of Europe. How he bore the first years of his exile from all he loved best—the theatre, the world of literature, the cosmopolitan and stimulating atmosphere of European cities—we can only guess. Of what he found in New Jersey nothing was familiar except the heavy debts and numerous creditors he quickly acquired.

After two years exile in the provinces da Ponte could stand it no longer, and he returned to New York, still hoping to make a living for himself and his family—now increased to five children by the birth of a third son, Charles, in Elizabethtown in 1806—by giving Latin or Italian lessons. He found that the inhabitants of New York showed complete indifference to Italian, which he said was 'as well known there as Turkish or Chinese', and that they considered Americans could teach Latin as well as if not better, than could an Italian. If it had not been for a chance encounter in a bookshop one day he might well have been obliged to return to his grocery.

Lorenzo could never resist either books or bookshops, and all his life he had suffered from bibliomania. When he was well off he would buy books, and when he was poor he would stand in shops for hours just looking at them. As a small boy in Ceneda he had stolen and sold odd bits of leather from his father's shop in order to buy books; as a grown man whenever he had to leave a country in a hurry the only possessions he ever took with him were his books. One day in New York as he was walking along Broadway, da Ponte noticed Riley's bookshop there, and of course immediately went inside to ask if there were any Italian books for sale. He began to chat with the bookseller and to sing the praises of the works of his compatriots for which, he was told, there was no demand. As he was talking, a young American, obviously a cultured and intelligent man, came up and joined in the conversation. After a long discussion about Italian literature—of which, da Ponte perceived with regret, his companions were very ignorant—he asked whether they considered that a teacher of Italian would have any chance of success in New York. Both the young man and the bookseller thought that there was a need for such a teacher, and offered da Ponte their assistance in finding pupils; in fact, the young gentleman said that he would like to take lessons with da Ponte himself.

The young American who thus met da Ponte in Riley's bookshop was Clement Clarke Moore, then twenty-eight years old; he was later to become a most distinguished Hebrew scholar and lexographer, the founder of the General Theological Seminary, and a Trustee of Columbia College. He is probably better remembered now, however, not for the imposing positions he occupied, but rather as the author of a charming children's classic, *The Night Before Christmas*. Clement Moore's father, Bishop Benjamin Moore, was no less distinguished than his son, and ultimately became President of Columbia; it was in his house that da Ponte gave his first lessons in New York. Clement Clarke Moore, although much younger than da Ponte, became his close friend and patron, and did a great deal to make life in America easier and more agreeable for him. He was of a very different temperament to the poet, having written at the age of twenty-five that he regretted that 'more of the well-disposed among his young countrymen do not devote their leisure hours to the attainment of useful learning, rather than to frivolous amusements or political wrangling'. Moore was a scholarly, pious, serious-minded young man, the same kind of person as Father Huber, da Ponte's Jesuit friend in Dresden.

Da Ponte's first pupils included two young men who both later became professors at Columbia, Nathaniel F. Moore and John M. MacVickar, and several other members of distinguished American families. The classes proved very popular; the number of pupils grew rapidly, and very soon Nancy also began giving lessons to female students. As the number of pupils increased, so the scope of da Ponte's classes expanded; in a year's time the 'Manhattan Academy for Young Gentleman' had come into existence, at which students had facilities for learning not only Italian, French and Latin, but 'writing and ciphering . . . English grammar, geography and other juvenile rudiments' as well. In addition, da Ponte stated in his advertisements, 'Every attention will be paid to the morals of those entrusted to his care'. At 'The Manhattan Academy for Young Ladies' Nancy taught French and Italian and 'the art of making artificial flowers'; teachers were also engaged to give lessons in drawing and music.

Da Ponte had always had real gifts as a teacher; as a very young man, in the seminaries at Portogruaro and Treviso, this had already been apparent. Full of intellectual enthusiasm himself, he had the great gift of transmitting it to others, and he fired the imagination of the young Americans with whom he came into contact to such an extent that they remembered his lectures for the rest of their lives. Arthur Livingston, the American editor of da Ponte's *Memoirs*, considers that The Manhattan Academy for Young Gentlemen was of great significance; 'There is no doubt that this was an important moment for the American mind', he writes. 'Da Ponte made Europe, poetry, painting, music, the artistic spirit, classical lore, a creative classical education, live for many important Americans as no one, I venture, had done before.'

For all his love of literature and learning da Ponte was anything but a dry pedant, and he succeeded in giving his students that desire to learn without which no teaching has any value. He never made the mistake, so common with teachers of foreign languages, of giving beginners third-rate books to read, but always insisted that they should read the great Italian writers from the start. His brother Paolo sent him copies of the Italian classics from London, and his students even gave some performances of Alfieri's *Mirra* before an audience in da Ponte's own house. Although this performance was on the whole a great success, it nevertheless shocked some members of New York society, who still had strong puritan prejudices against theatricals of any kind, professional or amateur, more especially if their own daughters took part in them.

In 1811, Lorenzo da Ponte became an American citizen. His own country no longer existed as an independent State, and although since the fall of the Venetian Republic he had been, technically, an Austrian citizen, he had never considered himself a subject of the Hapsburgs. Although he never lost his love for Italy in general and Venice in particular—on the contrary, as is so often the case, exile from his native land made him far more patriotic than he had ever been before—he became a true American, not only according to the letter of the law, but in spirit as well. Indeed, long before he had ever set foot in the New World he had had many American qualities—his tremendous energy, his freshness of approach to every problem, his capacity for making friends, his adaptability, his strong enthusiasms, his love of novelty. Politically, too, he had much sympathy for the young republic. In his youth in Venice he had been accused of 'radicalism' and 'revolutionary activities'; in point of fact his political opinions had been those of most intelligent young men of his day who were beginning to rebel against the old order in Europe, and who understood that a new, more democratic age was in the process of being born.

America gave da Ponte a home, a nationality, a future for his children, and a mission in life. Before he went to America he had never had any aim or purpose beyond the purely selfish one of satisfying his own desires and assuring his own material welfare; on his arrival in the States he discovered his true mission, that of making Italy and Italian literature and music known in the New World, and of supplying Americans with something which they sorely lacked: a knowledge and understanding of European culture. He took his mission seriously, and he served both his old country and his new one faithfully; da Ponte had every reason to be grateful to America, and both Italians and Americans have every reason to be grateful to him. Almost single-handed, he fought against ignorance and prejudice, and in his old age he achieved truly remarkable results. It is no exaggeration to say that he was the first person to introduce all the best that Italy has to offer in literature to the New World, and that it was largely through his efforts that Italian opera became known there.

Most unfortunately, da Ponte's initial activities as a teacher in New York were short-lived. In 1811, the same year in which he became an American citizen, his family persuaded him to leave the city and go to Pennsylvania. His father-in-law was still alive, and was living in Sunbury with his son Peter and his wife; also living in Sunbury were Charles and Louisa Niccolini, Nancy's sister and her husband who had been in London. Nancy's family persuaded da Ponte to visit Sunbury, and when he did so he fell in love with the place and decided to settle there himself. As he later realised, this decision was a dreadful mistake, and he paid for it bitterly. Whether he was tempted by the idea of an idyllic, peaceful old age in the country, a mirage which sometimes appears to essentially urban men in late middle-age, or whether he wished to be nearer the Grahl money in the hope of getting at least some of it on his father-in-law's death, will never be known—probably a little of both. In any case, in the summer of 1811 da Ponte, Nancy and four of his five children left New York for Sunbury, where they were shortly joined by da Ponte's eldest daughter, Louisa, and her husband, Miles Franklin Clossey, whom she had married in 1809.

II

When da Ponte went to live there, Sunbury was a charming small town set in a delightful countryside. Da Ponte had not lived in the country since his earliest childhood, and at first he was attracted by the rural life and the simple pleasures which the little town offered. He made friends with some of the local families—the Grants, the Halls, the Buyers—gave Italian lessons to their children, and to young people from the neighbouring town of Northumberland, where he tried, unsuccessfully, to found an 'Academy for Young Ladies and Gentlemen' similar to the one he had run in New York. But he found that he could not make a living by teaching and so, on his brother-in-law's advice, he set up as a trader, dealing principally in medicinal products and continental groceries.

It would be of no interest to recount in detail the various ups and downs of da Ponte's career as a grocer. He has done so himself in his *Memoirs*, and it makes very tedious reading; his account is little more than a catalogue of all the dishonest men who tricked him, abused his friendship and hospitality, and took advantage of his honesty and kindness. No doubt there were two sides to the story.

Although da Ponte was certainly not the naïf, kindly, honest simple-ton that he tries to make out, there is all the same something rather pathetic about his account of his struggles as a grocer—of how instead of writing odes to the crowned heads of Europe, he wrote out bills for sausages and dried prunes for the inhabitants of a Pennyslvania village. Although he must have found it extremely difficult to adapt himself to what was virtually a pioneer life, he did so fairly competently; he was probably never outstandingly success-ful as a business man, but he did not, apparently, do quite as badly in Sunbury as might have been expected. He even acquired a certain amount of property, and at one time owned no less than six horses.

If da Ponte's memories of Sunbury were mostly unpleasant, he at least left a good impression on some of the citizens of that town. One of them, who knew him intimately at that period of his life, described him as follows: 'A perfectly honest man, a delightful com-panion, unsuspicious and often led into trouble by rogues. . . . He was tall, well-built, very beautiful, and of highly-polished manners. He was very temperate and regular in all his ways.'

Apart from his groceries and his Italian lessons, da Ponte tried various other commercial ventures during his stay in Pennsylvania. In 1814 he opened a millinery store at 29 North 2nd Street, Phila-delphia—it will be remembered that he had contemplated a similar enterprise when he had been in the Low Countries, as Nancy was skilled in the art of making artificial flowers. He also ran a carrier service, transporting country produce from Sunbury to Philadelphia, and bringing back products of the city to the country; 'L. de Ponty's Wagon', as it was called, became a familiar feature on the road, and brought its owner a substantial income. At the end of 1814 he was able to build himself a three-story brick house—the only one in the county—and he was the second-largest taxpayer in Sunbury.

He also opened a distillery while he was in Sunbury. Although this seems as incongruous a profession for Mozart's librettist as making hats or selling sausages, it was one which was apparently in the blood of his family. To the present day, in the Treviso area of Northern Italy, distillers of the name of Conegliano-da Ponte are to be found, who are almost certainly descendants of da Ponte's half-brothers. It is not without interest that, in the course of time, the family seems to have reverted to its original surname without, however, dropping the name Geremia Conegliano had taken on his conversion to Christianity.

But da Ponte did not remember—or did not choose to record—the successes and the pleasant times which he did undoubtedly have during his stay in Pennsylvania. He was never truly happy there, principally because he was an intellectual in a totally unintellectual community, and because he was almost entirely cut off from all his own interests. He also experienced some keen disappointments there; one of his motives for going to Sunbury had been the hope that he might be able to acquire some of his parents-in-laws' money on their death, or on the death of his sister-in-law, Louisa Niccolini. In this he was not successful; Louisa Niccolini died in 1815, leaving $5,000 to her sister, Ann da Ponte, which was to be administered as a trust fund for the children. Louisa obviously knew da Ponte only too well, and had had the foresight to make it impossible for him to touch his children's money; he never forgave her for this.

Altogether da Ponte spent seven years in Sunbury—seven years of hard and sometimes profitable work, of financial ups and downs, litigation, and above all, of boredom. In 1818 he moved to Philadelphia, in the hope of being able to find enough pupils in that city to enable him to return to his true profession of teacher and poet; but he was not successful, and in April 1819, at the suggestion of his friend Clement Moore, he decided to return to New York.

CHAPTER XIV

THE PROPAGANDIST

WHEN da Ponte went back to New York he was accompanied only by his eldest son Joseph, for whom he wished to find a tutor. The other members of the family remained behind in Philadelphia, with the intention of going to New York if da Ponte could find some means of supporting them there. He was soon able to write to them that he had already found a number of pupils, and that the prospects in New York seemed extremely favourable.

Da Ponte had brought nothing with him from Philadelphia but a large quantity of Italian books. He had offered to sell some of these books to the civic library in Philadelphia, but after some hesitation the trustees had finally turned down his offer. Now, in New York, he made a gift of some sixty volumes to the public library, and suggested to his pupils that they should do the same. Da Ponte's gift, which included works by Parini, Ugo Foscolo and Cesarotti, laid the foundations of the collection of Italian books in that library which, until da Ponte's donation, had not possessed any of the Italian classics, let alone modern writers. Da Ponte's dream and ambition was always to found an Italian library in New York; he was not successful in creating a library exclusively for Italian books, but he did do Italian literature an immense service in founding departments for it not only in the New York Public Library, but also, later on, in the library of Columbia College.

It was in the autumn of 1819 that da Ponte made his first direct contact with Columbia College, when he entered his son Joseph as a student there. At the end of a year at Columbia, Joseph asked his father for permission to return to Philadelphia and to finish his studies there. Reluctantly Lorenzo agreed, but Joseph never completed his studies, for he died in 1821 of consumption, in his twenty-first year. At least three of da Ponte's five children were consumptive;

Louisa died of the same disease in 1823, and Lorenzo the younger, who survived his father, also fell a victim to it. Their parents were more robust; Nancy died at an advanced age of pneumonia, and da Ponte himself had an iron constitution. Apart from an attack of malaria as a very young man, he scarcely had a day's illness in the whole of his long life, and although in his old age he broke several bones as a result of a series of driving accidents and falls, he recovered with remarkable rapidity. After one of these accidents he was treated in Pennsylvania by two very eminent American doctors—Dr Physick and Dr Benjamin Smith Barton, both pioneers of American medicine.

Although da Ponte acquired a considerable number of pupils on his return to New York, he found that he was no longer the only teacher of Italian in that city. During his seven years' absence in Pennsylvania a number of new Italian emigrants had arrived who were not teachers by profession but who, like so many exiles, found that their only money-earning asset was a knowledge of their native tongue. These new emigrants viewed da Ponte's return to New York and to teaching with misgiving; apart from his truly remarkable gifts as a teacher, he had other assets which they could scarcely hope to rival, such as his glamorous past as poet to the Hapsburgs, his personal charm, his thorough knowledge of Italian literature, and his friendship with such eminent American families as the Moores and the Livingstons. However, if they could not compete with him as a teacher, his rivals realised that it would not be difficult to discredit him as a man, and thus discourage American parents from entrusting their children to his care. Some of the new Italian arrivals had known da Ponte, or known of him, in Italy, and were familiar with many of the less creditable details of his past; they did not hesitate to share this information with the citizens of New York.

One of these new Italian teachers was a certain Marc Antonio Casati; according to da Ponte, Casati was the person responsible for most of the more violent attacks which were launched against him at this time, and for many of the attempts which were made to discredit him as a teacher. Da Ponte also named such men as Ferrari, Aloisi, Strozzi and Sega as his enemies. Amongst other things, an anonymous pamphlet was circulated to the parents of da Ponte's pupils, in which he was specifically accused of twelve different crimes, including embezzlement, adultery, and homicide.

Whoever the author of this rather curious document was, he had got hold of some of the true facts about da Ponte's past—for instance, that 'he was obliged in his early life to quit Venice for his misbehaviour'—and had distorted others, saying for example, that: 'he wandered through the greatest part of Italy under a variety of different characters: composed plays, worthy of the actors who performed them, at the rate of two shillings a day. And his impudent assertion of having been appointed, by Joseph the second, poet of the Italian theatre at Vienna, is a ridiculous falsehood.' The author was apparently unaware of much of da Ponte's past—for example, of the fact that he had been a priest—for he had to go to the trouble of inventing crimes for his victim, instead of utilising those which he had, in fact, committed. Thus, in the pamphlet the following sentence appears under the heading *Adultery*: 'There is a young wench in the house, who is companion for the table, etc.!! . . . of either father or sons', but there is no mention of the Bellaudi incident in Venice, nor of the fact that, as he was a priest, da Ponte's marriage itself was highly irregular, to say the least. Three of the twelve accusations refer to dubious financial dealings, and may well have contained some truth; two accusations against his sons were almost certainly without foundation, for all reports agree that they were intelligent, hard-working, and eminently respectable young men.

The accusation against da Ponte of homicide was as follows: 'A young Miss Williams was sent to his house to finish her education. She soon became corrupted, and one day . . . (horresco referens!) . . . then in his rage so ill-treated this unfortunate girl, that she soon took to her bed, from which she never more arose. Dr Pascalis pronounced her illness occasioned by ill-treatment and want of food.' Although this accusation was quite without foundation—the young lady in question was, in fact, not only alive and well when the libel was published, but had by then become the mother of five children —da Ponte went to some trouble to deny it, and published letters from the girl's parents and from Dr Pascalis in his defence.

Although the accusations contained in this pamphlet were mostly so far beyond the comprehension of respectable citizens of New York that the majority dismissed them as the vile inventions of a poison-pen writer, da Ponte may have lost some pupils as a result. 'Calomniez, calomniez, il en reste toujours quelque chose . . .' In any case, if the truth about da Ponte had been known, there is no doubt at all that he would not have had a single pupil, for the truth was certainly no better than what his attacker had written about him. Fortunately for da Ponte, the whole truth about him never was known in his life-time, and very likely it never will be known.

At about this time—1821—da Ponte began taking students into his house as boarders. This new venture became known as 'Ann da Ponte's Boarding House' and had a long and successful life; it was still in existence in 1840, and appears to have been run, after Mrs da Ponte's death in 1832, by her daughter-in-law, the wife of Lorenzo da Ponte junior. The first boarder, and the person who gave da Ponte the idea of opening a boarding-house, was Henry James Anderson, a young man who was at that time a student of mathematics. In 1825 Anderson became professor of mathematics and astronomy in Columbia College, and in 1831 he married Fanny, da Ponte's younger daughter. Soon after he went to live in da Ponte's house he was joined there by his two brothers and some of their friends who, in their turn, recommended the establishment to other young people.

Apart from the attraction of such amenities as Italian and French lessons and conversation and an excellent continental cuisine, Fanny, da Ponte's younger daughter, probably also largely contributed to the success of the boarding-house; she was pretty, vivacious and intelligent, and the fact that her first marriage—to a certain Mr Freeman, of Bristol, Pa.—had recently ended in divorce probably made her seem even more interesting to the young men who lived in her father's house. It was, however, above all the background of European culture with which the da Pontes were able to provide their American guests which distinguished their boarding-house from the numerous other similar establishments which existed in New York at that time. Dr Johnson said that 'A man who has not been to Italy is always conscious of his inferiority', but not every cultured young American could afford the time and money necessary for a trip to Europe. Those who lived in the da Pontes' house felt that they had the next best thing. Da Ponte himself was an inexhaustible mine of European culture; his gifts as a raconteur brought Venice, Vienna and London home to his listeners as no books or pictures could; and the fact that he had known so many eminent Europeans personally made him a living and tangible link between his young American students and those great men of the past. His wife was well-versed in the domestic lore of the many European countries in which she had lived, and had brought up her children in the European tradition; young Americans felt that if they could not travel to Europe and see it for themselves the companionship of the young da Pontes, and their mother's *boeuf à la mode* with a touch of garlic in it, or her *pasta* with Parmesan cheese, brought them a good deal closer to it than anything else did in New York.

After the death of his son Joseph in the summer of 1821, da Ponte was invited by his friends the Livingstons to spend some weeks with them on their estate in the country. During his stay there a copy of Byron's *The Prophecy of Dante*, which had just been published, came into his hands. Da Ponte was very moved by the poem, and he decided to translate it into Italian *terza rima*; his version was published in New York in 1821, with a dedication to Miss Julia Livingston; there was also a long dedication to Lord Byron, both in Italian and Latin verse, and an English translation of the same by da Ponte's daughter Fanny; da Ponte's translation of part of the fourth canto of *Childe Harold* was also printed in the same volume. These translations of Byron—among the first that were ever made of his works—were highly praised in Italy; whether Byron himself ever saw them or read the dedication is not known, but da Ponte must be given the credit for being one of the first, if not the first, to make the poet's work available in Italian.

After he had made this valuable contribution to the knowledge of English literature in Italy, da Ponte returned to his primary mission of making Italian literature known in the New World. In spite of his age—he was over seventy—he was tireless in his efforts, and attacked the somewhat apathetic Americans with true missionary zeal. Nor were his exertions merely the useless activities of a semi-senile old man; they were, on the contrary, the constructive

and valuable products of an alert and intelligent brain. Amongst
other things, for example, da Ponte imported over a thousand Italian
books into America; having done so, and in spite of the fact that he
was unable to consult any books of reference or make use of normal
library facilities, he compiled a *catalogue raisonée* of the books in his
possession. Although da Ponte's catalogue undoubtedly contained
a good many errors and omissions, as he himself was the first to
realise, it was the only work of its kind available in America at that
time, and early American librarians and bibliographers must have
used it extensively, *faute de mieux*. The catalogue was taken by a
friend to Mexico, where it aroused so much interest that da Ponte
was soon receiving orders for the works of such Italian writers as
Macchiavelli and Filangieri from that country.

Da Ponte was not content merely to spread a knowledge of Italian
literature in America; he was also ready to defend it against any
attacker, and to avenge any real or imagined insults to the country
of his birth or to his compatriots. He considered himself—and to a
certain extent, with reason—the only champion Italy possessed in
the North American continent, and looked on it as his duty to defend
her traditions, her institutions, and her art against all attacks. In 1821,
for example, during the trial of Queen Caroline, the British press
was full of anti-Italian feeling, largely because of the corruptness of
certain Italian witnesses at the trial. Da Ponte was incensed by what
he considered a slanderous attack on the whole Italian nation, and
felt obliged to make an immediate reply on behalf of his country-
men. He therefore gave a lecutre, which he called an 'Apologetical
Discourse on Italy', before a numerous and elegant assembly in
New York, and later published it in pamphlet form. Dr Francis,
who was present at this lecture, recorded that da Ponte spoke in
English 'with all the earnestness and animation of a great speaker'.

In 1824 an attack was made on Italian literature, this time in an
American journal, the *North American Review*. Someone drew da
Ponte's attention to the article in question, and he of course immediately replied to it in a pamphlet which was published early in
1825. To his surprise, this pamphlet 'did not succeed in convincing
the still young athlete of his errors, but instead encouraged him to
publish another article which was even sharper, more bitter and

more full of mistakes and prejudice than the first'. The 'young athlete's' name was W. H. Prescott. The celebrated historian, who was then twenty-eight years old and relatively unknown, had written a long and very unfavourable review of English translations of Ariosto's *Orlando furioso* and Berni's *Orlando innamorato*, in which he had expressed the opinion that 'it hardly seems possible that an enlightened people should long continue to take satisfaction in poems, founded on the same extravagant fictions and spun out to the appalling length of twenty, thirty, nay, forty cantos of a thousand verses each.' Although such remarks naturally incensed da Ponte, he should have been delighted by Prescott's opinion of the poetry of his old friend Thomas Mathias: 'His poetical productions rank with those of Milton in merit', Prescott wrote, 'and far exceed them in quality.'

There is something humorous, pathetic, and at the same time magnificent in da Ponte's efforts to defend Italy. Undoubtedly, as he grew older, he became intolerably boring on the subject of Italian literature, for it became a veritable mania with him and he could talk of very little else; he imagined insults to his country where none existed, and defended third-rate Italian verse with as much love and enthusiasm as he defended Dante and Tasso. Yet, at that time, he was the only person in America to defend Italian letters against ignorance, prejudice and apathy, and he was the first person to make the great artistic heritage of Italy a living thing for Americans who had not visited Europe. A self-appointed cultural attaché of the country from which he was an exile, he did his work with energy, intelligence, perseverance, and above all, love.

Italians, who remember da Ponte—if they remember him at all—as a second-rate Casanova or a third-rate poet, would do well to recollect that, at one of the least creditable periods in the history of their great country and when she badly needed a champion, no one could be found to fulfil that function in the New World but the dissolute adventurer, the renegade priest, the converted Jew from the ghetto of Ceneda, and they should give him honour for having fought for their country's artistic reputation both nobly and fruit-fully. Without da Ponte's inexhaustible energy, without his infec-tious enthusiasm and his great gifts as a teacher, Americans might have remained ignorant of Dante and Petrarch, Ariosto and Tasso, of the Italian language and of Italy herself for very much longer than they did. Da Ponte deserves to be remembered by posterity quite as much for his missionary work in the New World as for his collaboration with Mozart in Vienna, and it is not too much of an exaggeration to say that he sowed the seeds in America from which, eventually, the poetry of Ezra Pound and T. S. Eliot was to grow.

III

In 1823 da Ponte began publishing his *Memoirs*; they appeared in four small volumes between 1823-1827. He had already published, in New York in 1807, a sketch of his life which was entitled *Storia compendiosa della vita di Lorenzo da Ponte*, but this had been little more than a pamphlet, and had been mainly concerned with his trials and tribulations as a grocer in New Jersey. Now, he felt, the time had come to give the world a more detailed account of his career and, at the same time, to refute some of the accusations which had been made against him by other Italians in America. Americans might really believe, for example, that he had never been Poet to the Imperial Theatres in Vienna, if he did not publish an account of his work there and his friendship with the Emperor. Da Ponte himself stated that he also wrote his *Memoirs* in order to provide a suitable Italian text-book for his American students; this may have been partly true, but there is no doubt that his principle object was to publish an *apologia pro vita sua*. The first edition, which contained some unfavourable references to Leopold II, was banned in Austria; it also contained a long and detailed examination of the various accusations which had been brought against the author in America and a bitter attack on certain Italians then living in New York. In the second edition, published in New York in 1829 and 1830, these passages were omitted, and various other minor alterations were made.

In spite of the exaggerated praise lavished on them by Lamartine, it must be admitted that the *Memoirs* are a very mediocre work. They cannot bear comparison, for example, with those of two of da Ponte's friends—Casanova and Michael Kelly—whose auto-biographies appeared more or less at the same time (Casanova's posthumously between 1822-1838, and Kelly's in 1825); and they are also greatly inferior to the memoirs of such men as Carlo Gozzi, or Goldoni. The fact that da Ponte's autobiography, written in the hope of showing the author in the best possible light, is full of inaccuracies, omissions, and falsehoods, has no importance from a literary point of view, although it has considerably complicated the task of da Ponte's biographers and editors. A far more serious criticism, from the average reader's point of view, is the fact that in his *Memoirs* da Ponte has largely failed to make either his epoch or his friends live again for posterity. This is chiefly due to his inordin-ate egotism; he was far too preoccupied with himself and with his own affairs to give an interesting picture of his friends and con-temporaries. Instead of telling us what Salieri or Metastasio were like as men, he devoted pages to proving his innocence in some trifling theatrical intrigue, or to describing how he had been cheated out of a few shillings by some insignificant and probably imaginary enemy. The reader is filled with disappointment and regret; if only he had told us something about his discussions with Mozart during the creation of *Figaro* or *Don Giovanni*; if only he had told us any-thing at all about *Così fan Tutte*! If only he had told us what Mozart looked like, what he talked about; if, instead of devoting pages to criticising his rivals, he had described his visit to Metastasio in detail; if only he had been able to give us a living portrait of Paisiello, of Casanova, of Gozzi, or of any of the other great men he had known! But the reader who hopes for some insight into Mozart's methods of work, or even for vivid descriptions of eighteenth-century life in Venice, Vienna or London, will be disappointed. Nor does da Ponte throw much light on early nineteenth-century America, although it was so different to the Europe in which he had been born and bred that it must have made an impression on him. He was not a good psychologist, and did not have the gift for describing detail which makes the reminiscences of Casanova or of the Prince de Ligne so fascinating. Even Kelly who, as da Ponte himself said, was not an educated or a cultured man, was able—with the help of a good 'ghost'—to give us far more interesting and valuable information about his epoch in general and about Mozart in particular.

As a historical document the *Memoirs* have very little value; they tell us next to nothing about the everyday life of the period, and nothing at all about the major historical events which da Ponte had lived through, such as the French Revolution, the Napoleonic era, the war between England and France. To scholars, the principal interest of the *Memoirs* is the faint light they throw on Casanova; the learned gentlemen who devote their lives to proving whether Casanova did or did not write his *Mémoires* have been able to find confirmation of at least three of Casanova's statements in da Ponte's book, which is presumably better than nothing. The portrait which da Ponte has left of Casanova would have more value if the adventurer had not already said almost everything there was to be said about himself in his own book, and if the Prince de Ligne had not admirably completed the portrait.

As to the picture of da Ponte himself which emerges from his autobiography, as usual he was his own worst enemy, and his self-portrait is not flattering. This was undoubtedly unintentional; da Ponte was not a Jean-Jacques Rousseau or a Leo Tolstoy, and did not aim at a completely objective self-portrait, however unflattering, in the interests of truth. Far from it—he does all he can to make himself out to be much better than he was, and he fails lamentably. He does not only fail to make himself seem an estimable character, but he also does himself less than justice. He emerges from the pages of his *Memoirs* as a sanctimonious prig, ever shrilly complaining about unfair treatment, an egocentric, petty individual concerned primarily with minor financial difficulties and squabbles, and interested in nothing beyond his own personal affairs. Undoubtedly much of this was true, but there was also another and far more estimable and attractive side to da Ponte's character which is not apparent from the *Memoirs*, and of which, perhaps, da Ponte was not aware himself. That he had real qualities cannot be doubted; such men as Joseph II, Father Huber, and Clement Moore would not otherwise have become his friends. If he had really been the self-complacent bore which he made himself out to be the Gozzis, the Memmos, Zaguri, and above all, Casanova, would never have thought twice about him. But he had many friends, many of whom were outstanding men in their own sphere; perhaps they sometimes found him aggravating and despicable, but he was always interesting. His undoubted charm is not apparent in his *Memoirs*, although it can occasionally be glimpsed in his letters, and it is vouched for by the testimony of those who knew him, both in Europe and America. Nor does da Ponte do himself justice as a teacher and disseminator of Italian culture; although he devotes many pages of the *Memoirs* to his activities in this sphere, he fails to make them interesting. As always, he insisted too much.

CHAPTER XV

THE PROFESSOR

IN March 1825 Lorenzo da Ponte celebrated his seventy-sixth birthday; he had reached a venerable age, an age at which most men are content to retire from public life and to rest on whatever laurels they may have been able to acquire in the course of it. For da Ponte, however, the year 1825 marked the opening of a new era of intense and exhilarating activity.

It was in this year that he published—in the *New York Review and Athenaeum Magazine*—his *Critique on certain passages in Dante*. Da Ponte was the first person to lecture on Dante in the New World, and the commentaries which he published in 1825 may well have been the first of their kind ever to be published by an American citizen. Nor were da Ponte's comments negligible; they were reprinted in Boston by the Dante Society in 1896, and anyone who has the curiosity to look them up will find them to be scholarly and useful, if not inspired.

In May 1825 the Trustees of Columbia College received a letter from da Ponte 'asking permission to instruct the alumni of the College in the Italian language and to make use of some part of the building for that purpose'. In September of the same year, and probably thanks to the influence of Clement Moore who was then a Trustee of Columbia College, it was decided to establish a Professorship of Italian Literature, and to appoint da Ponte as the first professor. The conditions of his appointment were as follows: he was not considered a member of the Board of the College, he received no salary from the College, but was entitled to receive 'a reasonable compensation' from any students who might attend his lectures, the attendance at which was to be voluntary.

Da Ponte received very little financial benefit from his newly acquired professorship; he had extremely few pupils, as modern languages were not much studied at that time, and in any case

French and Spanish were more popular than Italian. But he had, at long last, received some official recognition for his work in America, and this gave him consolation. In 1825, and again in 1829, he sold a considerable number of Italian books to the library of Columbia College; at one time he even offered to make a gift of a good many more if only the authorities could guarantee him a certain number of students, but this proposal was not accepted. Da Ponte himself had no illusions about his professorship; when invited to one of the annual functions of the college, a dinner which he was unable to attend, he sent the following lines to the students who had invited him:

> Sum pastor sine ovibus,
> arator sine bovibus,
> hortulus sine flore,
> lychnus sine splendore,
> campus sine frumento,
> crumena sine argento,
> navita sine navibus,
> ianua sine clavibus,
> arbustus sine foliis,
> taberna sine doliis,
> Olympus sine stellis,
> chorea sine puellis,
> artifex sine manibus,
> venator sine canibus,
> fons sine potatoribus,
> pons sine viatoribus,
> sacerdos sine templo,
> professor sine exemplo.

Although everyone at the dinner understood the last line, how many of them understood the allusion in the penultimate line?

In November 1825 one of da Ponte's fondest dreams was realised —he was able to witness the introduction of Italian opera to America and, later on, to hear one of his own libretti performed on the stage after an interval of about thirty years. If he was a little saddened by the fact that Italian opera was introduced to the New World not by

KX

Italian artists but by Spaniards, his joy that it was, in fact, introduced there during his lifetime amply made up for that slight wound to his patriotic pride. And in any case the quality of the Spanish singers, Manuel Garcia's company, was such that Italy might well have been proud of them.

Manuel Garcia had just concluded a successful season in London, where his daughter Maria had made a sensational début at Covent Garden at the age of seventeen. He had long cherished an ambition to take a company of singers to the New World, and at last he decided to embark on this hazardous and complicated venture. His task was considerably facilitated by the fact that he was able to recruit all his principal singers from his own family. He was himself a distinguished tenor of international repute and with much valuable experience to his credit; his wife, also a Spaniard, was a less distinguished singer—she had originally intended to become a nun, and had only studied singing seriously after her marriage—but was nevertheless capable of interpreting many of the leading soprano roles; his son, Manuel, who made his début in New York, was a baritone, but also on occasion took tenor parts when his father was indisposed; his elder daughter, Maria, who later became world-famous under her married name of Malibran, took all the contralto parts; his younger daughter did not sing during the American tour, being at that time four years old, but later she also became a famous singer under the name of Pauline Viardot, and she was also no less famous as the inspiration of the Russian novelist, Turgenev. The company which Garcia took with him to America also included the younger Crivelli, *secondo tenore*, d'Angrisani as *basso cantate* and Rosich as *buffo caricato*. It would have been far too expensive to transport a large number of singers across the Atlantic for the chorus, which Garcia hoped to be able to recruit on the spot in New York; as will be seen, he had the greatest difficulty in doing so.

The magnitude of Garcia's undertaking is not easily realised today. Quite apart from the long and hazardous journey which might last anything from about six weeks to three months, the conditions awaiting the artists on their arrival were extremely primitive and quite unlike what first-class artists were accustomed to in Europe. There were no full-time professional orchestras in New York at that time—indeed, in 1828 there was said to be only one oboist in the whole of North America, and he was in Baltimore—and when orchestras were needed they were recruited from what amateurs and professionals might be available at the time. Of necessity, the finer points of orchestration had to be ignored; not only oboes, but bassoons, trumpets and kettledrums were great rarities. 'In spite of this incompleteness', a scandalised German musician reported after a visit to New York, 'they play symphonies by Haydn, and grand overtures; and, if a gap occurs, they think "this is only of passing importance", provided it rattles away again afterwards.'

Garcia took with him from Europe a certain number of stage costumes, but obviously relied on finding artists capable of designing and constructing scenery on the spot in New York. He may have done so, but on one occcasion at least the press announced that 'The scenery, painted by one of the troupe, is of matchless vigour and beauty; displaying magnificent ruins, paintings, etc., so peculiar to modern Italy.' In fact, the singers had to lend a hand with all sorts of jobs back-stage which, in Europe, would have been dealt with by specialised workmen.

Financially, Garcia's expedition had the character of a wild speculation. As Italian opera had never been performed in America before, there was no knowing how the public would react to it, or what the production costs were likely to be. In Europe, although the production of opera was always a costly and risky business, artists knew that they could rely on a hard core of intelligent and wealthy opera-addicts to support them; in the States the public was totally ignorant so far as the grand Italian traditions of opera were con-cerned—although English ballad operas had been popular there for some time—did not understand Italian, and could not be counted on to take to such an exotic and foreign form of entertainment im-mediately. Would the Americans, in fact, take to opera at all? Garcia and his family were willing to risk it, and set off from England full of high hopes.

II

On 29th November, 1825, the first season of Italian opera in America opened at the Park Theatre in New York with a perform-

ance of Rossini's *Il Barbiere di Siviglia*. Da Ponte's excitement knew
no bounds; he had heard rumours that an Italian company was
coming to America, and on Garcia's arrival in New York he had
immediately gone to call on him. When he entered the singer's
room da Ponte introduced himself as the author of the libretto of
Don Giovanni and the friend of Mozart, and Garcia, no doubt
amazed and delighted to find such a relic of the past in New York,
embraced the old man with true Spanish fervour, singing *Fin ch'han
dal vino*—the drinking song from *Don Giovanni*—as he did so.
Whether da Ponte was present at the first performance of Rossini's
opera in New York is not known; he certainly attended the fifth
performance, and took a number of his pupils with him.

The *première* of Rossini's opera was one of the most brilliant
social occasions that New York had witnessed for many years; no
one knew quite what to expect—in fact, many people wrote to the
newspapers to enquire how they should dress for the opera 'in the
European manner' and what was the correct etiquette during performances—but everyone wanted to see and hear the Italian opera.
The critics were as non-plussed as the audience; one paper—'The
Albion'—preferred to refrain from detailed comment until it received a 'scientific critique' which had been promised by a professor,
while another newspaper referred to the music quite simply as
'monstrous'. On the whole, however, both Rossini's music and the
Garcias' singing were favourably received; the performance of
Maria Garcia (Malibran) as Rosina was especially praised. Manuel
Garcia junior made his operatic début at this performance in the part
of Figaro; he never became a great operatic singer, but he had a long
and distinguished career as a teacher—Jenny Lind was one of his
many pupils—and he died well within living memory, in 1906, at
the age of 101.

The orchestra which was assembled for this occasion was considered one of the largest that New York had seen; it consisted of
seven violins, two violas, three 'cellos, two double-basses, two flutes,
two clarinets, one bassoon, two horns, two trumpets and a kettle-
drum; a Monsieur Etienne 'presided at the piano-forte'. According
to da Ponte, Garcia sometimes conducted himself, but as he played
all the principal tenor parts this seems unlikely. The chorus was

recruited mainly from English factory-workers and mechanics who were used to singing in church choirs and were therefore able to read music.

The season continued with other works by Rossini—*Tancredi, Otello, La Cenerentola, Il Turco in Italia* and *Semiramide*; the first performance of Rossini's *Otello* in New York coincided with a production of Shakespeare's play with Kean in the title-role, and much interest was aroused by comparisons between the two productions. Two operas by Garcia himself were also performed.

Da Ponte did all he could to make Garcia's season a success. He carried on an energetic one-man publicity campaign for it, and insisted that all his pupils should support the new enterprise. In addition, he was most solicitous for the singers' comfort, and acted as host to them on their arrival in his adopted country. 'Knowing the delicate organisation of the vocalists', one of his pupils wrote, in the 1860's, 'he had taught a worthy American woman the mysteries of the Italian *cuisine*; so that soprano, contralto, basso and baritone, were agreeably surprised to find the viands and cookery to which they had been accustomed at home, provided in a New York boarding-house. The establishment retained its prestige long after the first, second and third operatic enterprises had failed; for no Italian or old habitué of that classic land, who had ever dined at Aunt Sallie's, was likely to forget the soup, macaroni, or red wine, to say nothing of the bread and vegetables—so like what he associated with the *trattorias* of Florence and Rome; indeed, to dine there, as was my fortune occasionally, and hear *la lingua Toscana in bocca Romana*, on all sides, with furious discussion of Italian politics and delectable praise of composers and vocalists or pictorial *critiques*—transported one by magic from Broome Street to the Piazza Vecchia or the Via Condotta. The death of Aunt Sallie a few years ago dispersed the few survivors of the circle that succeeded da Ponte's singing-birds; and the alimentive associations of his active and magnetic sojourn have no more a local habitation.'

Da Ponte followed the progress of Garcia's season with the closest interest, taking any adverse criticism almost as a personal insult and enjoying the praise as much as if his own operas were being performed. And indeed, he thought, why should his own operas not be performed? Rossini was all very well, but one can have too much of a good thing, and he had a great desire to see 'his' *Don Giovanni* on the stage once more before he died. He suggested to Garcia that Mozart's opera should be added to the repertoire, and Garcia was delighted at the idea; there was only one major difficulty, and that was the absence of a singer suitable for the part of Don Ottavio. In his enthusiasm da Ponte promised not only to find a singer, but also, when the manager of the theatre objected to the additional expense, to pay him.

On May 23rd, 1826, the greatest ambition of da Ponte's old age was realised, and his *Don Giovanni* was performed in America for the first time. What excitement and emotion he must have experienced as, after an interval of over thirty years, he once more saw the play he had written for Mozart come to life on the stage! Did he compare Garcia junior's Leporello with that of Benucci, Malibran's Zerlina with that of Mombelli? Instead of M. Etienne at the piano, did he once more see Mozart conducting in his crimson pelisse and gold-laced cocked hat? As the octogenarian poet sat in the Park Theatre in New York the solid young Americans around him began to fade before his eyes, and their places were taken by a crowd of ghosts.

They were all dead by now, the companions of his youth, all enshrined in encyclopaedias, they had all become part of history and were nothing but names to the American public; he alone survived, a lonely old man in an alien country. But to da Ponte the men and women who had been associated with the first performance of *Don Giovanni* were not just names: they were flesh and blood, his friends, and he remembered them not as the historical figures they had become, but as the human men and women they had been. Joseph II, the Holy Roman Emperor, the enlightened despot, was to him an ordinary man, with a dislike for pomp and ceremony and for having his portrait painted, with his sleeves patched at the elbows and his pockets full of chocolate drops. Salieri was not just an outmoded composer of opera, but the witty, explosive little man who had a passion for sweetmeats and could never pass a cake-shop without going into it. Casanova—who may even have written some of the words the Garcias were singing—was not, to da Ponte, merely the author of the most salacious memoirs of the eighteenth century, but his friend, the pathetic old man whom he had last seen at Dux, complaining about the servants' insolence. Mozart himself he probably thought of not as one of the greatest geniuses who ever lived, but as a remarkably small man, rather vain about his hair, and fond of punch and billiards. Almost all his friends were dead— Mozart, Salieri, Casti, Casanova, the Storaces, Martin. Kelly was still alive, but he died six months later; he had just published his *Reminiscences*, and they were advertised in America in the same issues of the newspapers which contained the announcement of the first performance of Mozart's opera. As he thought of his friends long dead and watched Don Giovanni on the stage being dragged down to Hell by the Commendatore's statue, did da Ponte perhaps think for a moment of his own approaching end?

Apart from having given da Ponte much pleasure and earned him new esteem from the citizens of New York, Garcia's season also benefited him financially. His son, Lorenzo da Ponte junior, made a translation of *Don Giovanni* into English, and the directors of the Park Theatre gave the old poet permission to print and sell the libretti, both in English and Italian, for his own personal benefit. His profits from the sale of the libretto cannot have been very great, but nevertheless, as he maintained, Mozart and Don Giovanni brought him luck and helped him to acquire quite a substantial sum by chance. He was in a bookshop one day, discussing the sale of his libretti, when the bookseller persuaded him to take a lottery ticket; he did so, and won five hundred dollars. He spent this money on importing various rare and important Italian books from Europe, books which eventually passed to the library of Columbia College.

Mozart's opera was received with great enthusiasm by the American public, and was repeated three more times before the end of the season, which continued until 1st October. The Garcias then left New York for Mexico, where they also gave a season of Italian opera before returning to Europe. Maria Garcia, however, did not accompany her family, but remained behind in New York. In the spring of the same year she had married Monsieur Malibran, a man considerably older than her own father. It was not a happy marriage; Malibran went bankrupt and was eventually sent to prison, and his wife was forced to earn her living by singing in English operettas such as *The Devil's Bridge* and *Love in a Village*. In 1827 she decided to leave her husband and return to Europe where, under her married name, she became one of the greatest singers of the epoch.

Financially, Garcia's opera season in New York was a success: for the seventy-nine performances which were given, the gross takings were $56,685. The Mexican season was also profitable, but unfortunately for Garcia he was attacked by brigands on his way from Mexico City to Vera Cruz and robbed of everything he possessed and of all the profits he had made during his North American tour.

CHAPTER XVI

THE IMPRESARIO

GARCIA's venture had proved that there was a public capable of appreciating Italian opera in the United States, and that such a venture could be a financial success. Other singers and impresarios began to think that, if Garcia had succeeded, there was no reason why they should not do so too, and da Ponte, who had been given a new lease of life by the production of his *Don Giovanni*, was filled with a desire to repeat the experiment.

For some months he had been in correspondence with his half-brother, Agostino da Ponte, whose daughter Giulietta was reputed to be a singer of great talent. Da Ponte suggested that his niece should visit America and give a series of concerts or, better still, appear in opera there. Towards the end of 1827 Agostino da Ponte wrote that he agreed to the idea in principle, but that he was having great difficulty in obtaining passports and in completing the other formalities required by the Austrian authorities. He did not, in fact, succeed in doing so for over two years; but finally, in February 1830, da Ponte had the immense joy of greeting his half-brother and his niece on their arrival in New York. He had been obliged to finance their journey, but the pleasure of seeing his own flesh and blood again after so long amply compensated for the expense.

The arrival of Agostino overwhelmed da Ponte with memories of his youth, of his family, of Italy. He sat up half the night talking to his brother, and when he did finally go to bed his dreams were of his father, of Ceneda, of Venice, of his childhood in the little village in the Dolomites, of that distant past, almost eighty years ago, when he had been Emanuele Conegliano, 'the clever dunce'. When he awoke the next morning it was some time before he could readjust himself to America, New York, and old age.

Giulia da Ponte made her début in New York at a 'Grand Concert of Vocal and Instrumental Music' on 31st March, 1830. A month later one of her uncle's dearest dreams was realised when she appeared in his *L'Ape Musicale*, that same *Pasticcio* which he had originally written for La Ferrarese in Vienna in 1789. It was not a success; Giulietta was a mediocre singer—'She was not made for the stage, nor the stage for her' her uncle said tactfully—and *L'Ape Musicale*, which had been a witty, topical and highly personal revue in Vienna forty years ago, must have seemed quite incomprehensible to an American audience.

On May 10th, 1830 Giulia da Ponte sang at a concert given by the Musical Fund Society at the City Hall, to an extremely large audience—a thousand to twelve hundred people. The programme included works by Mozart, Rossini and Weber, and the overture to *Zaire* by da Ponte's old associate, Winter, was also given. Although these classical works were applauded, what really pleased the audience above all was the trumpet-playing of a Mr Norton who played a 'Concerto' in which the 'Star-Spangled Banner' and the 'British Grenadiers' were incorporated. The Americans at that time were extremely partial to 'the noisy part of the orchestra', a taste which shocked not only visiting foreigners but also at least one American critic, who wrote that if this marked preference were to continue much longer 'New York would be blown away'.

Giulietta proved a great disappointment to her uncle; not only did she do him little credit on the stage, but she showed no gratitude to him for having financed her journey from Europe and her appearances in America. Shortly after her arrival in the States she married a man named Stafler and left the stage, and in 1832 she returned to Trieste with her husband, without even taking the trouble to bid her aged uncle good-bye. It was a great grief to him, more especially as he had boasted about his niece's great gifts and bored everyone with his talk about her for two whole years before her arrival, and he felt he had been made to look a fool by her.

Da Ponte was now over eighty, but his physical and mental powers were by no means declining. Old age had changed him remarkably little; it had only slightly exaggerated both his physical appearance and his mental characteristics. His face had always possessed rather strongly marked features, and extreme old age made him a caricature of himself when young. His nose, always prominent, became dominant; his eyes, always piercing and brilliant, became burning lights in their deep sockets; the humorous lines around his mouth had become deep ravines surrounding his tooth-less jaws; his long white hair gave him the aspect of some inspired Hebrew prophet. In character, old age intensified both his faults and his virtues. He became more querulous about his enemies, more touchy and even quicker to take offence; his financial dealings became more and more complicated, and he was for ever borrowing money from anyone who was foolish enough to lend it to him. His missionary zeal and his efforts to spread a knowledge of Italian literature became a true obsession, so that his friends would tactfully slip away from him at the very mention of Italy, fearing the inevitable lecture on Dante or Petrarch which would follow. The affected mannerisms which people had laughed at in his youth had become, in his old age, the polished and courtly ways of the *ancien régime*, and greatly impressed the Americans, who considered him a typical European aristocrat. Age had, perforce, much modified his attitude to women; he had once been ardent, now he was courtly; he had once been licentious, now he was correct; he had once been active, now he was passive. The man whose youthful loves and lusts were enough to fill a thick and heavy dossier in the Venetian State Archives was reduced to such harmless and semi-senile gallantries as calling all his female students by the names of different flowers and writing odes to them, which he himself translated into English:

> '. . . When in the garden, beautiful and fair,
> The jasmine blossomed, planted by my care,
> The vi'let, the narcissus and the rose,
> The lily, type of virtue and repose,
> The stately tulip and the fleur-de-lis,
> Adding their beauty to the scenery,
> While flowers of fairest and of richest hue
> Upon the air their sweetest perfume threw—
> Spring into freshened life at my command,
> Planted and raised and cultured by my hand. . . .'

In December 1831 Nancy da Ponte died after a short illness. She was some twenty years younger than Lorenzo, and her death was an unexpected blow and a great grief to him. They had been together for almost forty years, and they had been happy; da Ponte had staked everything on his happiness with Nancy, and he had won. For her he had abandoned Italy, Europe, the Catholic Church and, so far as the Church was concerned, his chances in the next world as well; it had been worth it, and he had no regrets. Now the great adventure of matrimony was over, and he was once more alone and free—free to make his peace with the Church before his own death. Although he was eighty-three years old he did not feel that this was a pressing matter, but considered that it could quite well wait for another few years.

In memory of his wife da Ponte published, in 1832, his *Sonetti per la morte di Anna Celestina Ernestina da Ponte*; in the same volume he included another précis of his own *Memoirs*. In these sonnets, as one of his pupils remarked, 'the heathen mythology was singularly blended with the Roman creed, although at the close St Peter was made to acknowledge that the virtues of the excellent *sposa* entitled her to heaven, independent of all ecclesiastical dogmas—she being an angel even while on earth'. The same pupil told a friend that da Ponte's faith 'was sometimes a question with his intimates on account of the inconsistent views he expressed'; in fact, one of the most consistent things about da Ponte was his lack of faith in anything except himself.

After his wife's death the old poet went to live with his son Lorenzo L. da Ponte, and his wife Cornelia. Lorenzo L. da Ponte had inherited some of his father's gifts and tastes, and if he had only inherited his robust constitution as well he might have made a distinguished career. He became professor of Italian at Maryland University, and then in New York (1832-1836) and he also gave private lessons in Italian. He was a fine Greek scholar, and wrote a number of learned works, including a *History of the Florentine Republic*. He also translated some of his father's works into English. Unlike his father, the young Lorenzo was a dreamy, absent-minded person; he was much liked by his friends and pupils, and his early death—in 1840, when he was only thirty-six—was deeply mourned. Of his four children, only one—John Durant da Ponte—survived infancy; he was brought up in New Orleans, and himself gained distinction in that city; he died in 1894. Da Ponte's line in America descends through him and through the Andersons, the children of the poet's second daughter, Fanny. His youngest son, Charles, may also have married and had children, but very little is known about him.

II

Nancy's death was a great grief to da Ponte, but it in no way curtailed his activities. He continued to produce a vast amount of poetry, pamphlets and articles, he opened a bookstore, and went on with various schemes for promoting Italian opera in America. In 1829 he had tried, through his half-brother Agostino, to persuade Domenico Barbaja, director of the San Carlo Theatre in Naples, to bring a company of artists to New York, but his efforts had not been successful. In no way discouraged, he next tried to interest Jacques Montrésor, a tenor and impresario from Bologna, in his pet scheme. This time he met with more response; he had a long correspondence with the French singer, who very naturally wished to have as much information about conditions in America as possible before embarking on any definite undertaking, but who was inclined to think that if Garcia had been able to make a handsome profit in the New World, he could too.

The permanent establishment of Italian opera in New York was one of the greatest desires of da Ponte's old age; he may, therefore, have sent Montrésor rosier descriptions of theatrical conditions in the States than were warranted by the actual state of affairs. Nor did he forget his own personal interests entirely; he assured Montrésor, for instance, that Mozart and Rossini were certainly the composers of opera most popular with Americans—omitting to add that the New World had not had the opportunity to hear the works of any other composers sung in Italian—and suggested which operas he should bring to America. Out of the sixteen operas da Ponte proposed, all but two by Rossini belonged to the period of his own youth, about half a century ago, and no less than six of the libretti were by himself. Montrésor did not follow his advice, except about Rossini, and even then he did not bring the operas da Ponte had specified.

Da Ponte's correspondence with Montrésor lasted almost two years. The old poet continued to give glowing accounts of America in general and of opera audiences in particular, but also warned the impresario that he should bring with him from Italy a first-class violinist, an oboist, a horn player, 'un maestro al cembalo', and a prompter, none of whom were obtainable in New York. He also advised him to bring a scene-painter, because although they were to be found in America, their fees were enormous, as were those of the music copyists; he should also bring with him a good stock of violin and 'cello strings and of music paper. As to chorus singers, da Ponte did not know what to say—there were only too many of them available in the United States, but most of them were far better as teachers of Italian than as singers; it would be as well to bring some good ones if possible. Montrésor followed da Ponte's advice, and did bring some first-class orchestral musicians with him; many of them subsequently settled in America, where they formed an important addition to the orchestras which were then coming into being there.

Finally, all the preparations were made, and Montrésor collected a company of singers who were willing to cross the Atlantic with him. Among those whom he mentioned to da Ponte was a Signorina Mombelli; she was the daughter of the Mombellis who had been singing at the Vienna opera when da Ponte was there (her mother had been the first Zerlina), and he had of course known her parents well. He was delighted at the prospect of seeing the daughter of his old friends again, and at the prospect of hearing her sing, perhaps, in one of 'his' operas.

Montrésor and his company finally arrived in New York in 1832, and their season opened at the Richmond Hill Theatre on 6th October with a performance of Rossini's *La Cenerentola*. There were several good singers in the company—including Pedrotti, Fornasari and Corsetti—and the orchestra, in particular, made a great impression; it was considered the finest that had so far performed in New York. In all, thirty-five performances were given, and the repertoire included *L'Italiana in Algeri* of Rossini, Bellini's *Il Pirata* and Mercadante's *Elisa e Claudio*—but none of da Ponte's operas. The company then went to Philadelphia, accompanied by da Ponte, and gave twenty-four performances of opera there, as well as several concerts.

In spite of da Ponte's efforts—he had obtained some $8,000 in subscriptions in Philadelphia alone—the season was not a financial success; the novelty of Italian opera, which had attracted the public to Garcia's performances, had worn off, and Americans had come to the conclusion that although Italian singers might be very gifted musically, grand opera was less indigestible when sung in English and 'adapted' to American tastes. Both da Ponte and Montrésor lost a good deal of money during the season, and they had quarrelled bitterly by the end of it. Da Ponte gave his version of the story in two pamphlets, but it must be taken with a grain of salt; on his side, Montrésor obviously found that collaboration with an extremely active and self-assertive octogenarian had its disadvantages.

Disappointed, but in no way discouraged, da Ponte retired to the seclusion of his son's house once more, and began making plans for an even more ambitious project. In spite of overwhelming evidence to the contrary, he remained convinced that Americans really desired Italian opera on a grand scale, although they perhaps did not realise this themselves. The last season had been a failure because it had been badly organised—if only his advice had been followed everything would have been quite different—and also because the theatres available had not been suitable for grand opera. What New York really needed, da Ponte decided, was an opera house; if only opera could be performed under the proper conditions, as it had been in Vienna or in London, Americans would flock to hear it.

Da Ponte was, of course, putting the cart before the horse; what was needed was not an opera house, but the people to fill it, and it was to be many years before the Americans finally overcame all their prejudices and took Italian opera to their hearts. Ever since its conception, opera had always been the prerogative of a rich and cultured aristocracy centred around European courts; in America, although people were beginning to be rich, there was no court, no aristocracy, and very little culture. In addition, the puritan outlook of the original settlers in the New World died hard; although, by da Ponte's day, the theatre was established in the United States, by no means everyone approved of it. Thomas Hastings (1787-1872) an eminent American teacher and writer on church music, in his *Dissertation on Musical Taste* first published in 1822, expressed the following opinion on opera, and the vast majority of Americans agreed with him:

> 'If the question be asked as to the influence of operas, we answer that, as splendid pieces of composition, they cannot fail, in some limited circles, to promote the increase of musical learning and refinement. As to their moral influence, we class them, of course where they belong—among other dramatic works. In our country this species of composition is unknown. It appears among us only as an exotic from other climes, which is a circumstance on the whole not much to be regretted.'

In addition to religious prejudices against opera in general, there were also nationalist prejudices against foreign opera in particular. Like all young countries, America was beginning to resent foreign domination in artistic spheres, although she had, as yet, been unable to create any national art of her own. During da Ponte's life-time Americans were still too dependent on foreign musicians to show their resentment against them openly, for almost all orchestral players and teachers of music were fresh emigrants from Europe or, at most, had been in the States for one generation, and the first music-school in America was not founded until 1833; in a few years' time, however, Americans began to think that they could stand on their own feet in the world of art, and in an excess of patriotic enthusiasm and pride turned to attack the European sources of their culture.

The New York Philharmonic Society, which was founded in 1842, was one of the first organisations formed in America by professional musicians for the performances of instrumental music, and as such it had a high proportion of foreign, more especially German, members. By 1854 it was being sharply criticised in the press for its 'un-American activities', in other words, for performing nothing but foreign music. 'Now, in the name of the nine Muses, what is the Philharmonic Society in this country?' one critic asked. 'Is it to play exclusively the works of German masters, especially if they be dead, in order that our critics may translate their ready-made praises from the German? Or is it to stimulate original art on the spot? Is there a Philharmonic Society in Germany for the encouragement solely of American music?' The critics did not suggest what American music could be played instead of Mozart and Haydn, Beethoven, Rossini, and all the other foreigners, but instead went on to attack the German orchestral musicians without whose help there would have been no concerts in New York at all. 'If all their artistic affections are unalterably German, let them pack back to Germany, and enjoy the police and bayonets and aristocratic kicks and cuffs of that land, where an artist is a serf to a nobleman, as the history of their great composers shows. America has made the political revolution which illumines the world, while Germany is still shrouded with a pall of feudal darkness. While America has been thus far able to do the chief things for the dignity of man, forsooth she must be denied the brains for original art, and must stand like a beggar, cap in hand, when she comes to compete with the ability of any dirty German village.' Americans resented foreign orchestral music, but Italian opera sung in the original language was even more suspect, as the box-office receipts for the next half-century clearly demonstrated.

If da Ponte was aware of these various prejudices against Italian opera, he did not allow them to damp his ardour. In 1833, through his own personal efforts, he managed not only to persuade a number of Americans that they badly needed an opera house, but he also extracted large sums of money from them for that purpose. An association was formed, the theatre was built (at the corner of Church and Leonard Streets), and was opened in November under the management of da Ponte and an Italian acquaintance of his, Rivafinoli.

One of da Ponte's dearest dreams had been realised, and realised most magnificently. The new Opera House, the first ever to be built in New York, probably the first to be built in the States, cost $150,000, at that time a very considerable sum. The theatre was built on the European plan, with a tier composed entirely of boxes, and was lit by gas 'in a manner entirely new'. The accommodation was sumptuous, and no expense had been spared to make the interior a delight to the eye; the colour-scheme was white, blue and gold; there was a magnificent chandelier which illumined the dome and paintings on the walls made by artists specially imported from Europe; and the house was carpeted—a fact which aroused much comment. In addition, the acoustics were excellent, the artists' dressing-rooms were particularly large and comfortable, and the stage was 'vast'. The press agreed that 'the whole of this new and superb edifice is a credit to the taste and liberality of its founders'. They might have added that it owed its existence entirely to the energy, enthusiasm, and vision of an old man of eighty-four.

The theatre was opened on 18th November, 1833, with a performance of Rossini's *La Gazza Ladra*; the audience was so overwhelmed by the beauties of the new theatre that there was 'a consequent straining of necks from, rather than towards the stage', and they could scarcely take in the music at all. The press was almost universal in its praise of the new venture, with the exception of the *Albion*, whose editorial board complained that they had not been sent a press ticket and that as their reporter could not afford the high admission prices, they would not report on the performances. The season lasted until 21st July, 1834, and the repertoire included Rossini's *Barbiere di Siviglia*, *La Donna del Lago*, *Il Turco in Italia*, *Cenerentola*, and *Matilda di Shabran;* Pacini's *Gli Arabi nelle Gallie*, Cimarosa's *Il Matrimonio Segreto*, and an opera by Salvioni, the musical director of the company. The scenery and costumes were very splendid, and the orchestra was considered excellent. The singers were almost all Italian; the sopranos were Clementina and Rosina Fanti; mezzo-soprano, Louisa Bordogni; Schneider-Marconelli, contralto; Fabi and Raviglio, tenors; and De Rosa and Porto, basses. In spite of all these attractions, there was a deficit of \$29,275 at the end of the season, and the second season, which opened in November, 1834, was no more successful. In 1836 the Opera House was transformed into an ordinary theatre, the National Theatre as it was called, and shortly afterwards it was destroyed by fire.

So ended da Ponte's last and most ambitious venture. In spite of its lack of financial success, it was a most remarkable achievement, and one of which he could justly be proud. Not until the Metropolitan Opera House was built almost half a century later did America have any comparable theatre for the performance of opera.

Da Ponte lived on for another four years, which he spent relatively quietly. He published a number of poems and pamphlets, some of which he translated into English himself, and complained bitterly that he had not received due recognition for his work in America. 'Eighteen months have passed since I had a single pupil', he wrote in 1835. 'I, the creator of the Italian language in America, the teacher of more than two thousand persons whose progress astounded Italy! I, the poet of Joseph II, the author of thirty-six dramas, the inspiration of Salieri, of Weigl, of Martin, of Winter, and Mozart! After twenty-seven years of hard labour, I have no longer a pupil! Nearly ninety years old, I have no more bread in America!' It never occurred to him that he might be getting too old, that his long and active day was drawing to a close.

All the same, he had begun to think that it might be as well to make his chances in the next world a little more secure. Some years earlier, in 1831, he had opened a correspondence with Monsignor Jacopo Monico, the Patriarch of Venice. This 'foremost pillar of the portals of the Church of Christ', as da Ponte called him, had been Bishop of Ceneda, and may have known the poet personally. The Patriarch thanked him for some poems which he had sent him, and amongst other things expressed the hope that the distinguished poet might see his way to settling his affairs with the Church before he died. Da Ponte replied that the Patriarch's wishes had produced the desired effect in his soul; but he was in no particular hurry to take any more definite steps to return to the fold, and did not, in fact, do so for another seven years.

In August 1838 the old man felt unwell, and his doctor was summoned. There was nothing much wrong with him except old age, but it was clear that his life was at last drawing to a close. His mental faculties were in no way impaired by his illness, during which he translated a part of Hillhouse's *Hadad*, and Dr Francis, his physician, received from him, on the day preceding his death, 'a series of verses in his native tongue, partly in tone of gratitude, and partly to evince to his friends that, though speech had nigh left him, his mind was still entire'.

A Catholic priest was summoned, and at long last the Abbé da Ponte made his peace with the Church of Rome. As it was not generally known that he had been a priest, it was felt that it would be better not to draw attention to the fact at this late hour. Even though he had left it literally until the last moment, the prodigal had returned, and that was the principal thing.

On 16th August Dr Francis notified da Ponte's many friends and admirers that the poet was growing weaker, and they assembled to pay their last respects to him. 'It was one of those afternoons of waning summer', wrote one of his pupils who was present, 'when the mellow sunset foretells approaching autumn. The old poet's magnificent head lay upon a sea of pillows, and the conscious eye still shed its beam of regard upon all around him. Besides several of his countrymen were assembled some remnants of the old Italian (opera) troupe, who knelt for a farewell blessing around the pallet of their expiring bard; among them might be seen the fine head of Fornasari, and Bagioli's benevolent countenance. All wept as the patriarch bade them farewell and implored a blessing on their common country. The doctor, watching the flickerings of the life-torch, stood at the head of the couch, and a group of tearful women at the foot completed the scene . . .'

Did da Ponte himself take in this model final curtain, of which any dramatist might have been proud, or was he already busy with plans for spreading Italian culture in the next world and for writing libretti for Angelic choirs? At nine o'clock in the evening, on 17th August, 1838, Lorenzo da Ponte closed his eyes, gave a sigh, and embarked on his last and greatest adventure.

BIBLIOGRAPHY

I

Da Ponte's Memoirs

Memorie di Lorenzo da Ponte da Ceneda scritte da esso. Seconda edizione corretta e ampliata con note dell' autore e l'aggiunta d'un volume. New York, 1829-30. 3 volumes.

Les Mémoires de Lorenzo d'Aponte, traduits de l'Italien par M. C. D. de la Chavanne. With an introduction by Lamartine. Paris, 1860. (This is an abridged version of the *Memorie.*)

Memorie di Lorenzo da Ponte compendiate da Jacopo Bernardi, e scritti vari in prosa e poesia del medesimo autore. Florence, 1871.

Memorie di Lorenzo da Ponte, a cura di Giovanni Gambarin e Fausto Nicolini. Bari, 1918. 2 volumes.

Memoirs of Lorenzo da Ponte, translated with an introduction and notes by L. A. Sheppard, London, 1929. (An abridged version.)

Memoirs of Lorenzo da Ponte, translated by Elizabeth Abbott, edited and annotated by Arthur Livingston. Philadelphia, 1929.

Mémoires de Lorenzo da Ponte, suivis de Lettres inédites de Lorenzo da Ponte à Jacques Casanova, Préface et notes de Raoul Vèze. Paris, 1931.

In the present work the text of the *Memorie* used is that of the Gambarin-Nicolini edition; all quotations have been translated by the author.

II

Biographies of da Ponte

Marchesan, Angelo. *Della vita e delle opere di Lorenzo da Ponte.* Treviso, 1900.

Russo, J. L. *Lorenzo da Ponte, Poet and Adventurer.* New York, Columbia University Press, 1922.

III

Some other sources consulted

Part I—Venice

Baretti, Joseph. *An Account of the Manners and Customs of Italy*. London, 1768.

Bonora, Ettore (editor). *Letterati, Memorialisti e Viaggiatori del Settecento*. (Vol. 47, La Letteratura Italiana, storia e testi.) Milan—Naples, 1951.

Brosses (Président), Charles de. *Lettres d'Italie*, 3 volumes. Paris, 1799.

Burney, Dr Charles. *The Present State of Music in France and Italy*. London, 1771.

Casanova, Giacomo. *Mémoires* (édition originale). Leipzig, Paris, Brussels, 1826-38. 12 volumes.

Goethe: *Letters from Italy*. English translation, London, 1849.

Goldoni, Carlo. *Mémoires*. Milan, 1935.

Gozzi, Carlo. *Memorie inutili*, a cura di G. Prezzolini. Bari, 1910.
  Memoirs, trans. by J. A. Symonds, with essays on Italian impromptu comedy, Gozzi's life, the dramatic fables, etc. London, 1890.

Kelly, Michael. *Reminiscences*. London, 1826.

Kennard, J. S. *Goldoni and the Venice of his time*. New York, 1920.

Lee, Vernon. *Studies of the XVIIIth century in Italy*. 2nd edition, London, 1907.

Maynial, Edouard. *Casanova et son temps*. Paris, 1910.

Monnier, Philippe. *Venise au XVIII-ième siècle*. Paris, 1907.

Nicolini, Fausto. *La vera ragione della fuga di Lorenzo da Ponte de Venezia*. Archivo Storico Italiano, Serie VII, Vol. XIV. Florence, 1930.

Rousseau, Jean-Jacques. *Confessions*. Neuchâtel, 1790.

Sharp, Samuel. *Letters from Italy, describing the Customs and Manners of that country in the years 1765-1766*. 3rd edition (no date).

Venetian State Archives. *Esecutori Contro la Bestemmia. Processi, anno 1779, busta xxxvi (i)*.

Part II—Vienna

Anderson, Emily (editor and translator). *The Letters of Mozart and his Family.* London, 1938.

Beaumarchais, P. A. Caron de. *Théatre; suivi de ses poésies diverses.* Observations de Sainte-Beuve (no date).

Bergh, Herman van den. *Giambattista Casti, l'homme et l'oeuvre.* Amsterdam—Brussels, 1951.

Blom, Eric. *Mozart.* London, 1935.

Bombet, Louis-Alexandre César (Henri Beyle): *Lettres écrites de Vienne . . . sur Haydn, Mozart, Métastase . . .* Paris, 1814.

Burney, Dr Charles. *The Present State of Music in France and Italy* (see Part I above).
The Present State of Music in Germany, the Netherlands and the United Provinces. London, 1773.
Memoirs of the Life and Writings of the Abate Metastasio, 3 vols. London, 1796.

Casanova, Giacomo. *Mémoires* (see Part I above.)

Dent, Edward J. *Mozart's Operas,* 2nd edition, London, 1947.

Einstein, Alfred. *Mozart, His Character—His Work,* trans. by A. Mendel and N. Broder, London, 1946.

Fejtô, Francis. *Joseph II, Un Hapsburg Révolutionnaire.* Paris, 1954.

Holmes, Edward. *A ramble amongst the Musicians of Germany,* London, 1828.
Life of Mozart, London, 1845.

Jahn, Otto. *Life of Mozart,* trans. by P. D. Townsend, 3 vols. London, 1882.

Kelly, Michael. *Reminiscences* (see Part I above).

Lamartine, Alphonse de. *Cours familier de littérature* (Vol. V). Paris, 1858.

Lee, Vernon. *Studies of the XVIIIth Century in Italy* (see Part I above).

Ligne, Prince de. *Mémoires et Lettres.* Paris, 1923.

Maynial, Edouard. *Casanova et son temps* (see Part I above).

Molmenti, P. (editor). *Carteggi Casanoviani,* 2 vols. Palermo, 1917-1918.

Nettl, Paul. *The Other Casanova*. New York Philosophical Library, 1950.

Oulibicheff, Alexandre. *Nouvelle Biographie de Mozart*. Moscow, 1843.

Payer von Thurn, Dr R. *Joseph II als Theaterdirektor, Ungedruckte Briefe und Aktenstücke aus den Kinderjahren des Burgtheaters*. Vienna, 1920.

Pollio, J. and Vèze, R. *Pages Casanoviennes*. Paris, 1926.

Robertson, J. G. *Studies in the Genesis of the Romantic Theory in the Eighteenth Century*. Cambridge, 1923.

Scholes, Percy A. *The Great Dr Burney*. Oxford, 1948.

Wyzewa and Saint-Foix. *Mozart*. 5 vols. Brussels—Paris, 1912-1946.

Zagorski, M. *Poushkin i Teatr*. Moscow—Leningrad, 1940.

Ziliotto, B. *Lorenzo da Ponte e Giuseppe de Coletti*. Trieste, 1939.

Part III—London

Ebers, John. *Seven Years of the King's Theatre*. London, 1828.

Hogarth, George. *Memoirs of the Musical Drama*, 2 vols. London, 1838.

Kelly, Michael. *Reminiscences* (see Part I above).

Loewenberg, Alfred. *Lorenzo da Ponte in London, A Bibliographical account of his literary activity*, 1793-1804. Music Review, Vol. IV, No. 3, 1943.

Molmenti, P. (editor). *Carteggi Casanoviani* (see Part II above).

Mountedgecumbe, Earl of. *Musical Reminiscences*, London, 1827.

Newspapers, Contemporary.

Part IV—New York

Francis, Dr J. W. *Old New York*. New York, 1865.

Hornblow, Arthur. *A History of the Theatre in America*, 2 vols. Philadelphia, 1919.

Koch, Theodore. *Dante in America*, XVth Annual Report of the Dante Society. Boston, 1896.

Krehbiel, H. E. *Music and Manners from Pergolesi to Beethoven*. London, 1898.

Chapters of Opera. New York, 1909.

Mackinlay, M. S. *Garcia the Centenarian and His Times*. London, 1908.

Odell, George C. D. *Annals of the New York Stage*, 2 vols. New York, 1927.

Ritter, Dr F. L. *Music in America*. London, 1884.

Tuckerman, Henry T. *Lorenzo da Ponte*, Dublin University Magazine, Vol. LXXX, August, 1872.

Contemporary American Newspapers.

General Works of Reference

Loewenberg, Alfred. *Annals of Opera*. Cambridge, 1942.
Dictionary of National Biography,
Dictionary of American Biography,
Grove's Dictionary of Music and Musicians,
etc.

List of Lorenzo da Ponte's Principal Works

(Only the more important of his numerous
translations and adaptations have been included.)

1775-6 *Accademia poetica*. Fifteen poems in various metres, recited in the Seminary of Treviso at the end of the academic year 1775-6 (published for the first time in *Della vita e delle opere di Lorenzo da Ponte* (Marchesan), Treviso, 1900).

1779? ... A tragedy, translated from the German. Gorizia.
Il Conte di Warwick, translation of a French play by J. F. de la Harpe, perhaps made in collaboration with Girolamo da Ponte. (Performed Gorizia, 1779 or 1780; Trieste, autumn, 1791.)

1780 *Il capriccio*.
La gratitudine o sia la difesa delle donne.
Gorizia, 1780.

„ *La gara degli uccelli*, An ode. Privately printed for Count Guido Cobentzl. Gorizia, 1779 or 1780.

1781? *Salmi penitenziali*. Dresden, 1781 or 1782.

1783? *Lo Sposo deluso—o sia la rivalità di tre donne per un solo amante.* Opera buffa, music by Mozart (K. 430, unfinished). Many experts now consider that this libretto was by da Ponte. Mozart was probably working on it in the autumn of 1783.

1783   *L'Ifigenia in Tauride,* translation of French libretto by Guillard. Music by Gluck. First perf.: Dec. 14th, 1783, Vienna.

1784   *Il Ricco d'un Giorno, dramma buffo in tre atti.* Music by Salieri. First perf.: Dec. 6th, 1784, Vienna.

1785? *Davidde Penitente,* an oratorio, music by Mozart (K. 469). Mozart used the *Kyrie* and *Gloria* of his Mass in C minor (K. 427) for this oratorio, and the Latin text was probably translated into Italian by da Ponte. Probably performed in Vienna at a concert of the Society of Musicians during Lent, 1785.

1786   *Il Burbero di buon Cuore, dramma buffo.* (An adaptation of Goldoni's *Le Bourru bienfaisant.*) Music by Vincenzo Martin y Soler. First perf.: Jan. 4th, 1786, Vienna.

„   *Il finto Cieco, dramma buffo.* (Adaptation of an earlier libretto.) Music by Gazzaniga. First perf.: 20th Feb. 1786, Vienna.

„   *Le Nozze di Figaro, commedia per musica in quattro atti.* (Adaptation of *Le mariage de Figaro,* by Beaumarchais.) Music by Mozart. First perf.: May 1st, 1786, Vienna.

„   *Il Demogorgone ossia Il Filosofo confuso, opera buffa.* Music by Vincenzo Righini. First perf.: July 12th, 1786, Vienna.

„   *Una Cosa Rara, o sia Bellezza ed Onestà, dramma giocoso in due atti* (adapted from *La Luna della Sierra* by Luigi Velez de Guevara), music by Martin y Soler. First perf.: Nov. 17th, 1786, Vienna.

„   *Gli Equivoci, dramma buffo* (adapted from Shakespeare's *Comedy of Errors*), music by Stephen Storace. First perf.: Dec. 27th, 1786, Vienna.

1787   *Bertoldo, opera buffa* (adaptation of a libretto by Brunati), music by Francesco Piticchio. First perf.: 22nd June, 1787, Vienna.

„   *L'Arbore di Diana, dramma giocoso in due atti.* Music by Martin y Soler. First perf.: Oct. 1st, 1787, Vienna.

„   *Il Dissoluto punito o sia il Don Giovanni, dramma giocoso in due atti* (adaptation of a libretto by Bertati). Music by Mozart. First perf.: Oct. 29th, 1787, Prague.

1788   *Saggi poetici dell' ab. L. Da Ponte, poeta al servizio di Sua Maestà Cesarea.* 2 vols. Vienna, Imp. stamperia dei sordi e muti, 1788.

„   *Axur, Re d'Ormus, dramma tragicomico in cinque atti* (a translation of Beaumarchais' *Tarare*). Music by Salieri. First perf.: Jan. 8th, 1788, Vienna.

„   *Il Talismano, dramma giocoso in tre atti* (an adaptation of Goldoni's libretto of the same name). Music by Salieri. First perf.: Sept. 10th, 1788, Vienna.

1789   *Il Pastor fido, dramma in quattro atti* (probably an adaptation of an earlier libretto). Music by Salieri. First perf.: Feb. 11th, 1789, Vienna.

„   *Il Pasticcio o L'Ape musicale, commedia in due atti.* Music by various composers. First perf.: Feb. 27th, 1789, Vienna. (Also performed in Trieste, 24th Jan, 1792, and in New York, 1830.)

„   *La Cifra, dramma buffo in due atti.* (An adaptation of a libretto by Petrosellini: *La Dama pastorella.*) Music by Salieri. First perf.: Dec. 11th, 1789, Vienna.

1790   *Così fan tutte o sia La Scuola degli Amanti, dramma buffo in due atti.* Music by Mozart. First perf.: Jan 26th, 1790, Vienna.

„   *Nina o sia La Pazza per Amore.* (A translation from the French of Marsollier.) Music by Paisiello and Weigl. First perf.: April 13th, 1790.

„   *La Quakera spiritosa* (adaptation of a libretto by Palomba). Music by Guglielmi. First perf.: Aug. 13th, 1790, Vienna.

„   *La Caffettiera bizzarra.* Music by Weigl. First perf.: Sept. 15th, 1790, Vienna.

1791   *Il Tempio di Flora e Minerva,* cantata. Music by Weigl. First perf.: Jan. 17th, 1791, in Prince Auersperg's palace, Vienna.

„   *I voti della nazione napoletana,* cantata. Music by Piticchio. First perf.: Jan. 1791, at the residence of the Neapolitain Ambassador in Vienna.

„   *Davide, oratorio sacro in quattro atti.* Composer unknown. (Possibly an adaptation of *Davidde Penitente?* see above). First perf.: during Lent, 1791, Vienna?

„   *Il Mezenzio,* a tragedy. (Written in collaboration with Luigi da Ponte?) First perf.: Autumn, 1791, Trieste.

1793   *Il Tributo del Core, Poesie.* London, 1793.

1794 *Il Don Giovanni*, a tragi-Comic Opera in One Act. Music by Sarti, Federici, Gazzaniga, Guglielmi, and perhaps Mozart. (Da Ponte made alterations and additions to Bertati's libretto, and included *Madamina* from Mozart's opera.) First perf.: March 1st, 1794, London.

1794 *La Vittoria*, cantata. Performed in honour of the 'Glorious First of June'. Music by Paisiello. First perf.: June 23rd, 1794, London.

1795 *La Scola de Maritati*, comic opera in two acts. Music by Martin y Soler. Sometimes performed as *La Capricciosa corretta*, *Gli Sposi in Contrasto*, or *La Moglie corretta*. First perf.: Jan. 27th, 1795, London.

„ *L'Isola del Piacere, or The Island of Pleasure*. Comic opera in two acts. Music by Martin y Soler. First perf.: May 26th, 1795, London.

„ *Six Italian Canzonetts*, with English translations adapted to the music with an accompaniment for the Piano-Forte or Harp. Music by Martin y Soler, Italian text by da Ponte, English translation by W. R. Lawrence. Corri, Dussek and Co. London, (1795).

1796 *Antigona*, serious opera in two acts. Libretto probably by, or adapted by da Ponte. Music by Bianchi. First perf.: May 24th, 1796, London.

„ *Il Tesoro, opera buffa* in two acts. Music by Mazzinghi. First perf.: June 14th, 1796, London.

„ *Zemira e Azore*. Comic opera, music by Grétry. Da Ponte seems to have made a translation of the original French libretto by Marmontel. First perf.: July 23rd, 1796, London.

„ *Il Consiglio imprudente*, comic opera in one act. Music by Bianchi. First perf.: Dec. 20th, 1796, London.

1797 *Evelina, or The Triumph of the English over the Romans*. Serious opera. (Translated from the French of Guillard). Music by Sacchini (as posthumous work). First perf.: Jan. 10th, 1797, London. (Published by L. Da Ponte, No. 134, Pall Mall, 1797.)

„ *La (sic) Nozze del Tamigi e Bellona*, an 'Entertainment of Singing and Dancing' in honour of the victory of Cape St Vincent. Music by Bianchi. (Da Ponte originally wrote this cantata for the marriage of the Prince of Wales with Caroline of Brunswick.) First perf.: March 11th, 1797, London.

„   *Merope*, serious opera in two acts. (Translated and adapted from Voltaire.) Music by Bianchi. First perf.: June 10th, 1797, London.

1801   *Saggi Poetici*, Parte I. London. Printed by and for L. Da Ponte, No. 5, Pall Mall, 1801. (Vol. II does not appear to have been published.)

1802   *Armida*, A Grand Serious Opera, in two acts. Music by Bianchi. First perf.: June 1st, 1802, London.

1803   *La Grotta di Calipso. Dramma in due atti.* Music by Winter. First perf.: May 31st, 1803, London.

1804   *Il Trionfo dell'Amor Fraterno;* or, The Triumph of Fraternal Love. A serious opera, in three acts. Music by Winter. First perf.: March 22nd, 1804, London.

„   *Il Ratto di Proserpina,* or *The Rape of Proserpine.* A Serious Opera in two acts. Music by Winter. First perf.: May 31st, 1804, London.

1807   *Storia compendiosa della vita di Lorenzo da Ponte, scritta da lui medesimo. A cui si aggiunge la prima letteraria conversazione tenuta in sua casa, il giorno 10 marzo dell'anno 1807, in New York, consistente in alcune composizioni italiane, sia in verso che in prosa, tradotte in inglese dai suoi allievi.* New York, I. Riley and Co., 1807.

1821   *Sull' Italia. Discorso apologetico in risposta alla lettera dell'avvocato Phillips.* New York, 1821.

„   *La profezia di Dante di Lord Byron tradotta in terza rima da L. da Ponte.* New York, 1821, and 1822.

1823   *Catalogo ragionato de' libri che si trovano al negozio di Lorenzo e Carlo da Ponte.* New York, 1823.

1825   *Alcune osservazioni sull' articolo quarto pubblicato nel 'North American Review' il mese d' ottobre dell' anno 1824.* New York, 1825.

„   *Critique on certain passages in Dante,* articles in the 'New York Review and Athenaeum Magazine', vol. i, pp. 156-58, 241-2, 325-7.

1825   *Scena Quarta del Quinto Atto di Adad* (Hillhouse) New York, 1825.

1823-   *Memorie di Lorenzo da Ponte da Ceneda scritte da esso.* 4 vols.
27   Published by Lorenzo and Carlo da Ponte, New York, 1823-27.

1827   *Storia della lingua e letteratura italiana in New York,* 1827.

1829- *Memorie di Lorenzo da Ponte da Ceneda scritte da esso. Seconda*
30   *edizione corretta e ampliata con note dell' autore e l'aggiunta d'un*
    volume. 3 vols. Vols. i and ii, 1829, vol. iii, 1830. New York.

1830 *Poesie varie.* New York, 1830.

   ,,   *Alcune poesie di Lorenzo da Ponte pubblicate da lui medesimo in*
    New York l'anno 1830. (Also known as *Mazzetti di fiori.*)

1832 *Sonetti per la morte di Anna Celestina Ernestina Da Ponte.* New
    York, 1832.

1833 *Storia della compagnia dell' opera italiana condotta da Giacomo*
    Montrésor in America in Agosto dell'anno 1832. *New York,* 1833.

   ,,   *Storia incredibile ma vera.* New York, 1833.

1835 *Frottola per far ridere.* New York, 1835.

   ,,   *Storia americana ossia Il Lamento di Lorenzo da Ponte quasi*
    nonagenario al nonagenario Michele Colombo. New York, 1835.

Bibliographical Note

Some reprints and new editions of Lorenzo da Ponte's *Memorie* published since 1956:

In Italian: *Memorie,* edited by C. Pagnini, Milan, 1960.
          Memorie e altri scritti, edited by C. Pagnini, Milan, 1971.
          Memorie: I libretti mozartiani, with an introduction by
          Giuseppe Armani, Milan, 1976.

Translations *Mémoires et livrets*, edited and annotated by Jean-François
in French: Labie, Paris, 1980.
          This is a new translation; the volume includes the three
          Mozart libretti in Italian and French. It also includes
          several critical essays by J-F Labie. Monsieur Labie is kind
          enough to say that he has used my book extensively; I can
          only reply that he has made good use of it, and that his
          essays and annotations are both valuable and stimulating.

Reprints   Elizabeth Abbott's English translation (New York, 1929),
          the only complete edition in English, was reprinted in
          1959 and 1967.
          G. Gugitz's German translation (1924) was reprinted in 1969.

Mozart   has proliferated to such an extent since 1956 (the bicen-
scholarship: tenary year) that those interested should consult the
          extensive bibliographies in *The New Grove*, London 1980.

INDEX